Raj Khosla

Raj Khosla

THE AUTHORIZED BIOGRAPHY

AMBORISH ROYCHOUDHURY

with ANITA KHOSLA & UMA KHOSLA KAPUR

hachette
INDIA

First published in 2025 by Hachette India
(Registered name: Hachette Book Publishing India Pvt. Ltd)
An Hachette UK company
www.hachetteindia.com

1

All images except for those specifically credited to their sources are courtesy the personal collection of Raj Khosla's family.

Section opener image courtesy Dafont.

The old names of some places such as Bombay, Poona and Madras, and others have been used only to maintain the historicity of the information or the references used.

All QR codes included in the book lead to video links which belong to the respective channels/video platforms that have posted them. Their availability is subject to the period till the respective channels/video platforms continue to feature them.

Subsequent edition/reprint specifications may be subject to change, including but not limited to cover or inside finishes, paper, text colour and/or colour sections.

ISBN 978-93-5731-770-2

Hachette Book Publishing India Pvt. Ltd
4th & 5th Floors, Corporate Centre
Plot No. 94, Sector 44, Gurugram – 122003, India

Typeset in Minion Pro
by Mukul Chand, Delhi

Printed and bound in India by
Manipal Technologies Limited

FSC
www.fsc.org
MIX
Paper | Supporting responsible forestry
FSC™ C043100

Contents

Foreword

The Light That Lingers

It was 1969, and I was 20 years old when I first walked into Mehboob Studios, trembling with ambition and nerves. A burly watchman stopped me, sizing me up – tight pants, side locks, Bata rubber slippers. 'Where are you going? You're not allowed in.'

I stared him down. 'I'm here on Mr Raj Khosla's invitation.'

Something in my voice must have rung true, because he relented. I walked past him into the chaos of the studio, its air thick with the smell of paint, sweat and possibility. Stage after stage buzzed with technicians, junior artistes and booming voices. I snaked my way to Raj sahab's office, my heart pounding as I imagined what awaited me – a college dropout seeking a place in the world of cinema.

Inside, I found a man with a thin moustache and a disarming smile, still shaking off sleep after his afternoon siesta, which he fondly called his '40 winks'. It was a ritual that rejuvenated him, readying him for the long hours ahead. He sat beneath a framed image of Guru Dutt. 'Do you know anything about filmmaking?' he asked, not bothering with pleasantries.

'No, sir,' I admitted.

He grinned.

'Ah, zero is a great place to start.'

That was Raj sahab – the man who believed in beginnings, no matter how bleak. And with that began my journey into the world of movies, a journey that saw him rise again from the ashes of failure with *Do Raaste*. It was the film that not only cemented his place in the pantheon of directors but also brought Rajesh Khanna to the pinnacle of stardom.

I remember vividly how, after the premiere, Raj sahab urged me to accompany the legendary editor Waman Bhonsle to add the iconic song 'Bindiya chamkegi' to the film's tail end, ensuring the audience left on a high note. We raced from theatre to theatre across Bombay, physically inserting those precious few feet of celluloid into reels already spinning. The gamble worked; the song became the magic touch that turned a success into a phenomenon.

With *Do Raaste* behind him, Raj sahab embarked on *Mera Gaon Mera Desh*, his first 'Eastern Western', shot in the rugged landscapes of Udaipur. I was a second-unit assistant director, star-struck by Dharmendra, Vinod Khanna and Asha Parekh, and overwhelmed by the sheer scale of the production. The film, another resounding success, catapulted Raj sahab back to the top, cementing his legend.

But all great rivers twist and turn. There came a time when I had to part ways with him and carve my own path. My journey was strewn with failure – flops that nearly erased me before I began. Yet I drew strength from the memory of Raj sahab, a man who had clawed his way back from nothing and dared to rise again.

And rise I did, with *Arth*, *Saaransh*, *Janam* and *Naam*. Success brought its own burdens, and the young man once fetching drinks for his master found himself navigating the treacherous tides of fame.

Years later, I met him again at the Sea Rock Hotel in Bandra. My mentor. My master. The man who had once defied failure and soared was now slipping once more, this time into the shadows of irrelevance. 'Fetch me a drink,' he commanded. I obeyed, as I always had.

As the party swirled around us, he looked at me and said, 'So, how does it feel to be riding the tide?'

'This is not what I asked for, Sahab,' I replied.

He laughed, bitterly. 'Shut up. Four hits, and you're still not happy. Ask me what it feels like to taste it all and then beg for just one more hit to make your exit graceful.'

His words haunt me still. He likened fame to starlight – a glow emanating from stars long dead, their light journeying across vast distances to reach us. 'The light is the message,' he said, 'but the star, the messenger, is gone.'

Raj sahab is such a star. Though he is long gone, his light still shines through me. When I guide young filmmakers today, I hear his voice in my own. The wisdom I pass on to them is not mine; it's his. They say what you teach your children, you teach your grandchildren, and so his legacy ripples outward, carried forward by those who never even knew his name.

Raj sahab's story is larger than my memories, larger than any single telling. He was a magician, a creator of light and shadow, a man no biography could fully capture. But I salute the audacity of Amborish who has dared to do that.

Wasn't I privileged to sit in the front row and witness the magic of Raj sahab?

Thank you, Amborish, for giving him his rightful place among the greats of Indian cinema. He deserves nothing less.

– Mahesh Bhatt

Mumbai, 21 December 2024

Introduction

When I told my friends that I was writing a book on Raj Khosla, only the hardened film buffs amongst them showed any comprehension. Later, when I happened to post a collage of some of his songs, my inbox was flush with messages of the following nature:

> 'Wow! All these songs are from his films?'
> 'I didn't know all of these are by one guy!'
> 'This video gave me so much joy. It's unbelievable. He needs to be celebrated.'

And that pretty much sums up Raj Khosla and the state of his legacy. He wasn't adequately media-savvy, and didn't get featured enough to remain in circulation, like many of his peers. But his films and their songs continue to touch lives every single day. 'Lag ja gale' remains the definitive love song, played in pubs to this day. When Lata Mangeshkar passed away in 2022, every single tribute featured the song. YouTube vloggers from distant countries have made reaction videos on the song, and broken down talking about it.

'Achha ji main haari' and 'Maar diya jaaye' can still liven up parties. 'Yeh hai Bombay meri jaan', another blockbuster of a song, got a standing ovation in theatres when it was used in a goosebump-inducing scene in Nishikant Kamat's *Mumbai Meri Jaan*. 'Jhumka gira re' and its tune was rehashed and became a rage in the more recent *Rocky aur Rani kii Prem Kahaani*. A stray line of dialogue from *Anita* (1967) went viral on Instagram and TikTok a few years ago. 'Hai apna dil to awara' is the eternal, calming Hemant Kumar ballad, loved across generations. 'Jaane kya baat hai' would easily feature among the very best of R.D. Burman–Lata Mangeshkar collaborations. Could it be a coincidence that all these landmark songs just happen to be from one filmmaker's body of work? Of course, these represent the work of some of our best music directors and singers, but is that all?

While many of his contemporaries have had books and biographies on them, Raj Khosla has remained a significant footnote in books about Guru Dutt, including those by Nasreen Munni Kabir, Sathya Saran and Yasser Usman. The only televised interview that most Indians have seen him in was part of journalist Nasreen Munni Kabir's documentary on Guru Dutt. But no one has ever turned the arc lights on Raj Khosla himself. Yet he's no obscure filmmaker with one or two odd hits to their name. Raj Khosla had an enviable filmmaking career by any standards. No other filmmaker has, arguably, made so many iconic and path-breaking films. It is as if they are all from different filmographies. How on earth can the same director have made a *C.I.D.* and a *Do Raaste*? The same guy, without breaking a sweat, created *Main Tulsi Tere Aangan Ki* and *Dostana* within a span of two years. Such disparate kinds of films can only come from the stable of a director who is passionately in love with his work, and with cinema.

But was that what drove Raj Khosla? Was he in love with filmmaking? Did being on the sets make him happy? What made him tick? In truth, Raj Khosla was quite the enigma. This book only scratches the surface and hopefully encourages more conversation on the work of this charming, talented, prolific and yet deeply troubled and melancholic director.

Like his mentor Guru Dutt, a lot of Raj Khosla's later work was autobiographical. As with every sensitive artist, the trials and tribulations of his private life had a direct impact on his creative approach and output. As a biographer, I was intrigued: how did these sensitive aspects of his life impact his cinema?

But no relationship exists in a vacuum – there are always other people and other lives at stake. I tried to reach out and secure the requisite permissions so that those stories could be told, but to no avail. I must respect the wishes of those involved, and have hence steered clear of naming any names or going into more details than is absolutely necessary. In the precious few interviews that Raj Khosla has given in his life, he was refreshingly candid about his follies. I've touched upon them without getting into specifics. Rather than chronicle his life and see how his work was affected by it, I have tried to explore his work and see if some of that reflects the person he was.

– Amborish Roychoudhury

Prelude

Sunday, 9 June 1991.

It was the wettest day in the history of Mumbai. The Met department had never seen that kind of rainfall in 24 hours, in Bombay's recorded history. The main headline on the *Indian Express*'s masthead screamed, 'Incessant rains lash Bombay, 50 dead'.

The city was cut off from the rest of the country. Rail, road and air traffic were paralysed. Abhiruchi Hotel, promoted as 'the only floating restaurant in Asia', sank to the bottom of the Ambe Ghosale Lake. A one-and-a-half-foot tall Ganesh idol was rescued from another Thane lake. It was installed on the banks and even in the paralysing rains, people thronged to offer their obeisance to the deity. Three people were killed in a house collapse in Dombivli. In Turbhe, New Bombay (now Navi Mumbai), the bodies of a man and a child were recovered from a Maruti van, which had drowned in a roadside nullah. More than 3,000 people had been evacuated.

Hard rains are a regular occurrence in Bombay. But this was particularly intense; nobody had seen anything like it in their own lifetime. It was as if god was shedding copious tears, hell-bent on delivering the full magnitude of divine sadness. On this doomsday, a family tried to transfer the lifeless body of their patriarch from Jaslok Hospital in Breach Candy to their house in Pali Hill, Bandra. It was a struggle. There was no transport available, and in the middle of a seeming apocalypse where even the living found it impossible to get home, transporting the dead seemed like a Herculean task. But they had to try.

The next day's newspapers carried particulars of the mayhem in vivid detail. Among other news, they also reported that a giant of Indian cinema had died.

Raj Khosla, the veteran filmmaker, had breathed his last.

1

Origins: Punjab to Bombay

On the banks of the river Beas in Punjab, there was an ancient village called Ruhela. Around the late 1580s, Arjan Dev, the fifth Sikh guru, founded a city on the ruins of this old village. He populated it suitably, built it from the ground up and called it Sri Gobindpur. After Guru Arjan Dev's execution by the Mughals, the city changed hands and was ravaged and plundered. Arjan Dev's son, Guru Hargobind Sahib, fought the Mughals in the 1620s and reclaimed the city founded by his father. The guru got around 40 wells dug in the city, and it became one of the most prominent and sacred destinations for the Sikh people, eventually attaining the name of Sri Hargobindpur. Later, a prominent Sikh leader, Sardar Jassa Singh Ramgarhia, used the city as his capital.

It is believed that the sixth guru, Hargobind Sahib, brought a loyal migrant population with him to settle in this new town. These were members of the Khosla clan, who had thus far been living in other regions of Punjab, such as Talwan, Nurmahal and Rahon. They followed their guru to this place and since then, generations of Khoslas have made Sri Hargobindpur their home. But there was one among them who was destined to have a profound impact on Indian cinema and pop culture.

Three centuries after the migration of the Khoslas, Atmaram, an active member of the community and an enterprising young man, was getting ready to tie the knot. The bride-to-be was Saraswati Devi Bhalla. Saraswati was a force to reckon with. It is said that when she stepped out of her house, everyone was kept on their toes, because here was a woman who never failed to speak her mind. Her father, Bishan Das Bhalla, was a wealthy landowner and ardent follower of the Arya Samaj. Saraswati, though, was a devoted Sikhni who wore her *kada* with pride.

Atmaram Khosla held a position in the railways. Having a job in the railways commanded immense respect in those days. In the 1920s, the Indian Railways wasn't one integrated entity. The first passenger trains started running in the 1850s, and by the 1860s, the railway network had begun to connect various cities in undivided India. A plethora of railway companies had sprung up, which only managed certain routes. One of the more prominent companies among them was the Great Indian Peninsula Railway, with its headquarters at Bori Bunder in Bombay. It connected cities such as Poona, Nasik and Sholapur. There were other such companies too, including the Southern Punjab Railway, the Indus Valley State Railway and the North Western State Railway. The railway station in Ludhiana, which came into existence in the 1870s, soon became a major junction station. It was in Ludhiana that Atmaram Khosla was posted in the accounts department. With a cushy job in the railways and a respectable family background, he was the ideal prospect for Saraswati.

Once they were married, Atmaram and Saraswati set about building a family in Ludhiana, though they kept going back to the country house at Sri Hargobindpur – it was their *pind* (village) and nothing would change that. By the time Desraj Khosla opened his eyes and looked at the world around him for the first time, Atmaram and Saraswati had already given birth to three children – one son (Lekhraj) and two daughters. Another daughter, Sarla, was born after Desraj. He was the fourth of five siblings.

Raj Khosla was born 'Desraj'. This is the name he was known by in his close circles. To friends, he was Desraj or simply 'Des'. It was later that the name was clipped to Raj. But his close associates continued to call him Des even after he made a name in the industry as Raj Khosla.

Precious little is known of those early days. The extended members of the Khosla clan would keep visiting their country house in Sri Hargobindpur, and often stayed back. The Khoslas were accustomed to entertaining guests quite frequently, and their house – a palatial haveli with many rooms – just like their hearts, was large enough to accommodate everyone. 'It had 30 bedrooms,' Raj Khosla said in an interview many years after. 'We could ride our horses through the house.'[1] The Khoslas – particularly Raj – had a special connection with horses. He was fascinated by the beast. The haveli had its own stable and Raj learnt to ride when he was barely five. He took to it like a fish takes to water. He loved being around horses, and this stayed with him all his life. Years later, he would find ways to incorporate horses into his films.

Around 1928, when Raj was about three years old, the family moved to Bombay. Atmaram Khosla now had a job at the Great

Indian Peninsula Railway. Bombay was transforming into a bustling metropolis. The Khoslas' first home in the city was a rented accommodation in the newly formed Dadar Parsi Colony, set up in the wake of the infamous bubonic plague outbreak in Bombay in the 1890s. The Bombay City Improvement Trust was created in the aftermath of the epidemic, with the objective of improving living conditions and decongesting the heart of the city. All vacant lands were made available to the trust, and it opened up suburbs like Matunga for planned residences. Atmaram purchased one of these plots. He built a house there in 1935 and called it Khosla Niwas. The house still stands, 90 years later.

In Bombay, Raj Khosla attended Anjuman-I-Islam school, where he learned Urdu among other subjects. He would write and speak in it to the end of his days. His proficiency in the language drew him to Urdu poetry and its most celebrated practitioner Mirza Ghalib. It is because of his diction and command over the language that Guru Dutt would later employ his voice in one of his most iconic films.

But Raj Khosla's hero at this stage was not Ghalib. It was someone else. Kundan Lal Saigal had imprinted his name in the firmament of Indian cinema with Pramathesh Barua's *Devdas* (1935). He had had some successes like *Yahudi ki Ladki* (1933), *Puran Bhagat* (1933) and *Chandidas* (1934), but it was *Devdas* that truly consolidated Saigal's position as a star. His streak continued with blockbusters like *President* (1937) and *Street Singer* (1938). Saigal's voice rang through every street corner of the country. His singing was inspiring a whole generation of youngsters to take up music as their vocation. Among them were two young boys, Raj Khosla and Abhas Kumar Ganguly, soon to be christened Kishore Kumar.

Saigal was like a deity to Raj Khosla. A year before he died, Raj Khosla told journalist Rajiv Vijayakar about the precise moment of his birth in Ludhiana. He said that on 31 May 1925, when he was about to enter the world, his father was listening to a song by Kundanlal Saigal.[2] While this tale may have been apocryphal – Raj Khosla was about 10 years old when Saigal became a star – the anecdote foreshadows the filmmaker's obsession with music and with Saigal.

The singer was one of the earliest celebrities to move to Matunga. He became a resident of Radha Kunj, in an area of Matunga called Punjabi Gali. Radha Kunj was home to several legends over the years, including actors Manmohan Krishna and Madan Puri. Saigal was a sensation, and the house soon became a beacon for film lovers and music enthusiasts. Every evening, the singer would screen films on his terrace for friends and family. He would often sit by himself and perform his *riyaz*. Khosla Niwas was not far from Radha Kunj. Raj Khosla would often visit and listen to his idol singing, enraptured. He later said that on one of those occasions, Saigal told him, '*Jab tu gaayega, meri awaaz mein gaayega*. When you sing, you will sing in my voice.'[3] These words would prove prophetic in the years to come.

Raj Khosla's love for singing is well documented. His early escapades in the film industry had to do with singing. But a relatively lesser-known fact of his life is that he was well schooled in music. Pandit Jagannathbuwa Purohit took a young Raj under his wings to teach him the nuances of Hindustani classical music. Purohit belonged to the Agra gharana, one of the oldest and most prominent schools of Hindustani classical music. He learnt from Ustad Vilayat Hussain Khan and Mohammad Ali Khan. He served his gurus so earnestly and imbibed their teachings so well that he earned the moniker 'Gunidas'. Gunidas, aka Jagannathbuwa Purohit, trained some revered names in the Indian classical music scene, including Pandit Jitendra Abhisheki, Pandit Ram Marathe and Manik

Varma. This experience of learning under an accomplished maestro imbued Raj Khosla with a deep knowledge of and appreciation for Indian classical music forms, which held him in good stead. It also explains his command over singing, and the intense desire to build a career in it.

Khosla Niwas continued the legacy of the Sri Hargobindpur haveli, and the house was a hive of activity, bustling with people. Raj Khosla's parents were always entertaining guests, either from the extended family or 'from their village'. For Punjabi families back then, the concept of a village was expansive. Everyone from neighbouring villages, or from even the same district, had the right to say they were 'from their village'. Atmaram and Saraswati Khosla often organized soirees for music lovers and connoisseurs. On those music-soaked evenings, young Raj was wont to pull out the harmonium and sing the latest Saigal melodies.

Raj was a sporty child. While horseback riding no longer seemed an option in Bombay, cricket became his preferred game. He played for the school team. In fact, cricket became such an obsession that his father had to make him switch schools. From Anjuman-I-Islam, Raj Khosla was moved to a school where cricket was off the curriculum. He was a bright kid, so academics were never a problem.

The teenage Raj was also enamoured with the world of films, with cinema making an emphatic entry in his life about this time. Matunga witnessed the opening of a new theatre, Aurora Talkies. Over the years, Aurora would gain a reputation as the hub of Tamil cinema in Bombay, but in those early days it screened a host of Hollywood outings. This was the time when Alfred Hitchcock was coming into his own, with films like *The*

Lady Vanishes (1938), *Rebecca* (1940) and *Saboteur* (1942). Raj watched all of them.

When he joined Elphinstone College, the youngster discovered a newfound passion for theatre. He staged many plays, acted in and directed some of them.

Were the seeds of a career in storytelling sown in his college years? Maybe, but the idea of becoming a singer had consumed Raj Khosla. He was a devotee of the great Saigal, no less. He wanted the world to discover his talent as a singer. Filmmaking wasn't even a distant possibility. By this time, however, the nation was in turmoil. India's destiny was about to change, and with it, Raj's too.

2

Baby Steps: Radio, Singing and Acting

At the age of 16, Raj Khosla thought he had fallen in love for the first time. When he saw one of the girls in the village, his heart skipped a beat. 'It lasted three days,' he later revealed in an interview to *Filmfare*. 'I used to take a detour on the way to the bazaar, so I could pass by her house. On the third day, an old man shouted, "The road to the bazaar is from there. Don't think you're smart, we know what you're up to!"'[1] It was one of many infatuations.

In his second year of college, Raj fell in love again. He reminisced about this in an interview to journalist Khalid Mohamed for the May 1979 issue of *Filmfare*: 'Unfortunately for me and for her, she was a Muslim. She got married long ago, and settled down in Pakistan. Her father was also in the railways, so we both had first class passes.' The college-goer and his new girlfriend would travel daily from the Victoria Terminus station (present-day Chhatrapati Shivaji Maharaj Terminus) to Kalyan and back. The compartments were mostly empty, and the motorman would spy on the lovebirds. He knew their fathers, and spilled some beans. The families reckoned these young lovers were too naive to fathom the complications of a Hindu–Muslim marriage. The young man was promptly packed off to another college, where he would fall in love once again. This disposition would stay with him throughout his life and would reflect in his work.

Upon graduating from Elphinstone College in 1945, Raj Khosla's first work-related adventure was at the Punjab National Bank. He joined as an apprentice at their Mandvi branch in Bombay. The job was a concession to his father, who was then the financial adviser at the state transport department.[2] The banking career 'lasted about three months during which time he… messed up once or twice the clearance of cheques, and he broke away from the bank when communal riots broke out in the city'.[3]

In 1947, when two nations were carved out of the Indian subcontinent, more than 20 million people were directly affected, and countless others lost their lives. Wave after wave of migrants hit the major cities, including Bombay. Some of them had walked for days and weeks, braving the elements. It was the greatest mass migration in recorded history.

Riot-hit families from Punjab, Sind and various other places congregated in Bombay, creating a pressing need to record and document every person. The government-appointed officers couldn't have handled it alone, so young people from colleges and universities as well as fresh graduates were hired to help keep track of the refugees – where they were coming from and where they were being sent. Having left his job at the bank, Raj volunteered for the effort along with two compatriots, S.K. Kapur and Shankar B.C. Both would eventually make their way into films too. S.K. Kapur produced several films between the late 1960s and the late 1980s, including *Night in London* (1967) and *Insaaf Main Karungaa* (1985). Shankar B.C., on the other hand, became a producer–distributor of films, including the iconic *Laila Majnu* (1976).

Out on the other side, in 1948, Raj was at a juncture where he had to choose between two potential careers, neither of which ended up being his calling. He was shortlisted for the Indian Army and the All India Radio (AIR).[4] This was the golden age of radio. Every singer worth their salt was baptized through broadcasting before cutting their own records or albums. Singing was still important to Raj, and joining AIR seemed to be a shot at a career in music. He was recruited by the national broadcaster as an announcer at 80 rupees a month. Raj Khosla's voice had a rich timbre and one would think that the role of a radio announcer would suit him well. Whenever he had the chance, he also indulged in some singing. *The Indian Listener*, the programme journal of AIR, lists one song by him, which was broadcast on the Bombay 1 radio station at 7.30 a.m. on 7 August 1948: 'Phoola phoola phire jagat mein', a Kabir bhajan.

There was, however, a twist to this radio tale. In the mid-1970s, when he was an established filmmaker at the top of his game, Raj Khosla collaborated with radio icon Ameen Sayani on a popular show called *S. Kumars ka Filmi Mukaddama*. The show revealed the fact that in the early 1950s, Raj Khosla had been with Radio Ceylon for almost a year. As Sayani mentioned later in his immensely popular show *Geetmala ki Chhaon Mein*, Raj would sing the songs of Kundanlal Saigal on a weekly sponsored show called *Rang Tarang* on Radio Ceylon. In the show, Raj Khosla also spoke about his stint in theatre. As mentioned earlier, he had developed a penchant for the stage during his college days. Bombay had a thriving theatre scene and in the early days, when he was trying to find his voice, Raj directed some plays, maybe even acted in a few. Over the course of the show, the filmmaker said that he realized that Hindi and Urdu professional theatre in Bombay could never enjoy the popularity of Marathi or Gujarati plays. He added, 'I also realized that for good drama writing and direction, you needed to be as talented as Agha Hashar, and I wasn't.' He was referring to Agha Hashar Kashmiri, an Urdu playwright of immense repute.

Around the same time, Raj also landed his first job in the film industry. It was as a double for a heroine. Now how did that happen? In those early days, some friends told the young aspirant that he could make good money by riding a horse on a film set.[5] He was intrigued. It so happened that at around the same time, actor–filmmaker Bhagwan Dada was looking for a stunt double for his heroine. An outlandish scene in the film needed her to be dressed up as a bird and ride a horse. And so, Raj Khosla, in his first-ever film role, rode a horse, wearing a cape and a beak. His part was to avoid a branch hanging from a tree. He was paid 75 rupees for the stunt.

While Raj Khosla was on this quest to find himself, another story cooking among two young men in Poona was about to change the course of his career and destiny. One of them was born less than an hour's drive from the country home of the Khosla family.

In Gurdaspur, just about 40 kilometres from Sri Hargobindpur, a boy called Dharamdev was born two years before Raj Khosla. Dharamdev Anand, sometimes called DD by his friends, was fairly young when it was made clear to him how good-looking and attractive he was. His charm made girls gravitate to him and men do his bidding. In July 1943, having shed the 'Dharam' from his name, Dev Anand boarded the

Frontier Mail to go to Bombay and become a star. In less than two years, he bagged his first film.

Ostensibly in preparation for a life of screen acting, Dev Anand had been learning music and indulging in a little bit of theatre. He had a minor role in a play by the People's Theatre called *Zubeida*. The rehearsals were held in a hall adjoining the music classes where he was learning 'vocal music'. It was here that he met Masurekar, an amateur singer, who eventually became an integral part of Navketan Films, Dev Anand's home production company.

At Masurekar's insistence, Dev went to meet Baburao Pai, a partner of Prabhat Film Company. As expected, the charmer made quite the impression and was eventually cast as the leading man on *Hum Ek Hain* (1946). The film introduced several talents in various departments. Besides Dev Anand, actor Rehman debuted with this film. It was also the directorial debut for Pyarelal Santoshi (father of filmmaker Rajkumar Santoshi). The opening credits also mention one Guru Dutt under 'Dance Composition'.

Guru Dutt was born as Vasanthrao Padukone in Bangalore, but the family soon shifted to Calcutta. Dance maestro Uday Shankar's dance dramas were often staged in the city, and a young Guru Dutt was fascinated by the performances. Inspired by Shankar's unique style of dance movements, he wanted to be a dancer himself. With the help of some friends and his uncle B.B. Benegal, Guru Dutt managed to secure an entry into the famous dance academy Uday Shankar India Cultural Centre, in Almora. Between 1941 and 1944, Guru Dutt trained at the academy, learning various facets of dance, stage performance and lighting.

Following the outbreak of the Second World War in 1939, the foreign funding for Uday Shankar's academy dried up, and by 1944, the school had to be shut down. Guru Dutt was crestfallen. He wasn't sure where life would take him next. His uncle came to the rescue once again. B.B. Benegal had seen his nephew fiddling with his Bosch camera. He took the young man to Poona and introduced him to Baburao Pai. Guru Dutt was appointed as dance choreographer at the Prabhat Film Company, for 50 rupees a month. On several occasions, he doubled as assistant director, and even as an actor. He appeared as a dancer in Vishram Bedekar's film *Lakharani* (1945). He choreographed the dances for *Hum Ek Hain*, and this was where he crossed paths with Dev Anand.

At this time, Dev Anand was engaged in a clandestine affair with a young woman who occupied one of the rooms at the guest house where he stayed while he worked in the film. For one of their rendezvous, she insisted that Dev come all dressed up as it was her birthday. The next day, as he rummaged through his cupboard, the young actor realized that his best shirt wasn't there. It had been replaced by someone else's shirt; the washerman must have mixed them up. Cursing the man under his breath, Dev stepped out wearing the wrong shirt. As fate would have it, he bumped into Guru Dutt, the owner of the other shirt, on the studio floor. They had a good laugh over the laundry incident, and a great friendship began.

Meanwhile, Raj Khosla was offered his first shot at stardom. In 1941, Chand Lal or C.L. Dheer had come to India from East Africa, with the dream of making films. For a while, he interned with V. Shantaram at his studio Rajkamal Kalamandir, as associate director in films like *Dr. Kotnis ki Amar Kahani* (1946). At the time, Dheer used to live in the house of Pandit Sudarshan, a renowned lyricist and writer, in Matunga, not far from Khosla Niwas.[6] It was here, in the late 1940s, that Raj

Khosla met Dheer. Having learnt various aspects of filmmaking under his guru V. Shantaram, Dheer was now ready to start making films of his own. He was planning a film called *Raen Basera*, and he offered Raj Khosla a role in it.

Raj Khosla was more interested in singing, but an opportunity to act in a mainstream Hindi film was as irresistible then as it is now. The film also got him the opportunity to sing one of its songs, making it his first break as playback singer and actor.

Courtesy *Raen Basera*, Raj Khosla, unwittingly, also become the model for a personal care product. The *Indian Express* of 11 September 1946 carried an advertisement for Vaseline Pomade, which featured him. Raj had just turned 21 and looked very dapper. Alongside the headline copy ('For well-groomed hair') was a rectangular text box that screamed 'RAJ KHOSLA IN ASHA PICTURE'S "RAEN BASERA".'

There is no trace of *Raen Basera* today, apart from that ad and a still from the film with Raj Khosla wearing a bandana. Even C.L. Dheer's IMDb page doesn't list any film of that name. But the director's son, actor Pankaj Dheer (known for playing Karna in B.R. Chopra's *Mahabharat*), insists that the film was released. 'It was definitely completed and released. Jaswant was the hero and if I'm not mistaken, Balraj Sahni's first wife, Damayanti Sahni, was the heroine,' he told me in a telephonic interview. Jaswant was an actor as well as a partner in C.L. Dheer's production house,[7] and he may have something to do with the fact that *Raen Basera*, Raj Khosla's entry into the world of cinema, is now a lost film. Pankaj Dheer explained:

> Jaswant had married Geeta Bali's elder sister. Geeta Bali and my father were partners in seven films. There used to be a laboratory in Mahalaxmi, and most of the negatives were stored there. Jaswant decided to migrate to Pakistan. The negatives vamoosed from

> here overnight. My father realized much later that he took the negatives with him. By that time, Jaswant had already reached Lahore or Karachi, and we could not get to him there. My father died in 1984. Around 1988 or 1989, there was a knock on my door. I opened the door and there was an old man standing there. He said, 'I am Jaswant… you have played in my lap as a child. Where is my friend Dheer?' I told him that he is no more. He started crying. When I asked him about the negatives, he said they were in Pakistan. I told him, you could have left at least one print. I could have had something of my father.[8]

The film also prominently features in the reminiscences of Sardar Malik, who had just begun his journey as a music director and composed the tunes for the production. In such accounts, it is often mentioned that the film was released in 1947. At any rate, *Raen Basera* didn't do too well, and it didn't serve to propel the career of Raj Khosla either as singer or actor.

But the song he had sung may have opened the doors to more such opportunities. For a period, Raj Khosla worked as a singer at Ranjit Movietone, where he bagged his second playback number: 'Madhur suron mein suno jhamela' from *Bhool Bhulaiyan* (1949). The music director was Bulo C. Rani, and the film was directed by Taimur Behramshah. Raj Khosla's rendition, while mirroring the style of Kundanlal Saigal, is uniquely his own and almost flawless. It has comedic shades and certain parts of the song may remind one of Kishore Kumar's fun-filled ditties. *Bhool Bhulaiyan* has all but disappeared, but the song exists and can be enjoyed on YouTube.

'Madhur suron mein suno jhamela' from *Bhool Bhulaiyan* (1949).

His other surviving song is testament to a relationship that churned some classics and withstood many storms. If Raj, an eventual filmmaker, joined the industry with the desire to become a singer, Madan Mohan, a composer, wanted to be an actor in Hindi films. Madan Mohan would later talk about this: 'I had come to Bombay to join the film industry, not as a music director but as an actor. People producing films did not think of me as capable of acting.'[9] But he did consider it on the cards to be a singer–actor. While playing a minor role in the Dilip Kumar–Kamini Kaushal starrer *Shaheed* (1948), he sang his first duet with Lata Mangeshkar, which never made it to the final cut of the film. Eventually, Devendra Goel's *Ankhen* (1950) gave Madan Mohan his first film as a composer. Three people debuted with the film – Madan Mohan as music director, Devendra Goel as director–producer and Shekhar as hero. The composer employed Raj Khosla as singer and music assistant. This was an early endorsement of Raj Khosla's deep understanding of music. The song he sang was 'Rail mein jiya mora sananana hoy re', which he performed along with a chorus. Written by B.D. Mishra, it's a rather playful and fun romp about various communities travelling by train and their idiosyncrasies. *Ankhen* was the beginning of a friendship that would spawn some memorable songs. In fact, the first couple of songs one thinks of when the name Madan Mohan comes to mind are from Raj Khosla's films.

None of the songs he sung were superhits, but Raj Khosla was barely three films old and he could have continued to make an effort in singing. However, one incident around this time may have turned the tide and embittered him. Raj Khosla later explained in an interview:

> I came into the industry as a singer. I was with A.I.R and trying my luck in playback singing. But Mukesh

> and Mohammed Rafi were in their ascendency, and I couldn't get the better of them. Sardar Chandulal Shah [the owner of Ranjit Movietones] had liked my voice very much, so he called me for an audition. We did the rehearsals but when I went for the recording, I saw Mukesh singing the song. They'd changed their mind at the last minute. I was very upset, but I later realised that Ranjit studios was on the decline and they couldn't afford to experiment with a newcomer.[10]

Bulo C. Rani was the composer, he added in another interview. The song in question may have been 'Unki gali mein aaye hum keh de koi huzoor se', sung by Mukesh, from the album *Nazaare*. Mukesh, incidentally, was another ardent fan of Kundanlal Saigal.

But this rejection was a massive blow to Raj Khosla's ambitions. He went home and wept all night.

3

Learning the Ropes

During their stay in Poona, Dev Anand and Guru Dutt had found kindred souls in each other. Both were deeply enamoured of films and filmmaking. They watched a lot of great cinema together and rode their bicycles through the lanes of Poona, looking for books and magazines on their favourite subject. When they were back in Bombay, they would go shutter-happy with Guru Dutt's camera, Dev often posing as the model. On a particularly jovial occasion, they promised to work with each other once they had realized their dreams. While Dev was clear from the beginning that he wanted to shine in front of the camera, Guru Dutt was by now deeply entranced by the idea of creating whole new worlds on the silver screen. A mildly inebriated Guru Dutt, clinking his beer glass with Dev Anand's, promised him that if he were to turn a director, his dear friend would be his protagonist. In return, Dev gave him his word that Guru Dutt would be the director if he were to ever produce a film.[1]

Close on the heels of *Hum Ek Hain*, Dev worked on another Prabhat film: *Aage Badho* (1947). The company had fallen on hard times. A few years prior, the studio's legendary co-founder V. Shantaram had branched out to start his own venture –

Rajkamal Kalamandir. Baburao Pai, who had his own company called Famous Pictures, offered Dev Anand a lead role in *Mohan* (1947) under that banner. He also tasked his other protégé Guru Dutt to be an assistant director in the film. The friends were once again working together.

After the film, Guru Dutt's three-year contract with Baburao Pai was over. He went around doing odd jobs before being hired as assistant director to Amiya Chakrabarty on *Girls School* (1949). This was followed by a stint with Gyan Mukherjee on *Sangram* (1950). Though Guru Dutt wasn't credited in the film as an assistant director, Gyan Mukherjee did have a profound impact on him, and Dutt's early films were influenced by the veteran's style of filmmaking.

While all this was unfolding, Dev Anand was collaborating with his brother Chetan Anand to lay the foundations of their own production company. Chetan had proved his mettle as a filmmaker with *Neecha Nagar* (1946), which became one of India's first films to be honoured in an international film festival when it was awarded the Grand Prix at the first Cannes Film Festival held in 1946. With an emerging star actor as well as a director in the family, the venture was too good an opportunity to pass up. So, in 1949, the Anand brothers joined forces to establish Navketan Films, a new banner, named after Chetan's newborn, Ketan. Their first outing was *Afsar* (1950), based on Nikolai Gogol's *The Government Inspector*. It didn't perform as per expectations.

Navketan sorely needed a hit, and Dev was reminded of his friend and the deal they had struck. As a culmination of this promise, he now decided to hand over the reins of his next film to his old friend. Guru Dutt was still untested as a director, but his compadre had that thing that is said to move mountains: faith. The new project launched was *Baazi* (1951). While

Dev was the protagonist, the heroine was a newly discovered Kalpana Kartik. Geeta Bali had an interesting 'parallel heroine' role. S.D. Burman was roped in for the music, Sahir Ludhianvi did the lyrics and Balraj Sahni wrote the screenplay.

Around this time, branches of India Coffee House were springing up across the country, and becoming the hub of littérateurs, poets and the intelligentsia. The famous Calcutta Coffee House went on to find patrons like Satyajit Ray and Mrinal Sen, among others. It also became a very popular cultural and political institution in Kerala. But the first India Coffee House to come up was in Bombay's Churchgate, bang opposite Elphinstone College, in the 1930s. By the 1940s, it had gained popularity, and many prospective filmmakers, writers and actors spent their idle hours there, smoking and sipping endless cups of coffee.

It was at this coffee house that Raj bumped into Dev Anand. 'Anyone who wanted to be in films went there,' Raj Khosla said.[2] In his autobiography, Dev describes Raj Khosla as 'my coffee-house friend from the days I was working at the military censor office'. He adds:

> Raj had a deep grainy voice and was a blind admirer of K.L. Saigal's singing. He had also wanted to be a singer originally… Raj would often drop in at my place without notice, ask for a harmonium and sing songs that would delight us both. After having set the pace for a prolonged musical soiree, he would suddenly open the briefcase he always carried to dig out a bottle of scotch hiding amidst his numerous files, and take a swig.[3]

Raj remembered the birth of this friendship a little differently. Dev and he shared family history. According to Raj, their grandfathers were coworkers, and the Khoslas may also have been acquainted with the Anands as Pishorimal Anand, Dev Anand's father, was a renowned lawyer in the Gurdaspur area.[4] One of Dev's brothers, Manmohan Anand, who chose to adopt his father's vocation (after he tried his hand at lyric writing for Chetan Anand's *Neecha Nagar*), was at some point, taking care of the legal affairs of the Khosla–Bhalla clan.

But it is likely that Dev Anand and Raj Khosla got properly acquainted only when they met in Bombay. In an interview given to journalist Nasreen Munni Kabir, Raj Khosla said:

> In those days, I was trying to be a play-back singer. I knew Dev Anand and one day he told me, 'Raj, there's a friend of mine called Guru Dutt.' I remember that sentence, you know, 'a friend of mine called Guru Dutt'. Dev mentioned his name casually-and to imagine that one day that name would be world famous! Dev said to me, 'Guru Dutt is going to direct my next picture. Why don't you become his assistant? Come on, Raj, we'll work together, soon you'll be able to sing too.'[5]

By then, Raj had dabbled in everything. He had acted a bit, and sung for some films as well, but his career hadn't really taken off in the way he wanted it to. Dev Anand was already scaling the heights of stardom. Working with Navketan would mean learning on the job, exposure to the best filmmaking practices and, eventually, like Dev seemed to be indicating, maybe even a serious shot at playback singing. Finally, Raj Khosla agreed to meet Guru Dutt.

It was a momentous occasion, the two men meeting for the first time. Do those who shape history ever know what they are setting in motion? Did Raj Khosla and Guru Dutt know at the time that they would have far-reaching influence on the cinema of the subcontinent? But one would surmise that even without that foreknowledge, Raj was impressed by the sheer presence of Guru Dutt on their first meeting.

He was desperate to bag the job. As he narrated to Nasreen Munni Kabir:

> I met Guru Dutt and he asked me, 'Have you any experience in assisting?' I said, 'Yes, I have.' Tommy-rot, I knew nothing about film-making. The second thing he asked, 'Do you know Hindi?' I replied, 'Of course I know Hindi.' I couldn't actually write in Hindi. I'm from Punjab, Gurdaspur, so I knew Urdu. In those days, in the Punjab learning Urdu was very common; even now you will find that many Punjabis who are over forty know how to write Urdu, not Hindi. Guru Dutt said, 'Okay, start from tomorrow.'[6]

The whole thing about Urdu and Punjab is fascinating. Like Raj Khosla, composer O.P. Nayyar, too, was brought up in Punjab, hence he could read and write Urdu but struggled to read Devanagari/Hindi. The same goes for Dharmendra and Gulzar. The first thing Raj did after that meeting with Guru Dutt was to buy a book on the Hindi alphabet. He started learning the letters from scratch. By the time Guru Dutt put him to the test by asking him to copy out a few dialogue scenes from the script, Raj had already learned a bit. The perceptive Guru Dutt knew that something did not quite fit. Raj explained later:

> By that time I had picked up some Hindi. As I was writing a scene he asked, 'When did you start learning Hindi?'
>
> I said, 'On the day you asked me if I knew the language.'
>
> He said, 'Fine, it doesn't matter. Give this to Kuldeep

> (Guru Dutt's second assistant on *Baazi*), let him write them out.' We liked each other instantaneously.[7]

From that very first film, the learning was tremendous. Raj Khosla was ready for anything that was thrown at him, soaking in everything like a sponge. While shooting the iconic number 'Tadbeer se bigdi huyi taqdeer bana le', Guru Dutt entrusted him with the job of explaining the song to Geeta Bali, who had become a prominent fixture in Guru Dutt's films; the pair had met on the sets of Amiya Chakraborty's *Girls School*, in which Dutt was an assistant director. Geeta had to portray a unique situation in the song, and it was written and composed accordingly. The hero Madan (Dev Anand) is being sucked into the world of gambling. He shows unbeatable luck on the table, as the hustler Pedro (Rashid Khan) eggs him on. Suddenly, Madan sees one of the players hit a poor man mercilessly. Already unsure about this world, Madan decides to walk away. Seeing him go, anti-heroine Leena (Geeta Bali) strums on a guitar and croons:

> *Tadbeer se bigdi huyi taqdeer bana le*
> *Apne pe bharosa hai toh ek daav laga le*
>
> (Through your enterprise, beat destiny
> If you trust yourself, place a bet and see)

Raj Khosla later said in an interview, 'When I began briefing Geeta, she stopped me and said, "Don't explain anything to me. Just sing the song."'[8] The young man rarely needed more encouragement to break into song. He performed the lines in his own inimitable style, and Geeta Bali smiled. She had got it. No other explanation was needed. Raj Khosla was struck by the perceptiveness and clarity in this stunning actress. Eventually, when he was to make his own debut as a director, it is no surprise that he could see only Geeta Bali as the heroine.

Besides Raj Khosla and Guru Dutt, there is one other star who debuted with *Baazi*. By his own admission, Johnny Walker began working as an extra in films around 1948.[9] Balraj Sahni was witness to some of his rambunctious antics and brought him in to meet Guru Dutt. He was given a small but unmissable part in *Baazi*. He was still known by his given name, Badruddin. The name Johnny Walker doesn't appear on film till *Baaz* (1953).

Guru Dutt was probably aware of Raj Khosla's little acting adventure with *Raen Basera*, because he was given a cameo in *Baazi* too – the filmmaker's oldest surviving video footage. He appears as Inspector Ramesh's (Krishan Dhawan) superior, 'Superintendent sahab'. It's a short, rather simple sequence. Ramesh wants to show Madan's case files to the superintendent, because he thinks the hero is innocent. The superintendent examines the file and disagrees. In the scene, Raj Khosla steps in confidently, sits in a chair and coolly lights a cigarette. He whips out his glasses and examines the file. Then, taking off his glasses with finality, he says, 'I don't think so.' These seeming minutiae are important, because they demonstrate Raj's comfort with the physicality of acting and the craft of cinema. Incidentally, *Baazi* also featured a blink-and-miss cameo by Guru Dutt. In the opening scene, when Pedro emerges from his car, we see a man sitting with his back to the camera, only turning for a second or two. This is Guru Dutt. It was his second on-screen appearance after *Hum Ek Hain*. Interestingly, none of these cameos – Raj Khosla's, Johnny Walker's or Guru Dutt's – were credited in the film.

Baazi was a runaway success. Though much has been made about its similarities with Charles Vidor's definitive noir *Gilda* (1946), a closer examination would tell you that the parallels are only skin-deep. Only the first few minutes have similar beats as *Gilda*; eventually, *Baazi* is its own unique tale. Guru Dutt had proved himself as a director. The film was a huge success for Navketan as well. After the disappointment of their first outing, *Afsar*, *Baazi* reinforced their confidence to go on. For Raj Khosla, this was the first time that he was an integral part of an ensemble film that was also a superhit. Accepting Dev Anand's offer to work with Navketan had paid off. He had, in the process, acquired many new friends. Suddenly, he was surrounded by a coterie of like-minded people, who also happened to be incredibly talented.

When Chetan Anand and his wife, Uma, had first moved to Bombay in 1944, they came upon a bungalow in Pali Hill. The neighbourhood in those days was a far cry from the Beverly Hills-esque reputation that it has gained over time, what with many major film stars making it their home. The two were some of the earliest residents of Pali Hill and soon their bungalow became a landmark for a whole generation of artistes who were deeply interested in cinema, theatre and the arts. Many participated in the soirees at 41, Pali Hill, and some even made it their home. Balraj Sahni and his wife, Damayanti Sahni, alias Dammo, stayed there for a while. Among the frequenters of these sessions were Guru Dutt, Mohan Sehgal, Ayub and Nasir Khan (Dilip Kumar's brothers), S.D. Burman, Sahir Ludhianvi, Ali Sardar Jafri, Pandit Ravi Shankar, Manohan Krishna, Madan Puri and Raj Khosla.

Raj fit right in. He had a leaning for high literature in both Urdu and English, and was obsessed with Ghalib and Shakespeare in equal measure. In addition to a great talent for singing, he could quote Urdu couplets and verses off the top of his head. All in all, Raj had developed a charm that would hold him in good stead for the rest of his working life.

Despite the positive changes that *Baazi* brought in his life, Raj Khosla was still at a crossroads. Guru Dutt wanted him to join his team for *Jaal*, a new film he was working on. T.R. Fatehchand of Film Arts was producing it. Film Arts had just made *Buzdil* (1951), directed by Shaheed Latif and written by Ismat Chughtai. The same creative team of Latif and Chughtai were also behind Dev Anand's first big success called *Ziddi* (1948). Now Fatehchand was offering to produce Guru Dutt's next project. Guru Dutt wanted his *Baazi* team back, and that included Raj Khosla. What was he to do? Working on this project would mean bidding adieu to Navketan, which was already showing signs of becoming a film-producing behemoth. Everyone knew the Anands were talented, and nobody seemed to have any doubt that they would make something good of it. Besides, the long-term relation with the Anands had to be considered. Mindful of their shared history, Chetan Anand had already given Raj Khosla the offer to stay back at Navketan.

But Guru Dutt had made a profound impact on Raj Khosla. The young assistant director had turned into a gushing admirer of Guru Dutt, his persona and his filmmaking. Here was a man who was so taken up with his work that nothing else seemed to matter. Almost a saint, Guru Dutt seemed submerged in his own world, hardly ever indulging in gossip or small talk. He was obsessed with cinema and its intricacies. That's all he ever talked about. 'All the time, he was engrossed in trying to make movies of excellence,' Raj Khosla said to Nasreen Munni Kabir in an interview about Guru Dutt. 'So, he would often get lost from all the people he loved and then he would feel lonely. He was lonely, but he was never alone. He was always with his films, or the film that he was making.'[10] Raj had observed him work magic and if there was one person he wanted to continue to work for, it was Guru Dutt. Besides, Guru Dutt and Raj shared an abiding love of literature and music. The choice was clear. For the foreseeable future, Raj Khosla would continue to be an inseparable part of Guru Dutt and his world.

4

The Guru Dutt Years

'He used to come home. He had a car... his parents were well off,' the octogenarian artist Lalitha Lajmi, Guru Dutt's sister, said of Raj Khosla. 'He used to come in his car and pick up my brother for the shoot. He came and waited in the outer room. There was only one table and one chair, on which he used to sit. I used to meet him, bringing water and all that.'[1]

Lalitha was impressed by this eloquent, dapper man who spouted Urdu poetry and sang like a dream. 'He was a brilliant man,' she said.[2] Having grown up with a legend, birthing another (her daughter, Kalpana Lajmi, was an acclaimed filmmaker), and being quite the legend herself (she was a self-taught artist who held exhibitions across the globe), Lalitha Lajmi knew a thing or two about brilliant people.

Guru Dutt and his family were in Matunga at the time. Their flat was near Tejukaya Park, a well-known landmark in Matunga East. It was about a five-minute drive from Khosla Niwas. Raj Khosla would pick his boss up every day and drive him to the studio. During this time, Raj and Lalitha were also joint witnesses to a budding love story.

Twenty-six-year-old Guru Dutt and twenty-one-year-old Geeta Roy had first crossed paths at the rehearsal of a song for *Baazi*. Geeta Roy was in her prime, with audiences eating out of her hands. In the days and weeks that followed, Guru Dutt and Geeta Roy kept encountering each other at parties and gatherings. He was besotted by her ethereal Bengali beauty. Guru Dutt not only spoke fluently in Bengali, he also read its literature and was seeped in Bengali culture and music. He listened to one of her *adhunik gaan* (modern songs, a genre of non-film music popular in Bengal) on loop. Love tiptoed in and the two found that they couldn't have enough of each other.

Hopelessly in love, the pair would often set out on a drive to Powai Lake or Khandala. During these trips, their companions were Raj and Lalitha. Geeta Roy would often sing in unison with Raj. Lalitha reminisced:

> They used to have some tea and pick up some jalebis and bhajiyas on the way. It was like a picnic. Allowing these two (Guru and Geeta) to be by themselves, I spent time with Raj. He used to recite poems and talk literature all the time. He used to bring books and sometimes lend them to Guru as well. Also, Raj could sing, so when we were in the car together, sometimes he and Geeta would sing film songs. It was a lot of fun.[3]

Raj Khosla seemed to have found his tribe. He was happy with the decision to stick with Guru Dutt. He could see his future with this man. When Guru Dutt and Geeta Roy got married on 26 May 1953, Raj was overjoyed. Leading playback singers of the time were present at the wedding reception and as Yasser Usman mentions in his Guru Dutt biography, Raj Khosla convinced them to sing one song each from a Guru Dutt film.[4]

By now, *Jaal* (1952) – Guru Dutt's second outing as a director – had been released. Guru Dutt and Dev Anand were constantly exploring good films from across the world. One evening, they had happened to watch Italian filmmaker Giuseppe De Santis's neorealist classic *Riso Amaro*, aka *Bitter Rice* (1949), at the Excelsior cinema hall in Fort. It impacted both greatly. Guru Dutt wanted to make a film on it and Dev agreed to participate. The latter was enamoured of the grey character portrayed by the leading man, Vittorio Gassman. The film is about two small-time thieves Walter (Gassman) and Francesca (Doris Dowling) on the run. There, they hide among a group of rice farmers, who, despite living in penury, lead honourable lives. They run into the pretty Silvana (Silvana Mangano), who takes Francesca under her wings and teaches her their way of life. Silvana falls head over heels in love with Walter, which puts the rest of the story in motion.

Now, Guru Dutt picked up the seeds of this plot and based his new script on it, and *Jaal* was born. Instead of Italian rice farmers, he set the story among Goan fisherfolk and the movie was shot in the Malvan area of Maharashtra. Dev Anand and Purnima played the thieves Tony and Lisa respectively, while Geeta Bali portrayed the feisty Maria, a villager who shelters Lisa and eventually falls in love with Tony. In the original, unbeknownst to the peasant girl Silvana, Francesca is hiding stolen goods – a necklace. In Dutt's adaptation, the necklace became gold bars. Some characters were removed, while others were added, such as Carlos, Maria's blind brother, played by K.N. Singh. Unlike *Bitter Rice*, *Jaal* has a noirish tone and introduces religious elements in the plot. The ending was suitably changed to allow Dev's character to turn over a new leaf.

In his autobiography, Dev narrates elaborate tales of shooting the film, including one episode in which he got drunk on feni, the popular Goan drink, and almost drowned himself and Geeta Bali in the sea.[5] In another incident, while driving back from Malvan, Dev, Geeta Bali and his sister met with an accident. The actor almost broke his ribs, and spent a few days in the hospital, recuperating. His injury became such big news in Bombay that Frank Capra, the Hollywood legend known for his films like *It Happened One Night* (1934) and *Mr. Smith Goes to Washington* (1939), sent Dev a telegram wishing him a speedy recovery.

Jaal was the second film in which Raj Khosla was an assistant director to Guru Dutt. But the former's involvement with the film did not stop there. *Jaal* begins with a couplet by Mirza Ghalib appearing on the screen. There are two versions of the film available online: in one of them, Ghalib's lines are recited, courtesy a voice-over. In the other, the lines appear without narration. The quote is from a ghazal entitled 'Ibn-e-Mariam hua kare koi', and goes:

> *Na suno gar bura kahe koi*
> *Na kaho gar bura kahe koi*
> *Rok lo gar ghalat chale koi*
> *Baksh do gar khata kare koi*
>
> (Do not listen to words spoken in malice
> Do not respond to words spoken in spite
> Show the wayward the correct path
> Forgive those who transgress against you
> – translation by Mustansir Dalvi)[6]

This is followed by the narrator setting the context, declaring that the good and evil characters depicted in the film are not real, and can be found in any community or nation – a clarification ostensibly needed because all the characters in the film are Christians. The voice goes on to introduce the setting of the story, a colony of traders and fishermen on the western coast of India. No one is credited for the voiceover, and it has never been spoken or written of by film commentators or historians. None from the cast or crew is around to verify this, but the timbre and diction distinctly matches Raj Khosla's voice. His command over Hindi and Urdu may have been the reason behind the decision to assign him the job.

Raj also appeared in the film as one of two Arab traders who want to buy the contraband gold that Tony and Lisa have smuggled in – this time, his role was credited. Guru Dutt himself made an appearance as a fisherman in the song 'Zor laga ke haiya', his second uncredited appearance in his own films after *Baazi*.

Songs weren't just interludes for Guru Dutt, but contained stories of their own. Unlike most cinema of the time, songs in his films not only pushed the story forward, they also had narratives of their own. This was something that Raj Khosla picked up and artfully employed in his own films. Even in those early days, being in the shadow of a genius helped the young assistant director sharpen his own tools as a potential filmmaker.

All this while, the desire to sing hadn't left Raj. His journey in films, after all, began as a singer. Even when Dev brought Raj to Guru Dutt, he had hinted that being an assistant director could pave the way to Raj becoming a playback singer in one of the films he was working in. Guru Dutt knew this, and he offered Raj a shot at singing one of S.D. Burman's songs in *Jaal* – 'Yeh raat yeh chandni phir kahan'.[7] The song was one of the highlights of the album, and everyone seemed to have an opinion on who should sing it. While Guru Dutt wanted Raj, lyricist Sahir Ludhianvi voted for either Talat Mahmood or Mohammed Rafi. S.D. Burman himself was insistent on a new singer called Hemanta Mukhopadhyay, who later came to be known as Hemant Kumar.[8]

It is believed that a version of the song was recorded in Raj Khosla's voice, but the music director wasn't convinced. In an interview to Nasreen Munni Kabir, Raj said, 'He [Guru Dutt] wanted me to sing for *Jaal*, the song 'Ye raat ye chandni'; he even recorded me but I failed the test. S.D. Burman said, "Guru, not now. He's too raw, he can't make it." Guru Dutt was very upset as he had wanted me to sing that song.'[9] Ultimately, Hemant Kumar lent his voice to two versions of the song – one was a duet, the other a solo rendition.

This might very well have been the proverbial last nail for Raj's singing ambitions. But the desire to sing remained a part of his being till the end of his days. He would sing a cover version of Mukesh's song 'Toote na dil toote na' from Mehboob Khan's *Andaz* (1949)[10] – it was published later as part of an LP from a label called Young India, which was owned by V. Shantaram. Raj even surreptitiously included his songs in two of his iconic films, covered in later parts of this book.

When *Jaal* released, it didn't sweep the box office the way *Baazi* did, though Guru Dutt was showered with praise for his direction and the songs were a rage. One of the outcomes of the film was that Guru Dutt decided not to work with Dev Anand for his subsequent films. Yasser Usman writes in *Guru Dutt: An Unfinished Story*, 'According to Raj Khosla, Dev was steeped in his mannerisms while Guru Dutt wanted his performances to be more realistic.'[11] Dev Anand, the star, was on the rise and not even an old friend could make him behave otherwise. This would frustrate Guru Dutt – he wanted his actors to align to his vision of a more sensible, restrained cinema. His only choice seemed to be to don the greasepaint himself to show the world what he had in mind.

As he thought of plunging into producing his own films, Guru Dutt partnered with Geeta Bali's sister Hardarshan Kaur to form a new production house named H.G. Films, borrowing the initials of their names. The first production of this new company was to be *Baaz* (1953), an adventure on the high seas. This was a major departure from the theme of Guru Dutt's first two films, which were both noirish thrillers. And with this film, Guru Dutt also debuted as a leading man.

The film is set in the Portuguese-ruled Malabar of the sixteenth century. Geeta Bali is Nisha, whose father is imprisoned because he harbours a fugitive, a rebel against the oppressive Portuguese regime. When her father is tortured and killed, Nisha inspires a group of prisoners on a merchant ship to revolt and take over the vessel. They become pirates, with Nisha as their leader, looting Portuguese ships. During her adventures, she comes across a young man who joins their fight and who, unbeknownst to them, is the crown prince Ravi (Guru Dutt). Ravi and Nisha, very much in love, fight shoulder to shoulder and bring down the evil Portuguese general Barbarossa (K.N. Singh).

Baaz turned out to be Guru Dutt's first great fall. There is no evidence to suggest he cut corners in making it. Every ounce of the passion and zeal that went into *Baazi* and *Jaal* was present here, too. Yet, even the music didn't do as well. Instead of S.D. Burman, the music for *Baaz* was composed by Omkar Prasad, or O.P. Nayyar. He had just debuted as a composer with Dalsukh Pancholi's *Aasmaan* (1952) and it was Geeta Dutt, one of the singers in the film, who introduced him to Guru Dutt.

If one were to look for something to pin the blame of *Baaz*'s failure on, it would be the writing and the choice of Guru Dutt as the male lead. Writing was one of the things that Guru Dutt was burdened with while making *Baaz*. The dialogues were archaic and overly theatrical, and not suited for the screen at all. The story was a product of Guru's imagination, but it didn't have the narrative complexity that was a hallmark of his cinema. Also, both in terms of subject matter and the fact that he had to act as a swashbuckling hero, Guru Dutt was utterly out of his depth.

Acting was never one of the filmmaker's core strengths. Later on, in *Pyaasa* (1957), *Kaagaz Ke Phool* (1959) or even *Sahib Bibi aur Ghulam* (1962), what really worked for Guru Dutt were the pathos and melancholia wrought on his face, which, in retrospect, could have been drawn from what he was going through in his own life. Guru Dutt seemed to be on an eternal quest, constantly seeking something that even those closest to him couldn't quite fathom. Raj Khosla had seen Guru Dutt from close quarters during his brightest and darkest days. He had seen his Guru's life unravelling – the pining, the obsession, the alcoholism. And yet, one of his regrets was that he was unable to truly understand the man who was, literally and figuratively, his 'Guru'. 'I couldn't touch the core of his heart,' Raj kept saying.[12] Some of Guru Dutt's preoccupation found expression in his later films, because in real life, Guru Dutt wasn't the one to talk. In a strange sort of way, this had echoes in Raj Khosla's own life and career later.

Baaz was the penultimate film in which Raj Khosla was an assistant director to Guru Dutt. Unlike the first two films, he didn't appear on screen in *Baaz*, though during the filming, Raj was called upon to put his horse riding skills to use. In one of the long shots, he doubles for Geeta Bali astride a horse.

The film was a disappointment, but it was time to shake off the dust and move on. Even in an environment where films took months and often years to make, Guru Dutt was able to maintain an average of one film a year. He had already started work on what was the maiden film of Guru Dutt Productions, *Aar Paar* (1954). Nabendu Ghosh was writing the screenplay. He had just worked on *Parineeta* (1953) and *Biraj Bahu* (1954), and this was the first time he was breaking away from Bimal Roy's films to work as a writer.

Abrar Alvi was officially hired as the dialogue writer on *Aar Paar*. Jaswant, one of the principal actors in *Baaz*, had helped Abrar find work as an assistant to filmmaker C.L. Dheer in the film *Bahu Beti* (1952). To repay the debt he owed his cousin, Alvi would drive Jaswant to the sets of *Baaz* and back. It was on these sets that the former ran into Raj. In his reminiscences, Abrar Alvi often veers back to his run-ins with Raj.[13] Both men of letters and connoisseurs of art, they got along from the get-go. On occasion, Raj Khosla also sought advice from him for certain scenes in the film.[14] Alvi's inputs impressed Guru Dutt enough to subsequently hire him as a writer for *Aar Paar*. Despite being friends, Raj Khosla and Abrar Alvi would often lock horns on various creative aspects. According to the latter, about a third of *Aar Paar* had been shot when Raj Khosla was offered his first film as director.[15] And so it began.

5

Debut – *Milap*

In barely two years of starting work with Guru Dutt, Raj Khosla had become a significant member of his team. He was not only the chief assistant, but also acting in the films, lending his voice and being considered as a playback singer. His increasing importance was also an indication of his being a fast learner. Evidently, he made an impression and *Jaal*'s producer T.R. Fatehchand offered the young man an opportunity to direct a film. Twenty years later, Raj spoke rather matter-of-factly about this momentous break: 'Producers used to watch me assisting. I was sleeping on the terrace of my house, when a producer's [T.R. Fatehchand] son came over with an offer. The film was *Milap*.'[1]

To hand over the reins of direction for a big-ticket film featuring Dev Anand and Geeta Bali, the reigning stars of the time, to a rank newcomer like Raj Khosla couldn't have been solely based on his association with another talented filmmaker; Guru Dutt also had other talented assistants in his crew. T.R. Fatehchand's choice reflected his confidence in Raj as a prospective film director. So far, he had only hired young directors who had already proved themselves. *Buzdil*, the earliest-known film made under the producer's Film Arts banner, was helmed by Shaheed Latif who had proved his mettle with big hits like *Ziddi* and *Arzoo* (1950). For his second production venture, Fatehchand chose Guru Dutt, whose *Baazi* had already created a sensation. This was the first time that he was backing a debutante director. It is safe to assume that he had seen something in this 'assistant' that inspired in him the confidence to back him.

But before we get into that, a significant step in Raj Khosla's personal life needs to be recorded here. Just one day before the shooting of *Milap* (1955) began, Raj was married off. It was Saraswati Khosla, Raj's mother, who suggested the match. The prospective bride was the daughter of a friend of hers from Jalandhar. In a sharp contrast to Raj Khosla's liberal, unfettered upbringing, Usha Chopra was raised in a conservative environment. She was educated at home, and more of an introvert as opposed to Raj's flamboyant, boisterous persona. By now, Raj Khosla was in his early thirties and was increasingly found among the most desirable men and women in the country. Parents Atmaram and Saraswati may have feared that their son would fall into dubious company and acquire the 'bad habits' that could give them sleepless nights. So, Raj was married to Usha Chopra on 7 March 1954, and the couple started living with the rest of the family at Matunga's Khosla Niwas. The very next day, the shoot for *Milap* started.

Milap was also Raj's debut as a writer. The story and scenario of the film were written by him. Like his mentor, Raj Khosla was an avid movie buff and often sought refuge in the classics of world cinema. Besides Alfred Hitchcock, the other international filmmaker who had influenced him was Italian–American filmmaker Frank Capra. He based the plot of *Milap* on Frank Capra's classic romance *Mr. Deeds Goes to Town* (1936). *Milap* was the second Indian remake of the Hollywood classic, after *Nallathambi* (1949), which was in Tamil. It was later remade in Bengali as *Raja Shaja* (1960) and in Telugu as *Dagudu Moothalu* (1964). Nabendu Ghosh wrote the screenplay of *Milap*, basing it on Raj Khosla's story and scenario.

Many years later, Raj would tell his protégé Mahesh Bhatt about his deep admiration for Capra. As per Mahesh Bhatt, Frank Capra was Raj's idol. 'He,' Mahesh told me, 'used to say to me, "I learnt my craft from Frank Capra." Capra was all for the man who wins the world by remaining good, not the man who becomes bad and takes on the world. It was always about the triumph of the middle class.' In his autobiography, *The Name Above the Title*, Capra wrote, 'How powerful is the quality of honesty! Honest men, of any color or tongue, are trusted and loved… Such a man was Longfellow Deeds of Mandrake Falls.'[2] And this is the aspect that Raj also explored in *Milap*. The stand-in for Deeds was the country bumpkin Rajendra Sial (Dev Anand), who was honest to a fault.

This role was in complete contrast to Dev's carefully crafted on-screen image in the 1950s. He was always the street-smart city slicker, forced into a life of crime, only to eventually find redemption in the arms of a lover and turn over a new leaf. If Raj Kapoor excelled at playing the naive, morally upright simpleton who could do no wrong and Dilip Kumar's characters were mired in tragedy and self-pity, Dev Anand's roles were on the other extreme end of the spectrum. He was not the goody two shoes. But for *Milap*, the actor made an exception.

The village-bred Rajendra Sial lands a windfall inheritance when the wealthy Rai Bahadur leaves all his money to him. Rajendra and his friend Kalu (Johnny Walker) struggle to match the pace of city life. Greedy relatives and other opportunists circle them like vultures, waiting for a chance to pounce. The family lawyer Karamchand (K.N. Singh) also has his eyes on the riches. He plants the gorgeous Asha (Geeta Bali) as Rajendra's secretary, meaning to use her charms as a weapon to drain him of his newly acquired wealth. But what neither Karamchand nor Asha account for is love. Rajendra and Asha fall for each other, and she no longer has it in her to dupe him or take him for a ride. She rebels, which causes Karamchand to tell Rajendra that she has been fooling him all along. The betrayal hits hard and our hero spirals, deciding to squander his riches. He first tries to gamble them away and when that seems to be failing, he decides to give away all his money to the poor and the destitute. Karamchand, desperate to salvage the estate, conspires with Rai Bahadur's greedy relatives to prove to the authorities that Rajendra is losing his mind.

Dev Anand pulls off the role with aplomb, and manages to keep his charm intact, even without the urbane suave that's normally associated with him. But Geeta Bali is a live wire in the film, infusing every scene and song with her signature magnetism and allure. Her glamour doesn't take away from the incredible command over her craft. Raj Khosla's appreciation of her talent was clear:

> ... when I was directing her in *Milap*, where again she was a gangster's moll, who sets out to decoy a rustic simpleton (played by Dev Anand) but falls in love with him in the process, she had delineated the character to perfection with minimum briefing. Once when we were chatting, she told me, 'You are a carbon copy of your guru.' My guru was Guru Dutt, under whom I had worked for long. But Geeta was nobody's carbon copy. She was an inimitable original.[3]

Evidently, Geeta Bali and Raj Khosla had formed a mutual admiration society where he appreciated her craft and she could see the makings of a great director in him, just like his Guru. It was, of course, not easy to shake off the shadow of his mentor. Nasreen Munni Kabir writes, '[Raj Khosla] was more accustomed to working as Guru Dutt's assistant than as a director in his own right. On the first day of *Milap*'s shooting on 8 March 1954, when Murthy told him that the shot was ready, Khosla out of force of habit said, "Guru Dutt ko bulao" (Call Guru Dutt).'[4] *Milap*, in fact, featured Guru Dutt's regular cast and crew. Over the years, the filmmaker had assembled a coterie of artists and technicians he preferred to work with. Almost all of them were part of *Milap*. Headlined by Dev Anand and Geeta Bali, the cast featured other Guru Dutt regulars like Johnny Walker, K.N. Singh and Krishan Dhawan.

Despite Guru Dutt's influence on him, Raj brought in some new collaborators for this first directorial venture. The dialogues of the film were written by Rajinder Singh Bedi, a member of the Progressive Writers' Movement who worked with Raj Khosla again in *Bombai ka Babu* (1960).

Milap was also N. Datta's first Hindi film as an independent music director, although he had earlier composed the music for a Punjabi film called *Balo* (1951). Producer T.R. Fatehchand was impressed by the way Dattaram Naik, aka N. Datta, who was S.D. Burman's assistant in *Jaal*, contributed to the Goan beats of *Milap* (Naik was born in Goa). The movie ended up having some remarkable songs. The most popular is 'Yeh baharon ka sama'. The song has two versions, one sung by Lata Mangeshkar and the other by Hemant Kumar, which was in the album but not the film. It is said that Raj later regretted not including the song. Ostensibly to compensate for that mistake, the director later featured the most iconic Hemant Kumar–Dev Anand song in *Solva Saal* (1958): 'Hai apna dil toh awara'.

While not as popular as 'Yeh baharon ka sama', the other songs in *Milap* are impressive. Geeta Dutt lent her voice to four of the film's eight songs, out of which 'Jate ho to jao par jaoge kahan' is a real earworm. Sahir Ludhianvi's perky lyrics in 'Jate ho to jao par jaoge kahan' could work very well even in one of today's films. 'Humse bhi kar lo' also carries the signature Geeta Dutt playfulness. Asha Bhosle's 'Piya khulke na nain milaye re' is another song that leaves an impression. Interestingly, Asha Bhosle holds the distinction of singing both for Raj Khosla's directorial debut *Milap* and his swansong *Naqāb* (1989). Lata Mangeshkar, another Raj Khosla collaborator – some of their songs would go down in history – sang a song for the film too: the lilting *mujra* 'Dard ka saaz bhi hai dil ki awaz bhi hai'.

The soundtrack of *Milap* (1955).

While *Milap* is not often named in the same breath as some of Raj's other work, it does exhibit some of the quintessential attributes that his films came to be known for.

Great music, check. N. Datta's compositions were fresh, unique and quite hummable.

Fantastic song picturizations, check. Volumes could be written on how Raj imbibed the art of shooting songs from Guru Dutt and made it his own. Historically, songs have been an excuse for the audience to step out, have a smoke or take a breather. But Raj Khosla made an attempt to keep the viewer glued to the seat. Every song in *Milap* tells a story with a beginning, middle and end. From his very first film to his very last, he ensured that his heroines looked like a million dollars. Every frame complimented them, every song accentuated their mystique.

Strong female character, check. Geeta Bali is a formidable presence in the film. Her character is hardly a doormat. She is strong-willed and independent. For a while, she is forced to do the villain's bidding, but hits right back when she is pushed around. In a vast majority of mainstream Indian cinema, heroines exist in the film just to make the hero look cool and virtuous. Here, Asha is her own person – though she loves the hero, she refuses to let that love define her. And if we haven't said it enough, Geeta Bali is magnificent.

Nail-biting suspense, check. Raj Khosla has often been dubbed the Alfred Hitchcock of India. He did have a penchant for suspense à la Hitchcock, but closer examination would reveal that he may have been a nose ahead in one aspect. Just a nose. When you watch a Hitchcock film, despite the suspense, you know what you are in for. The stalwart made a lifetime of films, by and large in one genre. And like clockwork, he delivered every time. But with Raj Khosla, it is a little different – he traversed diverse genres and did everything from noirs to dacoit 'westerns', love stories, family dramas and mystery thrillers to action movies. But he managed to dissolve an element of suspense in all those different and diverse genres. Even within the microcosm of Hindi movies where you can predict the outcome almost every time, he infused suspense in a way that kept the audience on tenterhooks. *Milap* is not primarily a thriller. It is more of a social drama with a commentary on greed and avarice and how money can make you do terrible things. But there are certain moments – like during the song 'Jate ho jao par jaoge kahan', when Asha tries to distract Rajendra while Karamchand's minion is in his room stealing cash from the *tijori* – when everyone knows what is likely to happen, yet the suspense is all too real.

Some of the trademark humour was there too. Curiously, Raj Khosla – or rather, his voice – appears in the film as a radio announcer. When Rosy (Indira Billi) is flipping through a magazine, the radio booms in the background, with Raj saying in his impeccable diction, '*Iss samay raat ke 10 baje hain, ab aap hamaara Hindi drama* Khooni Aashiq *suniye*.' Hilarity ensues as Johnny Walker, aka Kalu, walks in and assumes that the sounds of gunfire emanating from the radio are all too real and he is being shot at.

Alongside everything else, *Milap* also features an abiding obsession of Raj Khosla – horses. There is a racecourse Asha takes Rajendra to, and later, when he is determined to squander all his money, he heads over there to gamble and lose. The exact opposite happens. He bets on the losing horse and wins. Raj loved horses and going to the races. He once narrated how Sahir Ludhianvi caught him leafing through a racing book.[5] 'Is this filmmaking? This is what you are studying?' the poet admonished him. Raj thought it might be a good idea to take him to the racecourse one day. 'So, I took him to the races. He put 10 rupees on a horse, it gave him about 250 rupees. He was so happy, he said, "Raj, this is excellent."' The very next day, Sahir Ludhianvi scolded him again, for taking him to the races!

Milap is also important because from his very first film, Raj had begun assembling his team of collaborators. Akin to his mentor who often nurtured future filmmakers who branched out to have long, successful careers, Raj himself took many aspirants under his wings. One of them was Bhappi Sonie, who went on to direct iconic Shammi Kapoor blockbusters like *Janwar* (1965) and *Brahmachari* (1968). Sonie debuted as an assistant director on *Milap* and continued to assist Raj in two more films. The other assistant was B. Padmanabham, who worked with Raj Khosla for the next 14 years, and then made the Dharmendra–Tanuja starrer *Do Chor* (1972), with Raj Khosla as producer. Pramod Chakravorty, Geeta Dutt's brother-in-law, was also one of the assistants in *Milap*, and he continued to assist Raj Khosla in *C.I.D.* (1956), before debuting as a director, with Guru Dutt as the hero, in *12 o'clock* (1958).

Pramod Chakravorty would later launch a new star called Akshay Kumar with *Deedar* (1992).

An actor who debuted with *Milap* was Jagdish Raj, arguably one of the most identifiable faces in all of Hindi cinema who built a name for himself as an on-screen policeman. In this film, he played one of the greedy relatives who tries to take all of Rajendra's money for himself.

Milap, which was released on 4 February 1955, did not work at the box office. In retrospect, this is disappointing because the film is an immensely entertaining romp with some great performances and lilting music, and the emergence of a new voice on the scene. It is difficult to pinpoint a reason, but it could be that the audience couldn't accept Dev Anand as a docile simpleton. Despite the commercial failure, *Milap* did garner some good reviews. *Filmfare* was all praises for the directorial chops of the debutant filmmaker:

> Though this is his initial essay on the screen, Raj Khosla, the young and enterprising director, has not betrayed any unfamiliarity with the megaphone anywhere in the film. On the contrary, his deft directorial touches in it could do credit to a veteran.[6]

In the meantime, Guru Dutt's *Aar Paar* had been released and was a massive hit. The songs were on everyone's lips and Guru Dutt seemed way more confident as an actor now. Having fiddled a little with the director's chair, Raj Khosla was back to his mentor, hoping to get back to assisting him. Little did he know his Guru had other plans for him.

6

On the Rise – *C.I.D.*

Much before he made it as a film director, there was a period right after his stint at Prabhat Films, when Guru Dutt was looking for work in Bombay. Every day, he would make the rounds of production houses, often facing rejection. So far, both at Uday Shankar's dance school and then at Prabhat, Guru Dutt had found a creatively stimulating atmosphere, and he had taken to it like a fish takes to water. But now, the struggle he was going through and the constant rejections weighed heavy on his mind. While waiting at the offices of Pramukh Pictures, one of the production houses he visited often, Dutt wrote a story about the struggles of an artist and how the world tries to put him down. He called it *Kashmakash*, and promised himself that he would make a film on it. This is the story that eventually morphed into *Pyaasa* (1957).

Around the mid-1950s, after having made several successful films, Guru Dutt was finally toying with the idea of *Pyaasa*. But it was an intense film. So far, the projects he had worked on were either films noir or romances, which were seen as commercially viable subjects. This would be an inward-looking film, which wouldn't necessarily have the trappings of conventional mainstream Hindi cinema. While he mulled over it, he was conscious that he would have to get another film with better box-office prospects on the floor. Dutt already had a subject in mind. Submerged in *Pyaasa*, he needed someone else to direct the other commercially feasible film. It had to be a noir, and he knew his protégé Raj Khosla had learned the ropes of making a good thriller.

But there was also another reason to offer *C.I.D.* (1956) to Raj. 'He had a contract with somebody,' Raj told Nasreen Munni Kabir in an interview. 'Some very skilful manipulator had bogged him down to three films. The only escape from the contract was if somebody else directed it for him. So he told me, "Raj make a film for me." I said, "Fine." He told me about this plot. "This title will be a hit," he said, 'title is enough, Raj. *C.I.D.* is enough."'[1]

But there was somebody else waiting in the wings. Guru Dutt's brother Atmaram had been assisting him since *Jaal*, and had remained by his side when Raj went away on his own adventure. Atmaram felt that if there was anyone else who deserved to direct the next Guru Dutt production, it was him. Lalitha Lajmi said of him, 'We always felt that Atma never had that talent in him to make a Hindi film. I don't know what it is… some people have it, others don't. He was very good at documentary filmmaking – he won many international awards for them. But Guru Dutt felt he was not capable of making a commercial Hindi film. This was discussed many times at home between Guru and my mother.'[2] But Atmaram was not pleased that his brother chose someone else over him. In a huff, he left Bombay and went away to make documentary films for Burmah Shell in London. To be fair to him, after a few years of making acclaimed documentary films in the UK, Atmaram did come back and made several Hindi commercial movies like *Shikar* (1968), *Ye Gulistan Hamara* (1973) and *Aarop* (1974).

Raj later said that his Guru offering him a film was one of the most thrilling moments of his life.[3] He had already directed a film, but his mentor bestowing his faith on him was all the validation he needed. Yet, for someone who craved validation from his mentor, Raj Khosla could also be quite headstrong and unyielding in certain matters. One of the centrepieces of any discussion on *C.I.D.* is the face-off between Guru Dutt's team – primarily Raj Khosla – and a new actress called Waheeda Rehman. Dutt had been at a distributor's office in Hyderabad when there was a commotion outside. To his amusement, he saw some fans chasing a new girl who had just shot a dance sequence in a new Telugu film. The film was *Rojulu Marayi* (1955), and the girl had danced to a song called 'Eruvaaka sagaroranno chinnanna' (this song had a special significance in a future Raj Khosla film). Guru Dutt's interest was piqued when he learned that she was fluent in Urdu. He arranged a meeting with her and her mother. They spoke for about half an hour and went their respective ways. Waheeda Rehman narrated the following events to me in an interview:

> There was no news for around three or four months. At the time I was living in Chennai [then Madras]. One day, a man called Mannu Bhai Patel came to meet us. He rang the bell and then said that he was from Bombay. We were wondering who would have come from Bombay. He explained that he was there on behalf of Guru Dutt. It took us some time to process. We had heard of Dilip Kumar, Dev Anand or Mehboob Khan. Who was this Guru Dutt? Then he reminded us of the Hyderabad meeting and said that Guru Dutt wanted me in Bombay. We told him we'll think about it and let him know.

For the next two days, while Mannu Bhai Patel waited in Madras, Waheeda and her mother consulted friends and elders of the family. Theirs was a conservative south Indian family, so it wasn't easy to say 'yes' to a summons all the way from Bombay, that too from a film director. Finally, Waheeda Rehman reached Bombay and met Guru Dutt at his office in Famous Studios. Sitting with him was Raj Khosla. 'We spoke for some time, and then they took some of my still photographs. Then they said, we'll do a three-year contract with you, and you will be on a monthly salary. But Raj Khosla added, "*Magar aap ka naam bahut lamba hai*, change *karna padega*. You have a long name, we must change it for the screen."'

Today, if one were to think about the incident with Waheeda in detail, one would see that it was the meeting of two headstrong, proud people who didn't see eye to eye on certain aspects. Raj Khosla was a no-nonsense man trained in the ways of the film industry. It was the norm for most heroines to take on more 'acceptable' names, which is why Kokila Kishorechandra Balsara became Nirupa Roy, Harkirtan Kaur was Geeta Bali and Mumtaz Jahan Dehlvi was Madhubala. Waheeda Rehman, however, didn't want to change her name at any cost. She was all of 17 but didn't mince her words. She was clear about what she wanted and what she didn't want. 'Why should I change the name my parents have given me?' she protested. She was still a minor, so her mother was accompanying her. They took a day to think about it but didn't change their stand. Waheeda also wanted to add a clause about costumes. If the clothes were not to her liking, she reserved the right to refuse to wear them. Raj Khosla was furious – in his world, newcomers didn't throw their weight around. This girl was just getting started! If she was throwing such tantrums already, who would want to cast her? But his mentor could see a spark in her that Raj couldn't. Guru Dutt agreed to all her demands.

Waheeda got an 'introducing' credit in the film but *C.I.D.* also saw a whole bunch of other debuts. On the recommendation of Johnny Walker, Guru Dutt had signed up Mehmood to play his unholy brother in *Pyaasa*. Since *C.I.D.* was being filmed at the same time, Mehmood played a part in it too – that of a goon who kills a journalist in cold blood, and eventually shares his fate. It was one of his earliest major roles. *C.I.D.* was also costume designer Bhanu Athaiya's first film. She would, of course, go on to win an Oscar for her work in Richard Attenborough's *Gandhi* (1982). Here, she was credited as Bhanumati.

C.I.D. is also the first-known instance where Jagdish Raj donned a police uniform. For the next four decades, the man portrayed countless police officers and commissioners. Popular association of him with the role is evident – multiple sources on the internet (including many news websites) mention a Guinness World Record title in his name for the 'most typecast actor',[4] probably inaccurate because a search on the Guinness website didn't throw up anything.

Meanwhile, the same band of assistant directors that Raj had put together for *Milap* worked with him again: Pramod Chakravorty, Padmanabham and Bhappi Sonie. O.P. Nayyar, who began his journey with Guru Dutt from *Baaz*, and went on to deliver consistent hits with *Aar Paar* and *Mr. & Mrs. 55* (1955), was chosen as the music director. As far as Raj was concerned, he was quite fond of the song 'Preetam aan milo', a non-film composition by O.P. Nayyar, one of his earliest jobs. It was performed by C.H. Atma, for whom it was a career-defining number. The song was immensely popular, and 10 years later, when Nayyar was working on *Mr. & Mrs. 55*, he used the same track for the film. This time it was sung by Geeta Dutt, a self-proclaimed admirer of C.H. Atma. Whether it was the original version of the song that Raj heard on the radio way back in 1945, when it was first aired, or the second one, it was this song that Raj stated as the reason for taking on O.P. Nayyar as the music director for *C.I.D.*[5]

When the film went on the floor, Raj Khosla was confident and self-assured, miles away from the unsure man who directed *Milap*, constantly looking for the approving eyes of his mentor. This time, it was different. Raj spoke about the first day of shooting *C.I.D.* with Nasreen Munni Kabir:

> When we started the movie, he [Guru Dutt] was doing *Pyaasa* simultaneously, and I called him on the first shooting day of *C.I.D.* He came and looked at the shot, but he stuck on for a little longer than I thought he should. It was courtesy on my part and on his part it was affection. So, after he went away, I called the general manager, I told him, 'I don't want him on my sets again.' So Guru Dutt said: 'But Raj, you got upset? For what? You called me, I didn't want to come. I'll come on the last day… when you say it's the last shooting day, I'll come.' That's what he did… He never interfered in my work.[6]

With *C.I.D.*, Raj Khosla nailed the true-blue thriller that he eventually came to be known for. The film begins with the shot of a rotary telephone being dialled. What follows is a mini montage of conversations where it is instructed that a man be told to shut the hell up, or else… The instructions are passed on to the sombre and menacing Sher Singh (Mehmood). This is followed by a collage of conversations between some shady ne'er-do-wells. Inspector Shekhar (Dev Anand) from the Criminal Investigation Department (CID) gets a call from editor Srivastav of *Bombay Times*, saying that he has been receiving threatening calls from someone. Shekhar lands up at the *Bombay Times* office, but the editor is cold as ice by the time he does. Shekhar chases the killer for a while but partly due to the shenanigans of the dainty Rekha (Shakila), Sher Singh gets away. Unbeknownst to him, there is a witness to the murder: a petty thief/pickpocket called Master (Johnny Walker). The cops are on the verge of pinning the murder on him, when Shekhar tracks down Sher Singh and puts him behind bars. Despite his best attempts to make him sing, he is unable to extract anything from the culprit. Shekhar starts dating Rekha, who he finds, to his utter amusement, is the daughter of his boss, the police super (K.N. Singh). Meanwhile, Shekhar meets a mysterious woman Kamini (Waheeda Rehman) who wants him to release her *mitthu* (parrot), an obvious dig at Sher Singh. There are some gasp-out-loud moments; for example, when Shekhar discovers that the mystery woman, Kamini, is a friend of Rekha's. In a development straight out of a 'Breaking News' ticker on a news channel, Sher Singh dies in captivity and Shekhar is accused of extrajudicial killing. Deciding that the only way to clear his name is to avoid prison, he becomes a fugitive. The rest of the film is about how Shekhar proves his innocence and nabs the sinister people behind Sher Singh's dastardly act.

One of the many well-remembered aspects of *C.I.D.* is the song called 'Leke pehla pehla pyaar'. Raj Khosla reminisced about the shooting of the number:

> Dev Anand told me 'Raj, what am I doing in this song?' I said, 'The song is doing everything, you just walk.' So we started shooting. It was quite a long walk, you know. The song goes through its entirety for about three minutes and he just keeps walking. After a few shots, he said again: 'You want me to walk a mile or two

> or something. What am I doing in this song?' I said: 'You're walking. You're not going to sing.'
>
> 'Okay, you're the boss.'
>
> Typical of Dev, you know, he always wants to be active. Then the second thing I remember is that he had the habit of using his hands as he walked. 'You don't move your hands,' I told him. He said: 'I can't sing, I can't move my hands... I'm just supposed to walk?'
>
> I said: 'That's it, you are just supposed to walk and look handsome.'[7]

The song is unique in the sense that unlike a typical Hindi playback song, the ones who perform it are not the male and female leads. Despite the presence of Dev Anand and Shakila in the song, it is performed by Shyam Kapoor and Sheila Vaz. Vaz later told writer–filmmaker Karan Bali that the song, choreographed by Zohra Sehgal, was shot at Worli seaface in exactly two days.[8] Contemporary audiences and film buffs will recognize Zohra Sehgal as the 'cool grandmother' from a plethora of films in the 1990s and 2000s, including *Dil Se ... (1998)*, *Saawariya* (2007) and *Cheeni Kum* (2007). Back then, she was a teacher at Uday Shankar's dance school at Almora and had started choreographing dances with Chetan Anand's *Neecha Nagar*. Besides Sheila Vaz, the other performer in the song was Shyam Kapoor. He was one of the permanent fixtures in Guru Dutt's team and had also played a walk-on role in Raj Khosla's debut *Milap*. At this time, he was one of the assistants in *Pyaasa*. The tune of 'Leke pehla pehla pyaar' was later used by composer Ghantasala as 'Basthi dorasani' for the Telugu film *Abhimanam* (1960).

The other song that bears instant identification with *C.I.D.* is 'Yeh hai Bombay meri jaan'. O.P. Nayyar based the tune on 'Oh My Darling, Clementine', an American folk ballad. Over time, the song, sung by Mohammed Rafi and Geeta Dutt, became an anthem for the city it is named after. Anyone who has ever made the teeming metropolis their home would identify with some aspect of the song or another. Harmonica player Milon Gupta, who worked with O.P. Nayyar for many years, told his student Saikat Mukherjee about the making of the song: 'Me, O.P. Nayyar, Guru Dutt and Majrooh Sultanpuri, the lyricist, were sitting in Famous Studio. We were making the songs of *C.I.D.* O.P. Nayyar said, "Milon, *woh* tune *baja*. Milon, play that tune." I immediately knew which tune he was referring to. I played it, and Majrooh wrote the song almost instantly.'[9]

As Raj clarified on various occasions, Guru Dutt didn't interfere with the shooting of *C.I.D.* But he was ever present in Khosla's style of mounting songs. 'I am known for my song picturisations, that I picturise songs very well,' Raj Khosla once said, pointing to a portrait of Guru Dutt behind him. 'Actually it's Guru Dutt – it is his skill that I learnt.'[10] The fact that he had learned quite well is evident in how 'Yeh hai Bombay meri jaan' was shot. In Hindi cinema, comic actors have traditionally been employed only to provide relief from the intensity of the rest of the plot. Rarely have they been allowed a moment to turn inward and contemplate, show what they are capable of. In 'Yeh hai Bombay meri jaan', however, Johnny Walker is allowed that brief moment of contemplation in the midst of all the clowning around. As he mutters '*Milta hai yahan sab kuchh/ Ek milta nahi dil/ Insaan ka nahi koi naamonishan* (You'll find everything here/ What you'll never find is a heart/ No sign of humans either)', he pulls a street urchin into his arms and eyes are bound to turn moist. As the song progresses and Johnny Walker spouts witticisms about the selfishness, crime, corruption and violence in Bombay, his lady

The soundtrack of *C.I.D.* (1956).

love Kumkum joins him on the Victoria carriage, and contrasts his lamentations with a note of hope. She retorts, '*Bura duniya ko hai kehta/ Aisa bhola toh na ban/ Jo hai karta woh hai bharta/ Hai yahan ka ye chalan… Ae dil hai jeena asaan yahan* (You call the world evil/ Don't be so naive/ An eye for an eye/ That's the game here… O my heart, it's not so bad living here),' reinforcing that this city ensures you only get what's coming to you; it's not all bad. The song progresses like a well-written screenplay, with a build-up, conflict and denouement. By his second film, Raj Khosla had already found one of his very distinct signatures – of songs that, in addition to tugging at our heartstrings, become narrative devices. This song is proof of that. The song has in its own way inspired at least three Hindi films: *Yeh Hai Mumbai Meri Jaan* (1999), *Mumbai Meri Jaan* (2008), and *Ae Dil Hai Mushkil* (2016). It appeared towards the end of Nishikant Kamat's *Mumbai Meri Jaan*, when the city is shown to come to a standstill for a minute in mourning for the victims of the Mumbai train bombing of 2006. No other song could better capture that 'spirit of Mumbai', which makes its residents endure the most terrible tragedies and go back to their daily grind in a matter of days. For the second time, this classic from *C.I.D.* made everyone's eyes well up. Audiences all over stood up and applauded, as Rafi's velvet voice played out.

One of the songs of *C.I.D.* landed Majrooh Sultanpuri and the film's makers in trouble. Sung by Geeta Dutt, it went '*Jaata kahan hai deewaane/ Sab kuchh yahan hai sanam* (Where are you off to/ We have everything here, my love)', and continued with the refrain 'Fi-fi *kuchh tere dil mein/* Fi-fi *kuchh mere dil mein* (Fi-fi goes your heart/ And fi-fi goes mine)'. Film historian Manek Premchand wrote of the issue in his book on Sultanpuri:

> The draconian politician (Morarji Desai, the Chief Minister of Bombay at the time) summoned the film's

lead actor Dev Anand, its producer Guru Dutt, its director Raj Khosla, the music composer OP Nayyar, and lyricist Majrooh Sultanpuri to his office. 'Please explain to me what the words fi-fi mean in that song,' he demanded.

'They don't mean anything as such,' attempted Majrooh, 'these are meaningless fun words that I coined to sit in meter.'

'Hmm. We are censoring that song for suggestive words. Next time, please try using meaningful lyrics.'[11]

The song wasn't used in the film, but was part of the album and became almost as popular as the rest of the songs. It got a new lease of life when it was re-recorded and used in Anurag Kashyap's ill-fated Mumbai fable *Bombay Velvet* (2015).

Yet another *C.I.D.* song went on to become a cultural phenomenon. Shekhar and Rekha have just had their first lovers' tiff. They are on a date but avoid talking to each other. Yet love is prominent on their minds. In silence, they draw hearts in the dirt and on the bark of a tree. Rekha floats a paper boat. Shekhar tosses a pebble at her. Thus begins one of the most enduring love ballads, 'Ankhon hi ankhon mein ishaara ho gaya'. Mohammed Rafi sings just the opening stanza, the *mukhda*. The rest of the song is in the sublime voice of Geeta Dutt. The song breaks the ice between the mock-fighting couple, and they are relieved to finally smile and be in each other's arms. Who wants to fight anyway? The exquisite violin piece in the interlude is very similar to the one in a song from *Haar Jeet* (1940), 'Mast pawan shaakhein lehraye', which was composed by Raichand Boral.

One song in the movie even went on to become another reason for the young director and heroine to butt heads. Raj Khosla and Waheeda Rehman had seemingly moved on from their little disagreement. But midway through the shooting, they had another fight – this time over a costume. This was for the song 'Kahin pe nigahen kahin pe nishaana'. The hero Shekhar is in hiding in Rekha's house, recuperating from an injury, when the villain Dharamdas (Bir Sakhuja), her boss, comes looking for him. She is now sympathetic to Shekhar and his cause, and must distract the bad guy while warning Shekhar of the danger he is in. And that's how the song becomes a narrative tool.

In keeping with the song and Waheeda's role in the film (she was the gangster's moll, who was, in a manner of speaking, trying to seduce our hero), Bhanu Athaiya had come up with a long skirt and top. The blouse was lacy and Waheeda had an issue with it. She had made clear that she reserved the right to refuse the costume. She now refused to wear the blouse without a lining. Raj, miffed by what he saw as a young artiste throwing tantrums, tried to dissuade her. Waheeda told me:

> I said I needed a lining in the blouse, otherwise I am not even going on the set. To this, Raj said, 'What are you doing? You are a newcomer. *Aisa nahi hota hai* [It doesn't work this way]... don't make a fuss about it. *Itna lamba skirt hai* [It's such a long skirt]... what else do you need?' I told him the blouse was too lacy, and I didn't like it. I wasn't going to the set wearing that. Then they called Guru Dutt. He wasn't in town; he was somewhere in Khandala. A car went to fetch him, and he was brought there. Raj ji said, '*Bhai, yeh aap ki* artist *hain, aur aap* producer *hain* [Brother, she is your artist, and you are the producer]... she has a lot of demands. She is refusing to come on the set.' Guru came to meet my mother and me. I told him, this is probably the reason I had inserted that clause about costumes in the contract. He said, 'What do you want?' I replied, 'Lining.'

Bhanu Athaiya was summoned and asked to do it. But she said it would take her half a day to complete the task. Finally, it was Waheeda Rehman who provided a solution. 'Give me a dupatta,' she said. So, it was done. She wrapped a dupatta and the song was shot.

C.I.D. and its songs set the box office on fire. Every single number was a hit, and the film ran to packed houses. Raj Khosla had just delivered his first hit, and he was soon going to make a habit of it. The film went on to complete a silver jubilee (a 25-week run). Raj told journalist Sheila Vesuna in an interview:

> When *C.I.D.* completed its silver jubilee I got a call from Guru, asking me to go over and see him. When I went to meet him, he gave me a set of keys. They were the keys of a new car. I was overwhelmed. It was an automatic convertible. I got into it and drove around Bombay and felt as though I was flying. Guru had had all the papers transferred in my name. That is how thoughtful that man was.[12]

Within a short while, Guru Dutt was to offer him another picture to direct, with a staggering fee of one lakh. Raj hesitated – he was again at a crossroads.

7

Walking Out of the Shadows

Though Raj hailed from what he called 'the Guru Dutt style of filmmaking', there were significant ways in which their worlds diverged. This included their ways of handling actors. Raj Khosla's style presupposed an active involvement from the actor, while Guru Dutt believed in making his cast feel comfortable. Nothing illustrates this better than Waheeda Rehman's experience.

At one point, the actress worked almost simultaneously in two films being directed by the two talented men. But not only were *Pyaasa* and *C.I.D.* as different as chalk and cheese, the directors had very distinct styles. Waheeda elaborated:

> Raj Khosla was very lively, friendly and warm, while Guru Dutt-ji was a quiet person. But Guru Dutt-ji had the understanding of an artist – *ke inko* problem *kya ho rahi hai.* Not only with me, even with accomplished actors like Rehman saab, he was very patient and asked them if anything was troubling them. If they said they were not able to do things a certain way, he used to come up with an alternative. In my experience, no other director had it in him to say, '*Aapse ye nahi ho raha hai,*

> *koi baat nahi, aap aise kar lo*! If you're unable to do this, don't worry, do it like this! How are you feeling now, comfortable?' Guru Dutt was like that. On the other hand, Raj Khosla was very good as a director, but he had trouble dealing with a newcomer.

Difference in approach notwithstanding, Guru Dutt was obviously happy with what Raj had done with *C.I.D.* Dutt was now on his own journey, now that his vision of *Pyaasa*, a very personal kind of cinema, had been well received by the audience. This was all the validation that the man needed to embark on a new journey of self-discovery through cinema. But he was also conscious of the need to produce commercial hits of the kind he had been making so far. Guru Dutt Productions was a big team now and there were salaries to pay. With Raj having proved his mettle, he wanted this protégé of his to continue making blockbusters, so that he could focus on the films he really wanted to make. Guru Dutt asked Raj Khosla to make another film for him. An amount of one lakh was on the table, which was the director's for the taking if he agreed to make the film. But Raj had made his decision. It was time to chart his own path. He had been part of the Guru Dutt team for a while. It was now incumbent on him to establish his own identity, find his voice. Besides, he was now a married man. His wife, Usha, was part of his life now, and to provide for her was his responsibility. He had made up his mind.

Raj later told Sheila Vesuna about this encounter with Guru Dutt: 'I told him that a sapling could not grow under a big tree. Guru was a big name by then. He hugged me with tears in his eyes and said, "Carry on, but remember, Guru Dutt Films is as much yours as it is mine. Do make a film for me some other time." But that opportunity, unfortunately never came.'[1]

And so Raj began work on *Solva Saal* (1958). The movie is sometimes clubbed with a cornucopia of Indian films – *Nadan* (1951), *Chori Chori* (1956), *Nau Do Gyarah* (1957), *Chawa Pawa* (Bengali, 1959), *Chandrodayam* (Tamil, 1966), *Dil Hai Ke Manta Nahin* (1991) – that were inspired from Frank Capra's near-perfect romantic comedy *It Happened One Night* (1934), which in turn was based on a short story called 'Night Bus' by Samuel Hopkins Adams, featured in the August 1933 issue of *Cosmopolitan* magazine. Though *Solva Saal* shares some common plot elements, shoving it into this group might not be a fair assessment.

Movie credits attribute the story idea of *Solva Saal* to one Omkar Dogra. The deepest of online searches won't throw up anything about Mr Dogra beyond his connection with this one film. However, the screenplay of *Solva Saal* was co-written by Raj Khosla and an 'Omkar Saheb'. Interestingly, this Omkar Saheb is also supposed to have written the story and screenplay for Bhappi Sonie's directorial debut, *Ek Phool Char Kaante* (1960). In the absence of further evidence, one could assume that Omkar Dogra and Omkar Saheb were one and the same. Be that as it may, another theory behind the origin of *Solva Saal* is that it is based on a true story. A 1957 issue of *Filmfare* that reports Raj Khosla shooting the film at Bombay Central station conveys the same:

> Director Raj Khosla recently shot a location sequence for the film at Bombay Central... in it Waheeda is robbed by her boy friend, played by Jagdev, and Dev Anand, playing the role of a kindly journalist who comes to her help. Dev Anand and Waheeda Rehman give chase to the 'boy friend'. But it is a futile chase, at the end of which Dev Anand finds that Waheeda is a pleasant but embarrassing liability. Written by Bhappi,
>
> 'Solva Saal' is said to be based on an incident which took place a few years ago in a northern suburb of

> Bombay, where a rich young girl was duped by her boy friend. Vinod Desai produces the film.[2]

Solva Saal employed two different aspects of Raj Khosla, the storyteller. It fused a noirish tone with a timeless romantic motif that became an active ingredient of this director's oeuvre in the years to come. This kind of romance, in fact, became a mainstay in many of his future works. Shyam (Jagdev, who was a cousin of Dharmendra's) convinces Laaj (Waheeda Rehman) to elope with him in the dead of night. On the train, reporter Prannath Kashyap (Dev Anand) takes a keen interest in them. When Laaj's beau takes off with the jewellery she has brought along (ostensibly to fund their life together), the feeling of shame and betrayal gets the better of her and she decides to end it all. She jumps into the sea, and Prannath follows her. He saves her, and delivers the customary pep talk. They set about looking for Shyam together, encountering a series of amusing adventures along the way.

With the heros' story unfolding over the course of a night, Raj had ample scope to let the lens loose into the nightly ambience. The result was a glorious play of light and shadow that could only happen with black-and-white photography, and more so in films noir. In *Solva Saal*, Raj Khosla had an able cinematographer in Dwarka Divecha, who had just turned 40. Seventeen years later, near the end of his short life and career, this skilled technician would photograph the epic *Sholay* (1975).

The term 'film noir' came into currency only in the 1970s, though it was coined much earlier. It was used to describe a particular kind of film made in Hollywood in the 1940s and 1950s, distinguished by its preoccupation with dark themes, chiaroscuro lighting (a deft use of the contrast between light and dark), and certain conventions such as morally ambivalent protagonists, femme fatales and a general sense of fatality.

Many Indian filmmakers, especially the likes of Dev Anand, Guru Dutt and Raj Khosla, often looked to Hollywood for inspiration. They were inspired by the stylization and aesthetics of these films, and seamlessly blended them with Indian morality and sensibilities in their own work. As many of the films they watched happened to be the stylish American crime thrillers of the period, what came to be known as noirs, this was one of the first genres that Raj mastered.

Having used it most effectively in *C.I.D.*, he employed it in *Solva Saal*, too. The film has generous swathes of chiaroscuro-style shots, whether in scenes near the railway tracks or in the 'studio'. It also has other genre tropes, such as shots of characters smoking or Waheeda as a femme fatale (Waheeda's role in the film ticks most of the boxes for the character type: she is alluring and does land Dev's character in some very perilous circumstances). Even the hero Dev's initial motivation behind pursuing Waheeda and her beau isn't entirely selfless; he is in pursuit of a story. But Raj Khosla offset these elements of noir with the levity of a romantic comedy. And that is what makes the film more enjoyable.

Solva Saal, however, has gone down in history predominantly because of one song, a timeless classic that is still remembered and hummed by many. 'Hai apna dil to awara' became a youth anthem of sorts when it broke into the scene. Singer Hemant Kumar and Dev Anand were a rather unusual combination, considering the timbre of the singer's voice and the actor's youthful persona. But S.D. Burman repeated this combination in film after film, and more often than not, the result was exquisite, timeless and popular. Before *Solva Saal*, the duo was in 'Ye raat ye chandni phir kahan' from *Jaal*, and *House No. 44* (1955) and, subsequently, in *Baat Ek Raat Ki* (1962). While all other songs of this team are contemplative, 'Hai apna dil to awara' is unique in the sense that it is vivacious and full of life. The song also famously made use of a youngster by the name of Rahul Dev Burman, or R.D. Burman, who played the harmonica. H.Q. Chowdhury writes in his book *Incomparable Sachin Dev Burman*: 'Young Pancham played the mouth organ in the interlude music that became so popular that it was every young man's musical instrument of choice for many years.' He adds, 'If a survey for the most popular film song in the subcontinent is made, Hai apna dil would definitely be one of those.'[3] The movie soundtrack also had Mohammed Rafi singing for Dev in two instances – the delightful 'Yehi to hai woh' and 'Dekho mohe laaga solva saal'. But it is likely that even Raj Khosla himself was convinced that it was the tune by Hemant Kumar that would rule the airwaves; halfway through the film, Waheeda tells Dev Anand that his name should have been Hemant Kumar instead of Prannath Kashyap. And indeed, 'Hai apna dil' is one of the (at least) dozen songs from Raj Khosla's oeuvre that have not only survived the test of time but also flourished. This was the second such song in his directorial career, following 'Yeh hai Bombay meri jaan'.

The soundtrack of *Solva Saal* (1958).

Incidentally, Raj had a thing for hat tips and Easter eggs. *Solva Saal* is full of them. In one instance, a character played by Tun Tun remarks on how Prannath shares a resemblance with Dilip Kumar, while another character called Pehelwan says that Laaj looks like Madhubala, and offers her the role of a 'side-heroine'. This was the time when Dilip and Madhubala were both in their prime and believed to be in a relationship. In another scene, Tun Tun goes through the motions of 'comedy', which, in those days, meant making people laugh at one's own expense. In these situations, nothing that these actors ('comedians') did was to be taken seriously, even if they were in a pitiable state. But in the middle of this sequence, Tun Tun breaks into 'Kanhaiya tori murali bairan bhayi', a Lata Mangeshkar song from *New Delhi* (1956). Tun Tun sings it perfectly, and entirely in tune. How? Tun Tun was also Uma Devi, an accomplished playback singer, in another life. She was now a comedienne. That little scene may have been Raj Khosla's tribute to the great singer. Just like her, he had also wanted to make his name as a playback singer but was doing something else entirely.

The Easter egg featuring Tun Tun in *Solva Saal*.

Then, a considerable portion of *Solva Saal* unfolds in a movie studio, which allowed for a lot of self-referential – in today's parlance, 'meta' – humour. The studio in the film is called National Studio. The set seems to be the then newly formed Mehboob Studios (founded in 1954), which eventually became the centre of operations for both Raj and Dev. In a hilarious scene, Dev Anand talks to the receptionist Motiram while looking for Waheeda's gold-digger boyfriend. Motiram asks him to check out Stage No. 2, where they run into director Raj Khosla shooting his film (his own office in Mehboob Studios was also near Stage No. 2). As Dev and Waheeda's characters enter the studio floor, an assistant director casts them as extras for the film being directed by Raj Khosla. Raj briefly appears on screen as himself, and mouths instructions for the actors and crew. For the few minutes that he is on screen, the director exudes enough confidence to make one wonder why he didn't do it more often.

Finally, the lyrics of the title song 'Dekho mohe laaga solva saal', sung by Asha Bhosle, Mohammed Rafi and Sudha Malhotra, and written by Majrooh Sultanpuri, are uncannily

'Mohe laga solva saal' from *Mashal* (1950).

reminiscent of another song composed by S.D. Burman in the early days of his Bollywood career. *Mashal* (1950) features a song with a near-identical opening line, 'Mohe laga solva saal'. The rest of the song is, however, very different.

Speaking of songs, *Solva Saal* was one of three films that S.D. Burman composed for Raj, the other two being *Kala Pani* (1958) and *Bombai ka Babu* (1960). In all three soundtracks, as well as most others composed by the music director during this period, one singer was conspicuous by her absence. In their book *S.D. Burman: The Prince Musician*, writers and film buffs Aniruddha Bhattacharjee and Balaji Vittal say:

> In the late 1950s, S.D. Burman had a major setback in his career — a split with none other than Lata Mangeshkar. In the absence of any authentic or recorded account of the time, it is difficult to ascertain which film had driven a schism between the composer and the singer. By Lata's own admission to her biographer, Harish Bhimani, and subsequently to Nasreen Munni Kabir, the misunderstanding had occurred during *Miss India* (1957).[4]

The book quotes film historian Raju Bharatan as positing that the rift between S.D. Burman and Lata Mangeshkar began when she was supposed to go on a tour, and he expected her to record a song for *Sitaron se Aagey* (1958).[5] She didn't have enough time to manage the recording before the tour, she said on the call to Burman's then assistant Jaidev. S.D. Burman asked Jaidev to check with her if she would prioritize his recording after her trip. According to Raju Bharatan, the singer declined and this infuriated S.D. Burman. Lata Mangeshkar herself, however, remembered it a little differently. As she narrated to Nasreen Munni Kabir:

> I sang a song for a Nargisji film called Miss India. S.D. Burman asked me to sing it softly to create a sweet mood. A few days later, he called and said we had to re-record it. I asked: 'Dada, what's wrong with it?' He explained the character who would sing in the film was a kind of tomboy and the song was too soft and feminine. So I said: 'Fine. I'II do it again but I am a little busy right now.' Two or three days later, he sent someone to arrange a recording date. I later discovered this person went to Dada, and instead of saying I was busy, he said I had refused to re-record the song. Dada was upset and assumed I was being difficult and commented that he would not work with me again. I called him and said: 'I'll spare you the embarrassment, Dada. You don't need to say anything. I won't sing for you.'[6]

At any rate, the misunderstanding between the two legends led to the decision not to work with each other. This lasted till *Bandini* (1963), where R.D. Burman and Bimal Roy mediated a truce. In the intervening period, it was Asha Bhosle whom Burman Senior called upon for playback duties. She became the principal singer on most of his projects. *Solva Saal* was no exception. Asha Bhosle lent her voice to three of six songs in the film. Of them, the one that really stands out is 'Ye bhi koi roothne ka mausam hai deewane'. Playful, blithe and utterly joyous, it plays in the beginning of the film, where an exuberant Waheeda Rehman sings for her boyfriend Shyam.

Sixty-five years after the release of *Solva Saal*, sitting in her living room, listening to the song all over again, Asha Bhosle reminisced to me, '*Ek hi* music director *thha*, expressions *sikhaane waala*: S.D. Burman. There was just one music director who used to teach expressions: S.D. Burman. Raj Khosla used to come to Burman saab and say, "Show Asha your style, tell her how to do it your way." I was also relatively new, I had been singing in Hindi films since 1946, so it had been 10 years."' She drew attention to the words '*deewane*' and '*bhole-bhale*' in the song. 'Singing those words a certain way, making faces while singing them, this is what he told us to do. Only Burman saab used to experiment in this manner. He used to ask us to laugh during a song, for example. He was the only music director who did things like that. Nobody else.' About Raj, she added, 'He used to be there during the music sittings, and listen closely. He was also a singer, so he could articulate, I want this or that. He said these to the music director, not to us. To us, he only used to say, "This is the situation, and you would be singing for so and so. See how you would want to do it."'[7]

Another battle of minds affected the making of *Solva Saal*. The incident seemed to be an extension of the falling out between Raj and Waheeda while shooting for *C.I.D.* Despite the differences during their first film, Raj Khosla and Waheeda Rehman had remained cordial, even warm.

'He was always a warm, friendly person. He would always tell me, "*Tu meri chhoti behen hai*. You are like a younger sister to me." Raj, me and Dev had developed a friendship during *C.I.D.* So, I thought he knows me by now, what I can do and what not. Hence, I agreed to do *Solva Saal*,' Waheeda told me. But the feud, if one could call it that, was far from over. In the film, once Dev Anand's character saves Waheeda's character from drowning in the sea, they walk into a *dhobi ghaat* and request for a change of clothes. As they try on the new attire, with just a clothesline separating them, the two of them get into a conversation, which, for the first time, hints at a budding romance. It was an important scene, and Raj Khosla was, as usual, very particular about every detail. Waheeda Rehman was uncomfortable with the blouse she was asked to put on. She thought it was too revealing, and she spoke her mind.

Recalling the incident, she narrated:

> In the scene, the hero asks her, '*Aap ka naam kya hai*? What is your name?' To which she says, 'Laajwanti.' So, I asked, how can a girl like that wear these kind of clothes? That was my argument. Raj said, '*Nayi ladki ho, itni behes karti ho*, you shouldn't argue.' I said, 'I told you. I won't feel comfortable. I won't be able to perform, that's my problem. What can I do?'

They had a moment of disagreement but finally, Waheeda had her way and she wore a different blouse. The shoot went on and things went back to normal. 'Otherwise, he was a very friendly, warm, loving person,' Waheeda said about Raj. 'He was a very nice man.'

After *Solva Saal*, Raj Khosla and Waheeda Rehman continued to meet socially and enjoy each other's company, but they would cease to work together for 26 years.

When *Solva Saal* was finally released, it featured an A (adults only) certificate from the Central Board of Film Censors. It made no sense. Even by 1958 standards, it was a tame story. The girl does run away from home but ends up marrying the boy of her father's choice. The film would have spoken to a family audience. It was a fun romp, but the audiences kept it at an arm's length. Raj Khosla later said, 'Agreed (that) the concept was a little more advanced than other films being made at that time. But the censor board's giving the film an A certificate defeated the very purpose of the film. I wanted to tell the youth not to be rash in love and elope. But the censors wanted to keep the youngsters out of the hall… an A certificate kept half my audience away from the movie.'[8]

The disappointment of *Solva Saal* was more than compensated by the next collaboration between Dev Anand, Raj Khosla and S.D. Burman: *Kala Pani* (1958). The film, which won Dev his first acting award, was produced by Navketan. Raj, however, took a while to write the script. So, in the meantime, Dev Anand decided to make a film on a story read to him by his brother Goldie. It was called *Nau Do Gyarah*. In a demonstration of the faith that both Dev and the Navketan banner had in the directorial skills of the three films-old Raj, they wanted *Nau Do Gyarah* to be directed by him as well. But the young Goldie Anand, who had conceived the story, wanted to direct it himself. It finally went to him and a new filmmaker, Goldie, aka Vijay Anand, was born. (This was not the only time that a film supposed to be directed by Raj Khosla was given to Goldie, but more on that later.)

Mohan Churiwala, a long-time associate of Dev Anand and an authority on Navketan and the Anands, remembers it a little differently. According to him, Goldie, aka Vijay Anand, had written a story called 'Nau Do Gyarah' and everyone at Navketan was talking about it. Dev saab heard of it and asked Goldie to hand over the story to him. He was travelling to Mahabaleshwar, so he could read it on the way. But Goldie wanted to narrate the story to him personally. Come along with me to Mahabaleshwar then, Dev Anand said. On the way to Mahabaleshwar, Goldie narrated the story. His brother was so taken in by it that he wanted to make it immediately. Goldie insisted that he would allow his story to be adapted on one condition: that he be allowed to direct it himself. Around this time, Navketan was planning a film with Raj Khosla called *Khali Botal*. Dev made a trunk call to Bombay saying that *Khali Botal*, the script for which wasn't ready anyway, was to be postponed and *Nau Do Gyarah* be made in its place. Later, *Khali Botal* was renamed *Kala Pani*.

With *Kala Pani*, Raj had one of his team members leaving him for good, while a long-term collaborator began working with him for the first time. For Bhappi Sonie, who wrote the dialogues of *Kala Pani*, it was his last film with Raj Khosla. In the tradition of other great Indian filmmakers like Bimal Roy, Raj Kapoor and his own mentor, Guru Dutt, Raj, too, had nurtured and mentored a whole new generation of filmmakers. Bhappi Sonie was one of them. Sonie and his sisters had been adopted by Prithviraj Kapoor after their father died while directing a film with him in the lead. The kids didn't have anyone to look after them so the Kapoor patriarch, widely revered as 'Papa ji', took care of them. Sonie was raised in the Kapoor household along with the other children. Growing up, he was especially close to Shammi Kapoor. While the latter struggled to make his name as an actor, Bhappi Sonie took up a job as a ticket-checker on Bombay's local trains. He would operate from the erstwhile Victoria Terminus railway station (now known as Chhatrapati Shivaji Terminus). Shammi Kapoor would often land up at the station to relieve Sonie of his duties. Kapoor would don the uniform and stand in for Sonie while the latter watched a film at Capitol cinema next door. And then Sonie would return to work so that Kapoor could catch the next show. Later, Bhappi Sonie directed Shammi Kapoor in four films, including the iconic *Janwar* and *Brahmachari*, both key films in the actor's career.

But between his job in the railways and a successful career directing films, Bhappi Sonie assisted Raj Khosla in three films: *Milap*, *C.I.D.*, and *Solva Saal*, while also writing the dialogues for *Solva Saal* as well as *Kala Pani*.

Meanwhile, *Kala Pani* was the first time that the 35-year-old G.R. Kamat joined Raj's team. Gajanan Ramchandra or

G.R. Kamat had been working with veteran Marathi filmmaker Raja Paranjape on films like *Pedgaonche Shahane* (1952) and *Lakhachi Goshta* (1952). He also co-wrote Paranjape's Hindi film *Chacha Chowdhary* (1953). His very next project was *Kala Pani*, which was the beginning of a long and illustrious partnership. G.R. Kamat and Raj Khosla would continue to work together for 24 years, creating magic in milestone films such as *Mera Saaya* (1966), *Do Badan* (1966), *Do Raaste* (1969), *Mera Gaon Mera Desh* (1971) and *Kuchhe Dhaage* (1973).

The opening credits of *Kala Pani* say that it was 'based on a story idea by Anand Pal'. Pal was a young actor who had worked in a number of Navketan productions like *Afsar* and *House No. 44*. The idea may have been suggested by him, but the original inspiration for *Kala Pani* seems to have been a rather popular source material in the subcontinent. The stories of Archibald Joseph Cronin, or A.J. Cronin as he was popularly known, have been adaptation fodder for Indian filmmakers in several languages. By the time a British adaptation of his popular novel *Beyond this Place* was made (1959), it had already been adapted twice in India – as *Sabar Uparey* (1955) in Bengali and *Kala Pani* in Hindi. Eventually, other adaptations were made in Telugu (*Poola Rangadu*, 1967) and Tamil (*En Annan*, 1970).

Kala Pani follows the exploits of Karan (Dev Anand), who grows up under the impression that his father is long dead. One day, his mother reveals to him that his father, accused of murder, has been rotting in a Hyderabad jail for the past 15 years. The film, interestingly, begins after this revelation. Karan's mother has broken the news to him, and he's sitting crestfallen. That's where we start watching Karan's story. With the firm belief that his father cannot be a murderer, Karan takes it upon himself to clear his name. The charge against his father is of murdering a dancer named Mala, and there are witnesses who can prove his innocence. Among them is the grocer

Ramdas (Rashid Khan), and another dancer named Kishori (Nalini Jaywant). In an effort to dig more, Karan reaches the offices of the *Deccan Times*, where he meets the winsome Asha (Madhubala). He starts living in a boarding house, where Asha is one of the residents, alongside two slackers named Madhosh Miyan (Mukri) and Daulat Chand (Jankidas).

With *Kala Pani*, Raj was back to thriller territory, a major distinction between it and the other adaptations. Most of them are emotional dramas, but this one focuses on the murder and how the perpetrators are brought to justice. Beyond its thriller format, *Kala Pani* also tackles heavy themes, such as the corruption of public officials. Karan and Asha realize that the public prosecutor Jaswant Rai (Kishore Sahoo) was behind keeping the real murderer out of jail. He had been tampering with evidence and silencing witnesses. When a campaign in Asha's paper doesn't work, Karan starts propaganda on the streets, trying to raise public support for his crusade. Goons are sent to disrupt the gathering. Frustrated, Karan breaks into lawyer Jaswant Rai's house, resolved to kill him. Confronted by a furious Karan, and with a gun pointed at his chest, Jaswant is terrified but doesn't lose his cool. He manages to convince Karan that killing him is a bad idea and would never fulfil his purpose. If anything, it could be a hindrance. Karan is overcome with guilt and leaves the house. Jaswant is visibly relieved.

There is also romance and revelry along the way. Dev and Madhubala had by then built a successful partnership. She was one of Dev's most frequent co-stars. Before *Kala Pani*, they had appeared together in five films, most of which were fairly successful ventures. So, *Kala Pani* caught them at the height of their on-screen chemistry. Today, 65 years later, Madhubala continues to set screens on fire. Screen sizes have changed but her allure remains the same. To Raj, she was as effervescent on the sets as she was on screen:

> She was full of mischief, in a gentle sort of way. She would want, for example, to demoralize Dev Anand, her co-star. 'Why is the man so sober?' she would ask. And she would lay a mean plan to break him down, telling me about it beforehand and warning me with a grin that I would regret it if I don't co-operate. The shot would be ready for 'take'. Dev would arrive to do a perfectly serious scene. When I called 'Action!', Madhu would look at Dev and start giggling. I would say 'Cut'. Dev put up with it a couple of times more and then said between clenched teeth, in his perfect accent, 'Madhu, the shot is ready, I am ready, the director is ready, and if you don't mind...' At this she would giggle more and finally Dev would have to smile. [9]

The Dev–Madhubala chemistry is frozen in time, framed in one song which has been 'seen' nearly as often as it has been heard: 'Achha ji main hari, chalo maan jao na'. Madhubala serenading Dev in that song is one of the most recognizable visuals in Hindi cinema. By this time, Raj had elevated the song picturization skills he had learned from Guru Dutt to a fine art form. In this song, he lends both Dev Anand and Madhubala an ethereal quality that makes them seem otherworldly and angelic. The very specific pans, tilts and zooms make the artistes look like a million dollars. This was a special song, composed by Burman Senior. Asha Bhosle reminisced, laughing, 'When I used those expressions while singing "*Achha ji main haari*" and "*Maan jao na*", Dev Anand and the rest of the team were jumping with joy. We could see through the glass window of the recording room. They were jumping, going all crazy.'

The other significant song from the film is 'Hum bekhudi mein tum ko', a timeless Rafi ballad that oozes the syrupy niceness of Rafi's velvet voice. Anirudha Bhattacharjee and Balaji Vittal write in their S.D. Burman biography, 'For Hum bekhudi mein, Burman did away with almost every rhythm accompaniment, except for the duggi and tabla… This soliloquy of a song with minimal instrumentation, devoid of any extra embellishment, almost sounded like a hymn.' The song was based on an earlier Bengali tune by S.D. Burman that went 'Ghoom bhulechhi nijhum'.

The soundtrack of *Kala Pani* (1958).

'Hum bekhudi' is extremely popular and will comfortably find itself in the list of Mohammed Rafi's best ghazals. But interestingly, he wasn't the one to sing this song first. Within the film, there was someone else who did it first.

In *Kala Pani*, Madhosh Miyan and Daulat Chand, Karan's fellow boarders, often indulge in a bit of poetry and mirth. Madhosh Miyan, as his name would indicate, is a poet of Urdu verse and is known to break into a recital at the slightest provocation. One evening, as Karan sits writing a letter to his mother, Madhosh starts humming a ghazal he has just composed:

Hum bekhudi mein tumko pukare chale gaye
Saagar mein zindagi ko utaare chale gaye

The voice is uncanny, and in perfect tune. It is not the voice of Mukri, the actor, but one that sounds a lot like Kundan Lal Saigal's. It, in fact, belongs to Raj Khosla. This was the first time Khosla had surreptitiously used his singing voice in one of his own films. This is what he had always wanted to do after all. Sing playback in films. He had found a way to sing, though nobody really noticed. It wasn't so much as a footnote in any account of the film anywhere, and he didn't even credit himself.

But the voice is unmistakably his. He would use his voice again, but for a major superstar, 17 years later.

But making this movie wasn't all fun and games. Something that had been brewing in Madhubala's life reared its ugly head as Raj went about making *Kala Pani*. It was during the shoot of *Bahut Din Huwe* (1954) that Madhubala had first spat out blood. She was merely brushing her teeth. It was a Gemini film, being shot in Madras. Dilip Kumar immediately flew in with a doctor from Bombay. It was then that Madhubala learned that she had a hole in her heart. Things kept getting worse and there was a similar episode while shooting for a song of *Kala Pani*. Raj was caught unawares. Many years later, he said in an interview to Sheila Vesuna, 'During a dance sequence she was totally out of breath. At that time I did not know she had a heart ailment. It was only later that she told me that she was not allowed to dance.'[10] Ironically, it was the song and dance that made the film such a big success at the time.

But it wasn't just Madhubala who was going through a personal tragedy. Raj Khosla had just lost a son, and it was excruciatingly painful. Anitaa Padhye writes in her book *Goldie: The Man and His Movies*, 'Khosla suffered a personal tragedy with the death of his son while *Kala Pani* was being completed. It shattered him, and he was often seen crying in Navketan's office.'[11] He was barely in his mid-thirties and losing a child wasn't something he was prepared for. This loss would haunt him. Despite the windfall blessings of five daughters and much more to love and cherish, the tragic loss of his son seemed to echo through his work and life in multifarious ways.

Kala Pani was Raj's only film for Navketan for a good while, though there were other ideas. But nothing else worked out until *Shareef Budmaash* (1973), 15 years later. For now, Raj Khosla was about to join forces with Dev Anand to push the envelope of storytelling one more time. And we enter the 1960s.

8

Of Men from Bombay and Women from Bengal

It was 1960, and with the dawn of a new decade, Raj Khosla became a producer. For almost half a decade, he had been making films for others. His first film, *Milap*, was for Filmarts and T.R. Fatehchand; his second, *C.I.D.*, was for his boss, his Guru; *Solva Saal* was for Chandra Films and, finally, *Kala Pani* was for the Navketan banner. Maybe it was time to do something for himself, but he still wasn't confident enough to fly solo. He needed a collaborator, preferably someone who was his age and shared his creative sensibilities.

The young Jal Mistry, one half of the dynamic Mistry brothers, may have crossed paths with Raj at Navketan. Jal and his brother, Fali, are revered names in Indian cinematography. Self-taught, the brothers contributed to some iconic films in the history of Hindi cinema. While Fali Mistry photographed films like *Babul* (1950), *Nagin* (1954), *Ek Musafir Ek Hasina* (1962), *Guide* (1965) and *Johny Mera Naam* (1970), Jal Mistry worked on *Barsaat* (1949), *Uran Khatola* (1955), *Bombay to Goa* (1972) and *Naseeb* (1981). Jal, the younger of the two brothers, had worked on a Navketan project called *Aandhiyan* (1952), an experimental film by Chetan Anand. After the spectacular success of *Kala Pani*, Raj joined forces with Jal Mistry to make his boldest experiment yet: *Bombai ka Babu* (1960). They launched it under a new banner, literally called 'Naya Films'.

In December 1905, the latest O. Henry story was published in *Everybody's Magazine*, Vol. XIII. It was about 20-year-old Texas gunslinger Sprague Dalton, who prefers to be called the 'Llano Kid'. During a botched-up card game, a fight breaks out and the Kid shoots down his adversary, another boy of his age. The victim's friends launch a manhunt, and the Kid, though he is quite formidable and skilled with a gun, decides to take off to the north. Eventually, he reaches a town named Buenna Tierras on the coast of South America, where a corrupt US consul named Thacker makes his acquaintance. They hatch a plot to defraud a rich old couple whose son went missing as a child. The idea is to present the Kid as their son. Their plan seems to be going smoothly when the couple welcomes him into their lives and in their hearts. All the pair have needed to convince the old parents is to ink a tattoo on the Kid's left hand, identical to one the missing child had. The Llano Kid settles down in the old house, with thousands of dollars within arm's distance in the safe, but doesn't do much about it. When Thacker doesn't hear from him for over a month, he summons him to the consulate. But the Kid is a transformed man – he no longer wants to rob the old couple. The mother's love has made him turn over a new leaf. He has decided to stay back as their son and won't hesitate to kill Thacker if he tries to spill the beans. In the end, as part of the famous 'O. Henry twist', it emerges that there is one other reason he wants to stay. The boy he killed in the beginning of the story also had a tattoo on his left hand.

The plot of *Bombai ka Babu* is said to have been inspired by this O. Henry story. Though the broad strokes are similar, the story of the film deviates in significant ways. As the title would suggest, *Bombai ka Babu* is quite literally Babu's story. He shares some similarities with Karan, the protagonist of *Kala Pani.* Both grew up without a father, and both are on a quest to find that anchor in their life: family. Babu isn't just some trigger-happy young man. It's the vagaries of life that have made him choose the path of evil, and even in that he seems to have certain beliefs that stand out as redeeming qualities. For example, unseen by his gang members, he spends time with a group of street urchins, giving them hope for a better tomorrow and keeping them from committing petty crimes. His childhood buddy, the police officer Malik, thanks to Babu, was able to choose the high road early on in his life (it is indicated that Babu's sacrifices helped him secure his education and, subsequently, a respectable career). Moved by Malik's exhortations, Babu is tempted to turn over a new leaf, but his gang members will have none of it. One in particular, Balli (Jagdish Raj), is dead against Babu's move because he suspects he is going to rat them out to the cops. And that is when a fight ensues between the two young men. Balli lunges at Babu and ends up getting killed. Fearing retribution by the law, Babu flees and reaches the northern tip of the country. He bumps into Bhagat (Rashid Khan), who gauges that he is a fugitive from the law. Much like Thacker in the O. Henry story, Bhagat suggests that Babu should pretend to be the long-lost son of an old couple. The mother is now blind, having waited for and cried over her lost son. When Babu reaches their home, he realizes the man that he's pretending to be also has a sister, and that is going to be a problem.

'A Double-Dyed Deceiver', O. Henry's story, didn't have or need a romantic angle. It is the mother's naive love for someone she believes to be her son that changes the hero's outlook. In 1920, 15 years after the story was out, Jack Pickford starred in an eponymous silent film adaptation of 'A Double-Dyed Deceiver', in which the hero falls in love with someone in the family, which adds to his motivation to stay back. It is now a lost film, making it impossible to know who this 'relative' was. But it is clear that more than the short story, the film version may have had a greater impact on Raj Khosla's movie. The germ of this story was moulded into a screenplay by G.R. Kamat, who by now had begun to work with Raj Khosla regularly, and the dialogues were by Rajinder Singh Bedi. In their story, Babu falls helplessly in love with Maya, a woman who believes that he is her brother. This situation is quite unparalleled in the history of Hindi mainstream cinema, which has always underscored the sanctity of familial bonds in broad, thick strokes.

The role of Maya, the lead heroine, was first offered to Madhubala. Raj had just worked with her on *Kala Pani*, and she seemed the perfect choice for the role. *Kala Pani* was, after all, a grand success and there may have been that wish to replicate its success. Some early posters of *Bombai ka Babu* still survive with Madhubala in them. One of them announces the upcoming attraction: 'Raj Khosla and Jal Mistry present – Dev Anand, Madhubala… He lost a world but found a home…! Raj Khosla's *Bombai ka Babu.*' The poster shows a distressed Madhubala, with Dev Anand sprawled on a globe. Another poster features a happier Madhubala with Dev looking all menacing, wielding a stick.

But Madhubala's health was worsening every day. She had started turning down offers. One of the major projects that she had to decline was *Bombai ka Babu*. 'I think she had a premonition of the illness that was to interrupt her shining career,' Raj wrote. 'I was about to sign her for *Bombai ka Babu* when she said, friendly as ever, but with a touch of sadness in her voice, "I think you had better take someone else for your own good."'[1]

In her place came Suchitra Sen, the reigning superstar of Bengali films. Bengali cinema at this time was going through a veritable golden era. In the 1950s, Uttam Kumar and Sen were the king and queen ruling benevolently over their subjects, the Bengali-speaking audience. The kind of popularity the Uttam–Suchitra duo was experiencing was unparalleled. Even the big stars of the Hindi film industry didn't enjoy that kind of euphoria in Bengal. Having said that, Suchitra Sen was building a career quite her own, distinct from the pair. Her first Hindi outing had been Bimal Roy's *Devdas* (1955), where her depiction of Paro met with acclaim from audiences, her co-stars and critics. This was followed by a role in Hrishikesh Mukherjee's debut *Musafir* (1957) and Nandlal Jaswantlal's *Champakali* (1957). *Bombai ka Babu* was Sen's fourth film in Hindi. Jal Mistry was the cinematographer for *Champakali*, so he may have been instrumental in her selection for the role. Raj Khosla, like everyone else, was only too familiar with her stardom in Bengal. Also, her success in *Devdas* could have been a deciding factor.

Suchitra Sen, one would argue, pulled off the role of Maya with aplomb. One might consider the fact that in an era where impeccable diction in Hindustani and Urdu was not only expected but demanded, it is to her credit that she manages to seem convincing despite butchering entire words. Besides, she dances with abandon and much verve – despite the fact that the Bengali film industry that she was part of didn't have dance sequences at all. In fact, dance was such anathema to Bengali pop culture that one would struggle to find instances of any classic Bengali actor indulging in a dance sequence (with the rare exception when they were playing courtesans or breaking into a twist to underscore 'modernity'). Sen had never had to dance in a Bengali film till then, but as she swung to the beats of the Punjabi dholak in 'Dekhne mein bhola hai', she didn't seem like she had two left feet. Raj later said about her, 'She is in total command of her art, a very emotional artiste. Possibly, the secret of her success is her meticulous attention to detail.

In portraying a character she looks for the details that make a character come out as real.'[2]

Yet, in this film, too, Raj locked horns on occasion with his leading lady. According to him, most of the crowd at Kullu – where they were shooting – gravitated towards Dev Anand, and that would unnerve Sen, who was used to being the cynosure of all eyes wherever she shot in Bengal. What further intensified her annoyance was that Raj and his crew got into a celebratory mood when Dev Anand was to leave. The actor had finished his portion of the shoot and planned to leave for Bombay. The team decided to throw a party. The revelries went on till the dead of night, with local dholaks and musicians adding to celebrations. This disturbed the sleep of the Bengali superstar and her husband, who was also with her during the shoot. Her husband asked them to stop the noise. This snowballed into a big fight, and Suchitra Sen threatened to leave, with the film only 80 per cent complete. Not one to give in, Raj Khosla said that she was free to go, but the party would continue. Sen left. The wedding portions were left to be done, so Raj Khosla decided to use a body double. Halfway through the shoot, Sen was back on the sets, and quipped, 'You think she can act better than me?' She eventually completed the shoot.[3]

But another version of this incident exists. Actor Sanjeev Kumar had once recounted the incident differently: 'The crew of *Bombai ka Babu* had gathered at a hotel to celebrate a colleague's birthday. Coincidentally, they chose the same hotel where Sen was putting up with her husband.'[4] The couple couldn't sleep and Suchitra Sen went straight to the manager, expecting intervention. The manager was non-committal, too scared to ruffle feathers, and the lady decided to confront the revellers herself. Raj was there and became the target of her consternation. She may have been a little harsh in her demeanour. Offended, Raj asked her to leave:

> Many did their best to patch things up between the actress and the director, but neither would budge. Things took a turn for the worse when Sen filed a case against Khosla for not clearing her pending fee and Khosla retaliated by filing a counter-complaint at the Producers' Association against Sen for leaving the project incomplete. The judgement passed was in Khosla's favour and Sen was asked to complete the movie before claiming her due amount. Sen complied and the movie was completed.[5]

Much has been said about the theme of 'incest' in *Bombai ka Babu*. While it was not exactly incest, Raj did flirt with the idea. In the time-honoured tradition of Hindi films, families reunited after a long period of separation immediately accept each other without hesitation or taking any time to allow the idea to sink in. While Maya (Suchitra Sen) is expected to welcome her 'brother' Kundan, alias Babu (Dev Anand), into her life, she does seem to have a tinge of suspicion. At their very first meeting, she carpet-bombs him with questions – exactly when was he taken? Who took him? What did he do all these years? Why did he not think of returning before?

She settles into this newfound relationship with some discomfort at Kundan's demeanour, which, if she didn't know better, would seem like flirtatious advances. Kundan, the eponymous 'Bombai ka Babu', is instantly attracted to her and initially, it is all fun and games. But alongside a lingering sense of guilt at the idea of stealing from this kind and benevolent couple who shower him with parental affection, something that Babu is alien to (in the beginning of the film, we see that Babu had counted on his friend Malik's parents to accept him as their child but was betrayed by them), he also finds himself falling for Maya. Unlike her, he knows that in the real world, they are not related. He cannot resist making advances at her, yet there is something that holds him back.

This conflict pervades through the film. In the beginning, Kundan/Babu is clear that he must hoodwink the oldies and make off with their money. Along the way, it doesn't hurt to have a good time with the damsel. In a scene where Maya tries to pluck some flowers from a tree, Kundan salaciously surveys her body. But then things get muddled. He starts seeing Shahji and Rukmini (Nazir Hussain and Achala Sachdev, parents in perpetuity) as his real father and mother, and yet can't help falling deeply, hopelessly, madly in love with their daughter. He cannot stand to hear the word '*bhaiyya*' from her. Shocked at his behaviour, Maya follows him one evening as he meets Bhagat, who's getting impatient with all the delay in robbing the family and splitting the loot. She overhears their conversation, and the truth is revealed to her. She now not only knows that the man in their house is not Kundan at all but an imposter, she also knows that this imposter now treats her parents as his own and loves her to the end of the world. In a collage of emotions, all those moments come back to her. She doesn't have the heart to expose this fraud to her parents, but can she afford to watch silently and let it all happen? A song wafts in, mirroring her dilemma:

Aise mein kachhu kaha nahi jaaye
Apna hai ya begana, kaun mohe samjhaye
Anjaane se koi kaise reet nibhaye

(In moments like these,
Words fail me
Is he friend or foe – who's to say?

How am I to honour bonds
With someone I know not?)

Looking back at those shared moments where the fake Kundan tried to convey his feelings for her, is she now reciprocating them in some way, knowing that he is not really her brother? Raj Khosla keeps this bit slightly ambiguous.

Maya knows Kundan/Babu's real intentions about the family and she respects that. She also knows that he loves her. But all this while she has seen him as a brother. Can that change overnight? In the climax, Bhagat, tired of the delay, takes things in his own hands and breaks into Shahji's house, making off with valuables. Kundan goes to great lengths to bring the jewels back. He feels even more indebted to the family now that he knows that the 'boy' he supposedly replaced was actually Balli (Jagdish Raj), who he had killed.

In the end, as Maya is shown getting married, that iconic *bidaai* song starts playing – '*Chal ri sajni ab kya soche/ Kajra na beh jaaye rote rote*'. Over the years, this has become one of the definitive songs in this genre, which, to generations of Bollywood fans, has symbolized a father bidding a tearful goodbye to his daughter as she heads to her marital home. But the song, fascinatingly, plays out on two levels. While it contains a father's lamentation, it also contains the resignation of a companion:

Baabul pachhtay, haathon ko mal ke
Kaahe diya pardes, tukde ko dil ke
Ansoo liye soch raha door khada re

(The father stands weeping
Regretfully beseeching
Oh, why am I to send

My daughter to an unseen land?)

With that last line, the camera turns to Dev Anand and the words fit the character like a glove.

Nandini Ramnath, in her article dedicated to the song, says:

> The song turns the traditional ritual of the brother giving away his sister on its head. As Babu watches Maya leave her home, the real source of his pain is evident only to her. Maya keeps turning back to look at Babu, both with gratitude for having dumped his partner and saved the family honour as well as with something that approximates love. The frisson that has been crackling between the two throughout the movie finally has a name, but it's too late for both.[6]

Fellow film buff and filmmaker Udayan Ghosh draws a parallel with the song 'Hamesha tumko chaha', from Sanjay Leela Bhansali's *Devdas* (2002), where Devdas (Shah Rukh Khan) gives away Paro (Aishwarya Rai), even carrying her palanquin for a bit.[7] Was this an extension of Dev and Suchitra's situation in 'Chal ri sajni'? It's difficult to say but unlike Dev, Shah Rukh Khan in *Devdas* is under no compulsion to play-act as the brother. This situation doesn't exist in the original novel or any of the other adaptations, including Bimal Roy's 1955 version.

In the end, as she is about to get in the palanquin, Maya, in full bridal regalia, turns to Kundan/Babu to tell him that she knows. Babu, for the sake of the couple he once wished to hoodwink, just like the Llano Kid in 'A Double-Dyed Deceiver', decides to stay back as their son and never leave.

The ending of *Bombai ka Babu* was bold, even striking, considering the kind of films being made in the 1950s. Was

Khosla cognizant of the fact that he couldn't show the union of this pair because it might have seemed immoral to a conservative audience? Or was it because such a union would have contradicted the inherent rationality of the screenplay? After all, for more than half the film, Maya had treated this man as her brother. How could she, armed with the revelation from one stray incident, decide that he should no longer be her brother but a lover? It didn't make sense. But from the vantage point of commercial cinema, not to have the hero and heroine run into each other's arms was fraught with risk. Raj Khosla ran that risk, trusting the story and characterization, and believing that the audience would see that. Well, nobody did.

In a filmography littered with classics, *Bombai ka Babu* is the one film where Raj went out of his comfort zone and attempted something brave and different. But there were no takers for his quirky vision at the time, and *Bombai ka Babu* failed to garner the kind of success *Kala Pani* had.

The soundtrack of *Bombai ka Babu* (1960).

Nevertheless, the soundtrack, like all Raj Khosla films, contained some unforgettable songs. One of the most recognizable numbers from the film is the title song, 'Dekhne mein bhola hai'. For the lyrics of the song, S.D. Burman borrowed a refrain from a song in the Telugu film *Rojulu Marayi*. This was the same film in which Waheeda had debuted as a dancer in the song 'Eruvaaka sagaroranno chinnanna'. The music was by Master Venu, based on a Telugu folk song 'Ayyo koyyoda'. Burman Senior had heard this song and seen Waheeda Rehman dance to it. He wanted to use the tune of the *mukhda*, along with the word '*chinnanna*' ('little brother' in

Waheeda Rehman's debut as a dancer in the song 'Eruvaaka sagaroranno chinnanna' from *Rojulu Marayi* (1955).

Telugu). He got in touch with Waheeda, the song on his mind. As Waheeda explained to Nasreen Munni Kabir in her book, *Conversations with Waheeda Rehman*:

> Did you know that a Bombay music director copied that *Rojulu Marayi* song? And guess who? S.D. Burman! Sometime in the late 1950s, I got a call from Dada: 'You know that Telugu song of yours? Well, sing it for me.'
>
> 'Dada, how can I? I am not a singer.'
>
> 'I am not going to record you. I know you're not Lata Mangeshkar. Go on, sing!'
>
> I sang it for Dada a couple of times and he composed a song with the same tune for *Bombai Ka Babu*... Majrooh Sultanpuri wrote the lyrics and even used the word '*chinnanna*' from the original.[8]

Burman and Majrooh might have used '*chinnanna*' because it implies brother. '*Bombai se aaya hai/ Babu chinnanna...*'

The other song of note is 'Tak dhoom tak dhoom baje duniya tera dhol', performed by Manna Dey in the film. The tune gained wide popularity in Bengal later when S.D. Burman sang 'Ami takdum takdum bajai Bangladesher dhol'.

'Deewana mastana hua dil' is probably the second-most popular song of the film, and 'Saathi na koi manzil' is an unforgettable ballad by Mohammed Rafi. During an interview with me, while listening to the song 'Pawan chale to uthe nadi mein leher si', Asha Bhosle noted, 'This song is not by Burman saab. This was Jaidev. This was the distinctive style of Jaidev, who was assisting Burman dada at the time. Songs like "Nazar lagi raja tore bangle par" (*Kala Pani*) and this one, these kind of songs were all managed by Jaidev.' She added, 'All the snapping of the fingers that you see in the song, it was all Raj ji. He knew how to present the hero in a song. He used characterization in songs too. Whether it was us, the chorus singers, or anybody else, everyone was in character. He worked very hard to bring that mood in everyone.'

With *Bombai ka Babu*, it was as if an era in the filmography of Raj Khosla officially came to a close. Ever since his debut *Milap*, every film of his so far had had Dev Anand as the protagonist. Dev was in the prime of his life, deliberately choosing morally ambiguous characters, successfully making a mark as a leading man. In this phase of Dev's career, Raj Khosla is a glittering presence. He played to Dev Anand's strengths and mounted his persona in the best way possible, whether it was the officer in *C.I.D.* or the reporter in *Solva Saal*, or the drifting souls looking for an anchor in *Kala Pani* and *Bombai ka Babu*. The only other director who showcased Dev so well was Vijay 'Goldie' Anand.

The film also marked the end of Raj Khosla's collaboration with S.D. Burman. The composer had given Raj some of his most iconic hits in the three films they worked together on – 'Hai apna dil toh awara' (*Solva Saal*), 'Achha ji main hari chalo maan jao na' (*Kala Pani*) and 'Dekhne mein bhola hai' (*Bombai ka Babu*).

His stint with Guru Dutt, Navketan and Dev Anand ended, it was time for Raj to explore new avenues.

9

Ek Musafir Ek Hasina, and the Beginnings of the Sadhana Phase

Sashadhar Mukherjee may well be one of the least celebrated legends of Indian cinema. Considering how influential he was in shaping cinema in the subcontinent, precious little is known about his early life. He was the key figure in a major Bombay studio, founded two more, launched many careers, and was the patriarch of a family that boasts names like Kajol, Rani Mukerji and Ayan Mukerji.

According to screenwriter Nabendu Ghosh, Mukherjee was from an elite and prosperous family of Allahabad. At the Allahabad University, he became a student of renowned physicist Dr Meghnad Saha. He was a brilliant student and Dr Saha had high hopes for him. Mukherjee cleared his MSc with flying colours and started teaching, only to quit some time later, because he wanted to study abroad. In the interim, he took a job at Bombay's Famous Recording Studio. Just as he was about to set off for his stint abroad, Mukherjee happened to meet a young, passionate filmmaker named Himanshu Rai who wanted to set up a big studio to produce films. Himanshu Rai's passion was infectious, and Mukherjee cancelled his trip and plunged headlong into the business of making movies. Rai established Bombay Talkies in June 1934, and Sashadhar Mukherjee joined him. Soon, he brought his brother-in-law Ashok Kumar into the fold.

In the six years that followed, Mukherjee became one of the pillars of Bombay Talkies. After Himanshu Rai's untimely death, a power struggle erupted at Bombay Talkies, between the deceased's wife, Devika Rani, and Mukherjee's camp. The latter, along with his brother-in-law Ashok Kumar, Rai Bahadur Chunilal and Gyan Mukerji, left the studio in a huff and set up Filmistan, which became home to some of the greatest talents Hindi cinema had to offer, including Saadat Hasan Manto, Ritwik Ghatak, Nasir Hussain, Shammi Kapoor and Dev Anand. At Filmistan, while Ashok Kumar was often in front of the camera, Rai Bahadur Chunilal managed the finance and business side of things, and Mukherjee was in charge of creative output. However, following Chunilal's untimely death in 1950, Tolaram Jalan, a business magnate from Calcutta with a mind to be in films, took over. Mukherjee and Tolaram Jalan didn't see eye to eye on most aspects of film production. After working on the blockbuster *Tumsa Nahin Dekha* (1957), a film that catapulted Shammi Kapoor to stardom, Mukherjee left Filmistan, with the resolve of setting up another studio. And that is how he established Filmalaya in 1958.

Even in those early days, Filmalaya was a respected banner. By the early 1960s, Sashadhar Mukherjee was a formidable figure in the Hindi film industry. While Mukherjee was a veteran, Raj was a relatively new filmmaker, albeit one who had consistently delivered box office gold. He had made five films, of which only two weren't well received. And even when the films themselves didn't work, the songs were on everyone's lips. Although there is little clarity on how Raj Khosla came to be associated with Sashadhar Mukherjee, the two now decided to join hands. Raj always regarded Mukherjee as his second mentor after Guru Dutt. He held three men in high regard, and credited them for helping him lay the foundations of his career: his Guru, Dev Anand and Sashadhar Mukherjee.

The Filmalaya School of Acting was another institution that Mukherjee had built. Sadhana Shivdasani was trained here. Besides her, many well-known actors, including Sanjeev Kumar and Mac Mohan, came out of that school. But even before being trained at Filmalaya, Sadhana had appeared in two other films – as a dancer in *Shree 420* (1955) and as the heroine's sister in a Sindhi film called *Abaana* (1958). S. Mukherjee's son Joy was first seen in *Hum Hindustani* (1960) as Sunil Dutt's brother.[1] It was later that Filmalaya launched the 'sensational new stars' Joy Mukherjee and Sadhana in *Love in Simla* (1960). The film was a huge success.

Joy followed it up with a film by Nitin Bose, *Umeed* (1962), while Sadhana was inundated with a deluge of good offers. She ended up working in two Bimal Roy films – *Parakh* (1960) and *Prem Patra* (1962) – followed by *Man-Mauji* (1962) opposite Kishore Kumar who was at the top of his game, and a landmark Navketan film opposite Dev Anand, *Hum Dono* (1961). In just two years, she had managed to bag some coveted projects with leading production houses and filmmakers.

Two years after *Love in Simla*, Mukherjee wanted to feature the Joy Mukherjee–Sadhana pairing once again. He may have wanted to repeat the magic. And that is where Raj came in.

Fresh from his stint with Dev Anand, Raj was looking for something new and challenging. Partly because of the kind of image that Dev had been building those days and partly due to Raj's own inclination, the films the duo worked together in had crime as an important thematic aspect. Even in the garb of romantic comedy, *Solva Saal* had the element of crime. Now, after having made five crime films, Raj was aching to do something new. A diehard romantic, he always wore his heart on his sleeve. A connoisseur of Urdu poetry, Shakespeare and all the good things in life, it was natural for him to seek beauty and grace in everything he did. The heroines were supremely important in his scheme of things. In a stark contrast to his colleagues whose work was dominated by men, women were central to Raj's body of work. Women characters were given the kind of importance they deserved. A lot of his efforts were directed towards making his heroines look like goddesses. And one could safely say that this process began with Sadhana. She told radio legend Ameen Sayani on one of his shows some years later, 'His films are like poetry. He does romance on celluloid. He cannot make a film unless he completely glamourizes the heroine and makes her romantic.'[2]

When Sashadhar Mukherjee extended him an offer to direct *Ek Musafir Ek Hasina* (1962), Raj Khosla took it as an opportunity to prove that he could operate outside his comfort zone. He said to journalist Khalid Mohamed in a 1979 interview, 'By now I had also realized that I was depending on Dev as my hero all the time – if he's there, the project's there. I took the assignment, knowing Joy Mukherjee wasn't of the same calibre. I could shape him.' He added about Sadhana: 'Here was a girl who impressed me immediately. She was tremendous star material and would react to the slightest sign or guidance from me.'[3]

Ek Musafir Ek Hasina begins with two parallel storylines, guided by two voiceovers – of the hero and the heroine. Lieutenant Ajay (Joy Mukherjee) of the 5th Punjab Regiment is on a top-secret mission to Kashmir during the Kabali Raid of 1947, while Asha's (Sadhana) greedy uncle and aunt are getting her married against her will to a lout, in exchange for 15,000 rupees. Halfway through the rituals, there is an attack at the venue, and everyone runs for their life. The groom and his father drag Asha into a room, snatch her jewellery and leave her to die at the hands of the insurgents. Eventually, Asha manages to flee. She runs into Lieutenant Ajay who saves her from a band of Kabalis but injures himself in the process. She carries him into an abandoned shack and tends to him. When Ajay comes to, it is revealed that he has lost his memory. Asha nurses him back to health with the help of a street urchin Abdullah (Master Aziz) and a dog named Sheru. Robbed of his memory, Ajay has no concept of identity, nationality, family, allegiance or any sense of self. The only human connection he makes after this rebirth is with Asha, his benefactor. He holds on to her with all his might. Asha is taken aback.

This is one of the most elegantly handled bits in the film. In Bollywood of the 1960s, physical proximity was reason enough for a handsome man and a beautiful woman to be in love. Falling in love was a given. In *Ek Musafir Ek Hasina*, however, Ajay and Asha have their reasons to be drawn to each other. She has been betrayed by her own family and thrown to the wolves for a fistful of rupees. She can't imagine anyone having genuine feelings for her. Ajay, this new version of him, has known only one woman, one who has saved his life. He can't help but fall for her. And he tells her as much:

> *Main woh insaan hoon jiska koi thikana nahin. Woh musafir jiska koi manzil nahin. Kisi ghar, kisi zameen, kisi dharti se mera koi naata nahin. Tanhaaee ke iss phaile huye sehra mein agar koi mujhe jaanta hai, meri awaz ko koi pehchanta hai, toh sirf tum ho. Asha, mujhe na chhodna*!

(I am a man without an address, a traveller without a destination. I am not attached to any home, land or country. In this wasteland of solitude, if there is anyone who knows me, who knows my voice – it is you. Never let go of me, Asha!)

The plot of the film shares some uncanny similarities with Guru Dutt's *Sailaab* (1956), where the setting of the first half was Assam instead of Kashmir. In that film, the hero Gautam (Abhi Bhattacharya) crash-lands in Assam and finds love during a bout of amnesia.

Ek Musafir Ek Hasina ended up becoming a far bigger success than envisaged. It emerged as one of the biggest money-spinners for Filmalaya and gave Joy Mukherjee's career a fillip. Sadhana's position as the next big thing as a romantic heroine was further solidified.

And, as with a majority of Raj Khosla films covered in this book, the most memorable aspect of *Ek Musafir Ek Hasina*, one would argue, is its music. As always, whenever we speak of memorable songs in Raj Khosla's oeuvre, they can scarcely be detached from the visuals. This is true of every magical number in *Ek Musafir Ek Hasina*, making it nearly impossible to hum or listen to any of the songs without being reminded of the luminescent Sadhana unleashing her magic with Joy Mukherjee, the awestruck lover, lingering admiringly.

Evidently, music and music directors had a substantial role to play in Raj's film work. His deep knowledge and understanding of music, coupled with the insight that songs were often critical to a film's commercial acceptability, made him go to great lengths to try and ensure that the music in his films was top notch, even if it meant locking horns with the music director. Asha Bhosle agrees, and told me, 'Raj Khosla used to inspire us a lot during recordings. When things didn't work according to him, he would also get really angry and leave in a huff. It was a thing for him to inspire the singers to ensure they sing to his satisfaction. Though when the music director was saying something and he was saying something else, it used to really confuse us.'[4]

There are two different accounts about the music of *Ek Musafir Ek Hasina*. Writer, poet and anchor Jawaid Naseem speaks of a tiff between O.P. Nayyar and Raj while working on the songs.[5] According to this version of events, since Raj was a trained singer and had an understanding of music, it was he who would bring tunes to O.P. Nayyar and ask him to compose songs around them. When this episode repeated itself a few times, it got on O.P. Nayyar's nerves and the composer told Sashadhar Mukerji that he would like to leave the film. The worried producer wanted to know why. Nayyar explained his plight. 'If he is so insistent on giving music, why doesn't he quit directing and start composing?' Nayyar is supposed to have said. Raj was equally miffed when Sashadhar Mukherjee reached out to him, hoping for a truce. All he had done was try to contribute to the film to the best of his abilities. 'From here on out, I am not going to talk to Nayyar saab on anything whatsoever.' Once the film was completed, the two decided to part ways for good, and never worked together on any project again.

But if one were to believe Raj's own account, this is not how things panned out.[6] According to an interview given to journalist Sheila Vesuna, Raj came into the project when Mukherjee had already chosen a bouquet of songs composed by O.P. Nayyar. The composer and Raj had had a rather successful musical partnership in *C.I.D.* This time around, Mukherjee had signed O.P. Nayyar as the composer and chosen the songs.

The task assigned to Raj was to weave a film around the songs. More than anything else, the director's account describes a showdown with Mukherjee rather than Nayyar. 'We shot the songs in Kashmir,' says Raj, 'from where I sent the rushes of a few, many of which were close-ups of Joy and Sadhana, to Mr. Mukherjee. He sent back a telegram to me – "This could have been shot in Ghodbunder." It was signed S. Mukherjee. I sent back a cable saying – "These songs will be a lesson for all the dummies in Filmalaya."'[7]

The two also had another showdown regarding the chronology of the film. Since the film involved the loss of memory of the central character, Sashadhar Mukherjee suggested that the final edited version should start from the eighth reel and the rest could be rearranged. (For the uninitiated, films in the pre-digital days, were made on celluloid – hence the name 'film' – and one feature-length film would involve several 'reels'. Mukherjee insisted that Raj should re-edit the film and start it from a different point in the movie.) Raj played along and that was the order in which the film was released and screened at the iconic Maratha Mandir hall in Bombay.

When Raj visited the theatre, however, he heard stray comments like, 'Director *paagal hoga*. The director must be mad.' Raj rushed back to Mukherjee and insisted that the order be reverted to his original edit, or the film wouldn't make any sense to the public. 'To his credit,' Raj explained later, 'he understood my predicament and allowed me to make changes in the film.'[8] In the seventh week, the film was re-edited and they went back to the original structure.

The soundtrack of *Ek Musafir Ek Hasina* (1962).

Despite the creative differences, every little song in the film is a glittering pearl from the deep seas . The songs continue to be fairly popular to this day. The tune of 'Mujhe dekh kar aap ka muskurana' has a sublime, soothing quality, which has been replicated time and again: Telugu composer Pendyala Nageswara Rao, popularly known as Pendyala, repurposed it for the song 'O cheli kopama' from the film *Sri Krishna Tulabharam* (1966). More recently, music director duo Jatin–Lalit employed an uncannily similar tune for 'Mujhe raat din' from *Sangharsh* (1999).

Another interesting anecdote related to the film is about its most popular song – 'Bahut shukriya badi meherbani'. Raju Bharatan writes in his book *A Journey Down Melody Lane* that O.P. Nayyar called up fellow music composer N. Datta and told him point-blank that he wished to use the tune of his song 'Tere pyar ka aasra chahta hoon' from *Dhool Ka Phool* (1959) for one of his songs in *Ek Musafir Ek Hasina*.[9] Datta was only too glad to comply. Nayyar reused the tune for 'Bahut shukriya badi meherbani' and it went on to outshine Datta's original track. N. Datta too had been part of the Raj Khosla universe, having done the music for Raj Khosla's debut, *Milap*.

Another soulful number in *Ek Musafir Ek Hasina*, 'Humko tumhare ishq ne', bears an eerie resemblance to 'Tang aa chuke hain kashmakash-e-zindagi se hum' from Guru Dutt's *Pyaasa*. Did Datta's mentor S.D. Burman also get a call from O.P. Nayyar? Who knows?

This was the period when Nayyar and Asha Bhosle were a formidable team and all the songs in the film were by Asha Bhosle and Mohammed Rafi. Another triumph of the film and its album was 'Tumhe mohabbat hai humse maana'. Effortlessly sung by Bhosle, it was completely owned by Sadhana and the way she performed it. O.P. Nayyar was experiencing a lull in his career right around this time. The success of *Ek Musafir Ek Hasina* brought him back.

By this time, Raj had gone above and beyond his mentor in picturizing his songs. He had to. Unlike his mentor, Raj had to stay relevant through various eras and decades. But it might be a tad simplistic to conclude that he implicitly enjoyed the infusion of songs in his films, merely because of this and the fact that he loved music and wanted to be a singer at one point. On the contrary, he considered it largely unnatural, while acknowledging that it was a necessary evil. While writing about his filmmaking in the pages of *Filmfare* magazine, Raj explained, 'The director's biggest headache is the picturisation of songs. In the telling of a story, song is an unnatural intrusion, but in Indian movies songs are a "must" and the director has to blend the natural with the unnatural with such skill as to make a cohesive, stimulating and enjoyable whole. This certainly calls for maximum ingenuity, intense labour backed by knowledge and very subtle handling of the characters and situations.'[10]

This 'ingenuity', 'intense labour backed by knowledge', and 'subtle handling of characters and situations' would come into play in his next film, which remains one of his most recognizable pieces of work.

10

Woh Kaun Thi? The Woman in White? Or Not

In 1859, when *Household Words*, the magazine Charles Dickens edited, refused to publish a statement in defence of his divorce, the Victorian author decided to start his own journal. He called it *All the Year Round*, and its pilot issue in April 1859 featured the first instalment of *A Tale of Two Cities*. Other writers also contributed to the magazine, and one of its more popular serials published that year was a 'sensation novel' by 35-year-old Wilkie Collins. Called *The Woman in White*, the book is still widely revered as one of the earliest detective novels in the English language.

Collins had read law, and his book, in a thriller format, drew attention to the legal rights of married women. The story revolves around a young heiress called Laura Fairlie, who is betrothed to Sir Percival Glyde, a greedy man eyeing her inheritance. His partner in crime is the sinister Count Fosco. What complicates matters is the sudden appearance of a mysterious woman clad in all white, who shares an uncanny facial resemblance to Laura. One misty evening, this woman in white bumps into Walter Hartright, Laura's new drawing teacher. Walter is shocked at the resemblance. Eventually, the evil duo uses this resemblance to their advantage by killing one of the women and replacing her with the other. This may have been sufficient to fool the world, but the dashing Walter and Marian Holcombe, a half-sister of Laura, uncover the truth and ensure that justice is delivered.

The Woman in White was eventually published as a book in 1860 and inspired a stage adaptation that very year. When cinema appeared on the horizon, five silent films were adapted from the novel, with the first proper 'talkie' film released in 1948, in which the lissome Eleanor Parker played the dual role of Laura and her doppelgänger, with Gig Young as Walter Hartright.

Not long after, Guru Dutt was ready to produce an Indian take on the story. Guru Dutt Films announced the new film along with *Kaagaz Ke Phool*, calling it *Raaz*. The launch announcement named Waheeda Rehman in the dual role, with Sunil Dutt as the male lead.[1] The publicity booklet of *Kaagaz Ke Phool* contained an ad for *Raaz*, which stated that the film was 'fast progressing'. The ad also featured two new names as the director and music director: Niranjan and Rahul Dev Burman respectively. By this time, Raj Khosla had branched out with Guru Dutt's blessings. He was busy making *Kala Pani* and *Solva Saal* (both with Dev Anand). Niranjan was one of two people who had assisted Dutt in four films or more, the other one being Raj Khosla (not accounting for *Sailab*, the lost film for which crew information is unavailable). Niranjan had worked with Raj on *Baaz* and *Aar Paar*, and after the latter's exit, he had assisted Guru Dutt on two more films, *Pyaasa* and *Mr. & Mrs. 55*. Guru Dutt wanted to test the directorial chops of Niranjan – just like he had with Raj Khosla earlier – and *Raaz* seemed like a good opportunity for that.

Dutt also wanted to launch S.D. Burman's talented son with this film. 'After *Pyaasa*, Guru Dutt told me, I'm taking you for my next film. My father said, "Don't be silly, he hasn't started composing full-time yet"', R.D., the Rahul Dev Burman of the ad on *Raaz*, told Nasreen Munni Kabir in an interview. But Guru Dutt was adamant. R.D., aka Pancham, was just 19 years old but had impressed Guru with his work as an assistant to his father in *Pyaasa*.

With a cast and crew in place, the shooting of *Raaz* began in Shimla. Sunil Dutt was eventually replaced by Guru Dutt. But after shooting a few reels, Guru Dutt scrapped the film. As Pancham told Nasreen Munni Kabir:

> Niranjan worked hard; the film was fantastic. But after eight and a half reels were shot, I don't know what happened. Guru Dutt said he was shelving it, he didn't like it. I have witnessed him shelving six or seven films, so you can imagine what a whimsical person he was. He used to like a person in the morning, and after drinking, he would say, get out, I don't like you. Raj Khosla later took the story of *Raaz* and made it into *Woh Kaun Thi*.[2]

This story of Raj borrowing the idea to make his film was never ratified by the man himself. But the notion has been repeated so often that it has come to be the gospel truth. In fact, Raj once told Khalid Mohamed in an interview that N.N. Sippy – who was a typist when Raj was assisting Guru Dutt – came up with a 'suspense subject' that was the genesis of *Woh Kaun Thi?* (1964).[3] In an interview given to radio legend Ameen Sayani,[4] screenwriter Dhruva Chatterjee ratified this version of events when he reminisced that it was producer N.N. Sippy who brought the story idea to Raj Khosla. According to Chatterjee, Sippy had heard a three-line concept somewhere, which became the basis for Chatterjee's screenplay. Could N.N. Sippy have 'heard' of the novel by Wilkie Collins, or the 1948 Peter

Godfrey film? Pravesh Sippy, son of N.N. Sippy and himself a producer of repute, says, 'The contract and undertaking that he (Dhruva) had signed while handing over the script to the production house said that it was completely his original.'

Be that as it may, Guru Dutt's *Raaz* did share similarities with *Woh Kaun Thi?*, including the fact that the protagonists are doctors, which is a deviation from the novel, where Walter Hartright is an art teacher. Yet the two films were also vastly different. Guru Dutt's script had a sister to the heroine (Kum Kum was cast for the role), akin to Marion Halcombe who, in Collins's novel, was Laura's half-sister, companion and benefactor. The script that Chatterjee ultimately wrote had no such character. In fact, he introduced a character not there in the novel: the hero's first love, who is not the heroine. In the book, the only thing that motivates Walter in his actions is his deep affection for Laura – there is no other woman in his life. In *Woh Kaun Thi?*, after Dr Anand's (Manoj Kumar) first encounter with the mysterious woman clad in a white saree, we discover that he has a girlfriend called Seema and he intends to marry her. *Raaz* also had a sinister uncle, who was supposed to be the villain of the piece, with senior actor S. Nazir slated to play the role. In *Woh Kaun Thi?*, the villain was someone different.

'It was a suspense film, and I was the suspense in the film,' actor Prem Chopra said.[5] In mainstream Hindi cinema, it was easy to know at first glimpse if a character was up to no good. If it were Raj Kapoor, Dilip Kumar or Manoj Kumar, there was no chance of any monkey business. A Pran or Prem Chopra was a guarantee of wrongdoing. But in the early 1960s, Prem Chopra had only appeared as a hero in Punjabi films and a handful of Hindi films. He didn't have a set image, so when he made an appearance in the film, the audience had no reason to suspect this handsome young man of villainy. So, when he came out as the culprit, it was quite the shock. In that sense, he was indeed the 'suspense' in *Woh Kaun Thi?*.

Prem Chopra had a day job at the time. The film business still didn't pay enough for him to consider it a viable career option. He was an inspector/supervisor in the circulation department of the *Times of India*.[6] Like many aspiring actors of the time, he, too, frequented Gaylord, the central Bombay restaurant that was a regular haunt of film producers, directors and stars. It was here that N.N. Sippy first met Chopra and offered him the role in *Woh Kaun Thi?*. The actor says of the meeting: 'N.N. Sippy came to Gaylord and told me, "Come and see me tomorrow at my office." So, I went there, and the role was explained to me – a small role. They wanted a face that wasn't very recognizable.' It is likely that Raj was insistent on an actor who wasn't necessarily associated with a certain kind of screen persona. He didn't want to give away the ending by casting someone with a set image. The struggling artiste found 'Raj ji… a very mature director. I was very comfortable working with him. I was a little nervous, but he made me comfortable and encouraged me all the way.'

Nimmi was the original choice for the lead in *Woh Kaun Thi?*. She had been part of some exceptional hits of the 1950s, including *Deedar* (1951), *Aan* (1952) and *Uran Khatola* (1955). More recently, she had played sister to Sadhana, the heroine in *Mere Mehboob* (1963). *Woh Kaun Thi?* would have paired Manoj Kumar with Nimmi, a star on the wane. Raj Khosla didn't want that. To a *Filmfare* interviewer, almost 20 years later, he called it 'the worst possible combination', saying, 'Nimmi was on her way out… I still had *Bombai ka Babu*'s non-success behind me. But I had an ace up my sleeve – Sadhana.'[7]

In the early 1960s, Manoj Kumar and Raj had found kindred souls in each other. Kumar had a flair for writing and an understanding of how scenes should be constructed in a mainstream Hindi film. This talent came in handy to earn a quick buck in the early days. Many filmmakers and writers would rope him in to help write scenes. For every scene he wrote, the young actor, who didn't mind being deprived of credit, was paid 11 rupees. It was their love for cinema and common Punjabi roots that brought Raj and Kumar together despite the latter's string of flops until *Hariyali aur Rasta* (1962), the success of which, too, wasn't enough to make him a bankable star. Manoj was aware of the heroine situation in *Woh Kaun Thi?*. In March 2022, an emaciated, bedbound Manoj Kumar recounted to me: 'I was travelling to Delhi. Once I reached there, I returned to the Palam Airport [this was what the airport at Delhi was called] in the evening to receive the unit. I still didn't know who the heroine would be.'

The woman who emerged from the aircraft that day was Sadhana.

Raj wrote about Sadhana in November 1966. 'On the sets, she follows and trusts the director implicitly. This trust springs curiously from her trust in *herself* rather than the other person.'[8] Raj and Sadhana had worked out a sync by then, a rhythmic way of functioning. Well aware of each other's strengths, they were also conversant with each other's weaknesses. They were completely at ease with each other's families as well. Sadhana once described an evening during the shoot of *Woh Kaun Thi?* when she went to Raj Khosla's room. The director and his wife, Usha, were reading. Sadhana quietly slunk in and continued with her own reading, without disturbing the Khoslas. 'It was a comfortable silence,' she later said, 'the kind you only have with close friends.'[9]

Sadhana's natural allure and charm were great assets to *Woh Kaun Thi?*, and Raj worked on amplifying them. The film centres around the mystique of her character. In an interview to Sheila Vesuna, Raj narrated how Sadhana and he would deliberate on the different ways she had to smile in the film. 'The smile contributed a lot to the mystique of the character and the film. In fact, we actually sat down and worked out the kind of smile she would have to give for every shot,' he recalled.[10]

Unlike his Guru, Raj was quite obsessed with pre-credit sequences. *C.I.D* has one-and-a-half minute of intrigue before the title sequence begins rolling. *Bombai ka Babu* has shots of our (anti?) hero ambling out of jail, being picked up by his pal and followed by the police, interspersed with exterior shots of Bombay roads (quite unusual for Hindi films of the period). This continues for a good minute and 16 seconds before the title appears. Even for a romance like *Solva Saal*, the pre-credit sequence takes two-and-a-half minutes to set up the family that Laaj (Waheeda) is going to abandon. From this, Raj goes up to almost nine minutes – including an entire song – in *Anita*, and surpasses that in *Nehle peh Dehlaa*, which, in the tradition of 1970s revenge dramas, sets up the killing of a patriarch and separation of brothers before the title shows up.

Yet, it is quite possible that the pre-credit sequence of *Woh Kaun Thi?* might just be the most iconic opening scene not only in Raj Khosla's oeuvre, but in all of Hindi cinema. A car is braving its way through heavy rains on a country road. We find ourselves inside the car, the screeching of wipers loud and clear. Potholes and ditches are visible through the bumpy ride. Beyond the windshield, a white silhouette comes into view. It's a woman, draped in white. The driver slams on his brakes. He honks away, but she refuses to budge. The driver peeks out of window and says in the most velvety Manoj Kumar voice possible: '*Sunaai nahi deta*? *Raaste se hato*. *Kaun ho tum*? Can't you hear? Move out of the way. Who are you?' The woman in white (Sadhana), says she is no one. He asks again, '*Kahan jaana hai*? Where do you want to go?' Nowhere, she says. After a cryptic conversation, Kumar gives Sadhana a lift with the promise of no more questions. Kumar can't see a thing through the sheets of water, but she can. He notices blood oozing out of her finger. '*Mujhe khoon achha lagta hai*. I like blood,' she says. Eventually, she asks him to pull over next to a graveyard. As he wonders what business she could possibly have there, she reminds him of his promise. When she leaves the car, the wipers screech back into life. Kumar realizes that all this while, with the mysterious woman inside the car, the wipers had stopped moving. Sadhana casually walks into the graveyard, as the gate creaks open by itself. There is a bloodcurdling scream, followed by the song 'Naina barse rim jhim rim jhim', and the title, *Woh Kaun Thi?*, splashes across the screen.

This opening sequence is one of the most effective buildups seen in mainstream Hindi films, giving the viewer a taste of what's to come. It's eerie and delivers just the right dose of chills without underscoring the theatrics. There is something unique about the pace. It's not hurried, yet there is a sense of urgency, as if the events are unfolding at a rapid pace. It's not easy to place your finger on it. It finally clicked for me when Manoj Kumar explained. According to him, *Woh Kaun Thi?* was the first Hindi film that was 'cut to cut'. 'There were no fade-outs or fade-ins, no dissolves or wipes. *Likhi hi aise gayi thi*. It was written like that,' the actor told me. It was Raj Khosla's adroit sense of filmmaking and inventive editing that gave *Woh Kaun Thi?* its feverish feel. He was helped by editor Dattaram Pai, an alumnus of Filmistan and Filmalaya. The editor was shadowed by a 32-year-old who was already being noticed for his skills in cutting film: Waman Bhonsle. Waman and Raj later collaborated on a number of films.

From the outset, Raj was certain that this film needed a specific atmosphere. To establish the chilling, sinister feel, he decided to film it in Shimla. This was the early 1960s and the hill station was yet to become the darling of filmmakers. Despite this, the idea was stuck in his head. It wasn't cheap either, especially for a producer like N.N. Sippy, who was making his first film with A-list stars. 'N.N. Sippy was making small, stunt films then,' recalled Raj later, 'and couldn't afford to shoot in Shimla. Somehow, I persuaded him to raise funds, and we shot in the snows. This was very important to give that cold, eerie atmosphere to the film.'[11] Raj shot the film in one fell swoop, without any unnecessary retakes or reshoots. They couldn't afford any.

Early on in *Woh Kaun Thi?*, Dr Anand receives a call to see a patient in a dilapidated mansion near Versova post office. As he approaches the house, the doors swing open, allowing the camera to roll in and expand our view of the interiors. Cobwebs are aplenty and you can distinctly hear – and eventually see – a bat. It is suggested that the good doctor pick up a candle and light it. The man quietly complies and climbs up the rickety stairs to the patient's room. To his horror, this patient is the same woman he had driven to the graveyard the other night. But this woman is dead. While on his way back from the misadventure, Dr Anand is waylaid by two cops who claim that the house he has just been to is in fact abandoned. The doctor protests and leads them back into the mansion, only to find it truly abandoned. The only things in common with his last visit are the cobwebs. You could swear that the flying mammal is lurking in there.

Raj littered the film with such spooks. Not only do you have bats, cobwebs, screeching doors and repeated shots of a grotesque man holding flowers, Raj found a way of emphasizing the unearthly ambience with the help of the filmmaking devices at his disposal. After the somewhat shocking and untimely death of his girlfriend (Helen), Dr Anand's mother compels him into a marriage of convenience. Bizarrely, the heartbroken doctor, still mourning the loss of his beloved, discovers on his wedding night that his bride (whom he hasn't seen before) is the same mysterious woman he had dropped to the graveyard and also found dead in the abandoned mansion. To add to his woes, his new wife keeps breaking into the same song the woman in white sang as she disappeared into the graveyard: 'Naina barse rim jhim rim jhim'. As Dr Anand spies on his bride through a window, she begins to hum those lines. They sound faint at first, as if coming from a distance. As the camera – and the viewer – goes past the window and halts at the doorframe, the singing gets louder.

In another instance, Dr Anand walks out of his office into the hallway to investigate a noise. It is pitch dark and the camera follows him in a sluggish tracking shot as he ambles through the hallway, turning the lights on one by one. First. Second. Third. Fourth. As his hand inches to flick the fifth switch, a woman's voice rips through the silence, asking him not to turn this last one on. Almost instantly, a Venus de Milo appears in the frame. Dr Anand freezes, staring at it in disbelief as his wife emerges from behind the statue. Khosla employed such techniques throughout *Woh Kaun Thi?*, constantly inspiring the feel of a thriller.

'Naina barse' itself served as a musical motif in the film, following the mysterious woman that Sadhana portrays. For some time now, a version of the song, sung by Madan Mohan, has been doing the rounds of the internet. It contains only a few lines and isn't part of the final recording, which was sung by Lata Mangeshkar. Legend has it that

Madan Mohan's rendition of 'Naina barse'.

this version was played during the shoot, leaving the crowds in splits as they heard a woman singing in a man's voice. But what is not so well known is the fact that even Manoj Kumar, the hero of the film, was spooked by the song. Madan Mohan's son Samir Kohli broke it down for me:

> They are shooting in Nainital. It is the bank of the lake. He [Manoj Kumar] is sitting on a bench. The shot is of a boat moving on the lake – there's nobody in the boat – the oars are moving on their own, and the song plays in the background. Raj Khosla is on a hill far away from them. Manoj Kumar has not been told that the track that has been sent for the shoot is in my father's voice instead of Lata ji's. So, the moment it starts playing, he runs away from the set, shivering like a leaf. He actually thought it was a ghost!

Lata Mangeshkar, the nightingale herself, was not available that day. But since Sadhana's dates had been locked, they insisted that the song be dubbed for the shoot. The singer had to commute between several studios to record, and she couldn't dub the song just then. She told me that the shot was to be taken from a distance and all Sadhana had to do was to move her lips a bit. '*Madan bhaiyya ko maine kaha, iss waqt toh main aap ka gaana kar nahi sakoongi*. I told Madan *bhaiyya* that I won't be able to do your song at this time.' Her Madan *bhaiyya* reassured her that he would dub an *antara* of the song on track just for the purpose of the shoot. She could always sing it later.[12] Madan Mohan's singing talent is abundantly clear from the song but both the singer and Sadhana confirmed during interviews that some of the locals at the shoot were amused that a man was singing for a woman. They even commented '*Bakwaas* film *hogi*!'

According to Samir Kohli, the tune for 'Naina barse' was originally conceived by Madan Mohan more than a decade earlier, while composing the music of *Ankhen*, which was his debut and for which Raj Khosla even sang a song, 'Rail mein jiya mora sananana hai re'. Said Kohli, 'He [Madan Mohan] told me that "Naina barse" had been composed at the time *Ankhen* was being made… I believe Raj Khosla reminded my father of the tune he had made earlier, and insisted on using it as the theme for his own film.'[13]

Sanjeev Kohli, Madan Mohan's elder son, confirmed this: '… it was the very musically attuned Raj Khosla, who reminded Madanji of a haunting tune he had composed in 1949/1950, which was never used for a decade thereafter as many directors rejected it… That song became 'Naina barse', the theme song of the film. It would probably never have been recorded had Raj Khosla not recalled it.'[14]

'Jo humne dastaan apni sunayi' was another brilliant if underrated ballad from the film. After a series of disappearing and reappearing acts by his mysterious bride, an exasperated Dr Anand wants her out of his house and life. But when she delivers a monologue on the verge of leaving, his eyes well up. And here the song unspools. She asks:

The soundtrack of *Woh Kaun Thi?* (1964).

Jo humne dastaan apni sunayi
Aap kyon roye?
Tabaahi to hamaare dil pe aayi
Aap kyon roye?

(When I tell you my story
Why do you weep?
It's my heart that faces ruin
Why do you weep?)

The team of Raja Mehdi Ali Khan – who penned the precious lyrics outlined above – and Madan Mohan had joined hands with Raj for the first time. The pans, tracks and zooms through the song heighten the melancholy as these meticulously dressed lovers shed tears in a picturesque balcony. Raj Khosla had a thing for shooting songs in large, expansive terraces and balconies complemented by nature. This was repeated in *Mera Saaya*, *Anita*, *Do Raaste* and even *Sunny* (1984).

The piece de resistance, the film's crowning glory, happens to be an exquisite piece of music that has made whole generations swoon. But if Manoj Kumar is to be believed, Raj himself almost came in the way of one of his greatest musical artefacts. The actor reminisced, 'I got a call from Madan Mohan one day. "Raj Khosla has lost his mind," Madan said. "*Ek gaana sunaya. Usko pasand nahi aaya*. I made him hear a song. He didn't like it. You come and handle this please"'. Manoj Kumar didn't want to intervene. It was Raj Khosla's film, after all. He chose to speak to N.N. Sippy instead. There were only a few days left for the shoot and the song was yet to be finalized. What was to be done? Sippy concurred with the music director. He, too, wanted Manoj Kumar to approach Raj Khosla and sort this out. Meanwhile, Madan Mohan made Kumar listen to the song. Kumar was silent for a bit, then said, 'Don't tell me that Raj didn't like THIS song!' It was obviously a brilliant composition. One of Raj Khosla's great strengths as an artist and a filmmaker was the ability to appreciate good music. And he hadn't liked this? Kumar was flabbergasted.

Raj winced when Manoj Kumar told him about the song. 'Let's not talk about that song. It's really bad,' he said. No way was he going to give it a listen again. But on his lead actor's repeated insistence, the director reluctantly agreed to let Madan Mohan play the song to him once more. Raj was astonished – it was one of the best tunes he had heard. And this was a song he was about to let go? 'How incredibly stupid of me,' he exclaimed. According to Kumar, Raj even picked up his own shoe to hit himself. The song in question was 'Lag ja gale', a ditty that one might say continues to be Madan Mohan's most popular creation (with over 277 million views on YouTube). The incident was also an example of the filmmaker's keen instinct to spot and nurture talent. He had seen how good Kumar could be and allowed him a free hand to suggest and make changes. In turn, Kumar would often come up with ideas that would enrich the film. Once, when the crew was in Shimla and the shooting about to start, Manoj Kumar felt that the script could do with a bit of tightening. He reworked it and even wrote a few scenes.

As we have examined before, the music in Raj's films is inextricable from the visuals. Nowhere is this more evident than in 'Lag ja gale'. While the tune has developed a cult following of its own over the years, no one can think of it and not be reminded of the exquisite way in which it was shot. Raj and his team went to great lengths to heighten the mystery in Sadhana's character. In the song, as Sadhana pines over Dr Anand Manoj Kumar, the camera almost caresses her. The shadow of the coconut leaves on her face and the subtle moonlight lend her an ethereal quality. The song was shot at Filmalaya Studios, according to Manoj Kumar. Raj and the cinematographer K.H. Kapadia toiled for hours to get the right look. The high-contrast lighting and evocative play of light and shadow, chiaroscuro-like, is coupled with Raj's penchant for close-ups, an obsession that he inherited from Guru Dutt. The combination of these elements, along with the buttery camera movement gives 'Lag ja gale' the timeless visual appeal that the song so richly deserves. In an online discussion hosted by Film and Television Institute of India (FTII) commemorating Raj Khosla's birth anniversary, filmmaker and historian Karan Bali highlighted the Khosla–Kapadia magic in 'Lag ja gale', with specific emphasis on the low-key lighting: 'It adds to Sadhana's mystery, it adds to the confusion that Manoj Kumar is going through, and the way he Khosla makes Sadhana walk so that her face is always within light...' Bali went on to juxtapose how Raj Khosla lit Sadhana so richly compared to the relatively flatter cinematography of the Tamil (*Yaar Nee?*, 1966) and Telugu (*Aame Evaru?*, 1966) remakes of *Woh Kaun Thi?*, both of which featured Jayalalithaa reprising Sadhana's role.

Hindi film songs number in the tens of thousands, right from the first strands performed in *Alam Ara* (1931) to the latest Spotify sensations. But of all the songs that could be said to comprise the soul of Hindi film music, 'Lag ja gale' stands tall. In 2016, on her 87th birthday, Lata Mangeshkar listed six favourites from her glittering repertoire. 'Lag ja gale' was one of them. Sanjeev Kohli explained how even for the great Lata, it was a difficult song to pull off, what with all the *murki*s and the variations added by Madan Mohan and the singer herself.[15] Effervescent as a little schoolgirl, Lata ji told me, 'When we recorded the song, everybody was happy with it. Raj Khosla loved it. All of us were satisfied. Once the recording was over, Madan *bhaiyya aaye aur mujhe gale laga kar rone lage*. Madan *bhaiyya* came and hugging me, started crying. The song... created history.' History indeed. Today, six decades after release, the song still plays in pubs and clubs haunted by 20-somethings. Filmmakers have repurposed it variously in their films, including Karan Johar in *Bombay Talkies* (2013) and *Ae Dil Hai Mushkil*, and Tigmanshu Dhulia for the *Saheb, Biwi aur Gangster* franchise.

While its music caught on gradually, *Woh Kaun Thi?* itself was an instant hit, reinventing Sadhana and Manoj Kumar as mainstream stars, and establishing Prem Chopra as a baddie. The film turned out to be a major success and was bracketed as a horror film without giving in to genre conventions. So far, Raj had had an unbeatable run and proved conclusively that when it came to filmmaking, he indeed possessed the Midas touch. The success of *Woh Kaun Thi?* placed him among the most sought-after filmmakers of his generation. But the euphoria proved short-lived. Within eight months of the release, Raj Khosla encountered a crushing tragedy: the death of his mentor.

11

Mera Saaya – What *Jhumka*?

Dawn. Saturday, 10 October 1964. Bombay was still rubbing its eyes, yawning and pulling itself together for the drudgery of another long day. Meanwhile, a 39-year-old lay lifeless on his bed. He looked calm. The famously restless Guru Dutt was finally at peace. His sister Lalitha Lajmi later said he looked like he was about to say something.

Guru Dutt had always had things to say, only he preferred to say them through his films. Arguably, the most personal of these statements was *Kaagaz Ke Phool* (1959), a film that came a few decades too early. The audiences were blatantly unwelcoming of this indulgent, slow-burn of a spectacle. They rejected it, and Dutt's heart broke into a thousand pieces. As he wallowed in his misery, Raj was right there beside him. Like countless other evenings, the mentee gently offered his shoulder for his mentor to cry on. Guru Dutt looked at him, eyes brimming over, and said he had given birth to a stillborn child. 'He felt that the world had suffocated him,' Raj later told Nasreen Munni Kabir.[1]

Raj possibly shared the most precious components of Guru Dutt's enigmatic life – his silences. His silences were eloquent, Raj later said about his Guru. And that is what he missed the most. The two men shared many qualities and attributes. Both had a weakness for the bottle. Both had a penchant for the melancholy – Guru Dutt was known to be intensely emotional, and Raj could cry at the drop of a hat.

In 1988, when he got an opportunity to speak to veteran journalist Nasreen Munni Kabir about his mentor, Raj lapped it up with both hands. It resulted in one of two of his only surviving televised interviews, in which he waxes eloquent about Dutt, his process and their relationship. Despite how close they were, Raj couldn't touch the 'core of his heart', he said. Guru Dutt's untimely death left a hole in Raj Khosla's own heart that could not be filled till the end of his days.

Raj had a giant picture of Guru Dutt in his office. In the autumn of his life, it was not uncommon for journalists or assistants to walk in on him weeping in front of the portrait.

Despite the stupendous response to *Woh Kaun Thi?* at the box office, the film was snubbed at the Filmfare Awards that year. The only major award it won was in cinematography. The spectacular soundtrack by Madan Mohan and Raja Mehdi Ali Khan, too, did not receive a single nod at the awards. Composer duo Laxmikant–Pyarelal and lyricist Majrooh Sultanpuri won the top honours that year for *Dosti* (1964). Time has been kinder to 'Naina barse' and 'Lag ja gale', especially the latter. One would find stronger echoes of 'Lag ja gale' today than any other popular song released in 1964.

The lack of award recognition notwithstanding, Raj sought to recreate the magic of *Woh Kaun Thi?* and so, the team of Madan Mohan, Raja Mehdi Ali Khan and Sadhana were back in his next film, a story that originated in a semi-arid region of Maharashtra.

Author Jayant G. Deokule had written *Asha Parat Yete* (*The Return of Asha*) as part of a collection of mystery stories. 'Mystery stories' were all the rage in the 1950s and 1960s. Such stories, often with thriller and horror elements, were favourite travel companions in the pre-internet era and were often gobbled up in a single sitting. In Deokule's book, Asha, the wife of a lawyer, dies in her husband's arms but soon after, a woman, who's a spitting image of hers, appears and claims to be the wife. What's more, she seems to know intimate details about the lawyer that only a wife can be privy to. It seems like an impossible mystery.

Asha Parat Yete was lapped up by readers and caught the attention of Raja Paranjape, who liked the rather unconventional plot. Paranjape is counted among the most revered figures in the history of Marathi cinema, a position that is richly deserved. Not only was he, much like Raj himself, adept at straddling various genres, his films, marked by a naturalistic style, were fiercely popular among the masses. Besides directing some path-breaking films with progressive themes, he launched credible actors who went on to build names for themselves in Bollywood: Sachin Pilgaonkar and the thespian couple Ramesh and Seema Deo. As an actor, Paranjape was immensely prolific both on stage as well as on screen. He played Nutan's father in *Bandini* and Jaya Bhaduri's rustic uncle in *Piya ka Ghar* (1972), in addition to a plethora of films he both directed and acted in.

Raja Paranjape adapted Deokule's story into a film starring Kahinath Ghanekar as lawyer Balasaheb Phanse, and Bhavana as the wife Asha and her doppelgänger. He called it *Pathlaag* (1964), which literally translated to 'the chase'. It was so intense that Paranjape decided not to have too many songs. The movie just had two – 'Ya dolyanchi don pakhare' and 'Nako marus hak', both sung by Asha Bhosle, with music by Datta

Davjekar. The film caught the imagination of the masses and ended up being one of the most successful films in Paranjape's oeuvre. In addition to being a commercial success, *Pathlaag* was honoured with the National Film Award for Best Feature Film in Marathi. The very next year, it was remade in Tamil as *Idhaya Kamalam* (1965), with Ravichandran and K.R. Vijaya in the lead roles.

While he was a full-blooded Punjabi in most respects, Raj's feet were firmly entrenched in his *karma bhoomi* Maharashtra. Throughout his career, he would keep coming back to Marathi novels for inspiration (in *Do Raaste* and *Main Tulsi Tere Aangan Ki* [1978], for instance). His favourite screenwriter, his trusted confidante, was Marathi writer G.R. Kamat. As noted earlier, Kamat, who came to be known as Raj Khosla's resident screenwriter, actually began his career writing films – *Pedgaonche Shahane* and *Lakhachi Goshta* – for Paranjape. Kamat also wrote Paranjape's first Hindi outing *Chacha Chowdhary* and then went on to work on Raj Khosla's *Kala Pani* and *Bombai ka Babu*.

Raj Khosla worked with other writers for a short while, only to come back to collaborating with Kamat. One could surmise that Kamat was instrumental in Raj Khosla discovering, and eventually choosing, *Pathlaag* as a story apt to remake in Hindi. *Mera Saaya* (1966), Raj's next outing, was this remake.

The director and G.R. Kamat incorporated some crucial changes from the Marathi original. In *Pathlaag*, the husband seems inclined to believe the woman who claims to be his (not-so) dead wife. Around the finale, all it takes is for the woman to patiently explain her predicament for him to run after her and take her into his arms. For Raj Khosla, this was too convenient. A man who had lost his wife, who had seen her die before his own eyes, would scarcely believe anyone claiming to be her, no matter how closely she resembled her. So, in *Mera Saaya*, Sunil

Dutt's Thakur Rakesh Singh obstinately refuses to accept that the woman (Sadhana) is indeed his reanimated wife. At least not until the dacoit (Prem Chopra) himself spills the beans and explains that she is indeed the real deal. Raj also found a way to inject some humour into the proceedings via the jocular presence of Dhumal, who had also lightened the somewhat creepy atmosphere in *Woh Kaun Thi?*. The third major change in the Hindi adaptation was the plethora of songs. Despite the film being a thriller, Raj wanted to heighten the romance and the tender relationship between Sunil Dutt's character and his wife, which went a long way in accentuating the lead's fury when a stranger claims to be his wife. It also allowed for him to wallow in her memory, creating some precious moments that make this 'thriller' a little less dry.

What Raj Khosla had perfected by now was the art of making engaging thrillers with an emotional core. After exploring the tough, cynical world of *C.I.D.*, *Kala Pani* and *Bombai ka Babu* and dabbling with frothy romance in *Solva Saal* and *Ek Musafir Ek Hasina*, he was now cleverly meshing the two genres together. *Mera Saaya*, *Woh Kaun Thi?* and *Anita*, often dubbed the 'Sadhana trilogy', were all primarily love stories neatly wrapped in a thrilling exterior. At the heart of the mysteries were a man and a woman (actually two women – Sadhana had double roles in all three films) in love.

Arguably, it was the couple at the centre of *Mera Saaya* – lawyer Rakesh (Sunil Dutt) and Geeta (Sadhana) – that Raj invested with the warmest, most moving romance ever. In the aftermath of her death, Rakesh immerses himself in memories of the moments spent with Geeta. Interestingly, a wide expanse of filmmakers, from Satyajit Ray to Hrishikesh Mukherjee, have explored the depiction of conjugal love in bed – but not in the way you would think. All of them found the most sublime expression of love in the moments right after a couple wakes up, whether it is Soumitra and Sharmila in *Apur Sansar* (1959) or Amitabh and Jaya in *Abhimaan* (1973). But Raj, in an absolutely brilliant match cut, shows a solitary Sunil Dutt going to sleep alone, and then being cajoled out of bed by his resplendent wife. It's the same blanket and the same bed, but a different morning from the past, full of hope and tenderness. He takes her in his arms, they share sweet nothings in each other's ears, and he goes back to sleep. This time, he is woken by a gruff manservant instead of his wife. It was all a dream, evidently.

There are also flashbacks to happier times through songs, and Madan Mohan's music for *Mera Saaya* is as exquisitely beautiful as *Woh Kaun Thi?*'s was haunting. Whether it's the heart-rending title track – 'Mera saaya saath hoga' – based on Raag Nand, or the Bhimpalasi-based 'Naino mein badra chhaye', Lata Mangeshkar's 'Madan *bhaiyya*' was in peak form. But there was a mishap during one recording, which points at Madan Mohan's obsession with perfection. Lata Mangeshkar narrated the incident to me barely six months before she passed away:

The soundtrack of *Mera Saaya* (1966).

> *Jo baj raha thha woh achha nahi thha.* The music being played was not to his liking. I was singing, and it bothered him that the artiste was singing but the musicians weren't playing well. He lost his cool. He came out of the recording room – god knows what he thought. He punched on the glass pane of the door. It was a wooden door, but there was a glass pane – it was double-layered glass. He hit it, the glass broke and there was blood everywhere.[2]

They had to call a doctor and get him patched up before recording could resume. During our interview, Lata Mangeshkar couldn't recollect which song had prompted this reaction. Madan Mohan's son Sanjeev Kohli clarified during a discussion with *Filmfare* that the song was 'Nainon mein badra chhaye'.[3]

One of the abiding legacies that Raj's grandmother left him was a love for folk songs. She was fond of singing, and would often sing some folksy, rustic tune that would transport the young Desraj to a different world. One of the songs that she hummed was an old tune that went '*Jhumka gira re*/ Bareilly *ke bazar mein*.' Raj told Sheila Vesuna, '... she would sing some fascinating folk numbers. I grew up on a steady diet of those. And it was inevitable that a number of those haunting tunes should have influenced the songs in my films. For instance, 'Jhumka gira re' was a direct lift. She had a vast collection of such numbers.'[4] Around 1932, when Raj was seven years old, there was a version of 'Jhumka gira re' recorded in the voice of Dulari Bai, aka Miss Dulari, who hailed from Peshawar. Some 15 years later, Shamshad Begum sang a variant of it for the film *Dekho Ji* (1947). The lyrics of this version were attributed to Wali saheb, and the music directors were Sabir Hussain and Tufail Faruqui. While the tunes varied, the words of these two versions followed a similar pattern, and went roughly as follows:

Jhumka gira re
Bareilly *ki bazar mein*
Jhumka gira re
Saas meri roye
Nanad meri roye
Saiyyan roye re
Gale mein baiyan daal ke

(I lost my earring
In the bustle of Bareilly
I lost my earring good...
My mother-in-law cries over it
My sister-in-law cries too
My lover sobs through all of it
With arms around me)

One could surmise that this is how the original folk song went, though for a popular song, it is notoriously elusive.

But the most popular version of 'Jhumka gira re' happens to be Madan Mohan's creation for *Mera Saaya*, rendered by Asha Bhosle. Raja Mehdi Ali Khan added playful, skittish poetry to the traditional *mukhda* and made it entirely his own. There is another obviously apocryphal story attached to the lines – one that attempts to explain how Raja Mehdi Ali came upon those lyrics – that has to do with Hindi cinema's tallest superstar. His family, to be exact. Eminent poet and litterateur Dr Harivansh Rai Bachchan had lost his first wife, Shyama, to tuberculosis. Teji Suri mended his broken heart. It was in Bareilly that they met and fell in love. The story goes that when they were courting each other, fellow poets and teachers often enquired about their relationship and where it was going. On one such occasion when Raja Mehdi Ali Khan bumped into Suri at an event and made a similar enquiry, she responded, possibly alluding to the folk song, 'Bareilly *ke bazaar mein mera jhumka gir gaya*.' This incident is said to have inspired the lyricist to write the song for Raj Khosla's film. The story is unverifiable and probably largely untrue.

Regardless of its origins, 'Jhumka gira re' continues to be exclusively attached to *Mera Saaya*. Asha Bhosle's rendition went 'viral', so much so that according to Raj, whenever she ran into trouble with her audience during a live show, all she had to do was sing 'Jhumka gira re' and the crowds went crazy. Across the length and breadth of the country, the city of Bareilly came to be inextricably associated with the song. Fifty-seven years after *Mera Saaya*, the song found an echo in Karan Johar's *Rocky aur Rani kii Prem Kahaani* (2023) as 'What jhumka?', which bizarrely displaced the song from Bareilly to Raebareli.

But it would be grossly unjust to talk about the song without discussing Sadhana's breathtaking act in it. She was a sheer ball of energy, swirling and swerving, tambourine in hand. This was Sadhana in a completely different avatar. The portion featuring the song was important for Raj Khosla to establish a contrasting persona for the doppelgänger. As opposed to the demure disposition of the twin, this one was a livewire. To show off her histrionics, she had to dance with abandon. And dance she did! There was an assistant choreographer in the film that Sadhana befriended. She was so taken in by the dancing talent of this budding choreographer that she would soon give her a break as a dance director in her home production *Geeta Mera Naam* (1974). History would come to know this young choreographer as Saroj Khan.

Both Sunil Dutt and Sadhana were in peak form in *Mera Saaya*. In contrast with *Woh Kaun Thi?*, Sadhana not only had to accentuate the mystery in her character but also had to highlight the frustration of a wife who was once loved by a husband who now refuses to even recognize her. In the court scenes, when he virtually throws her a challenge, she realizes if she wants her life back, she has to fight him. The subtle shift of emotions in Sadhana's face underscores this.

Raj cast Sunil Dutt as the loving husband because he was, in the director's own words, 'an ideal husband in real life'.[5] Sunil Dutt had to play the man who loves his wife so dearly, so passionately, that he cannot conceive of any other woman claiming her mantle, no matter how much she claims to know him or resembles her. Sunil Dutt had a highly effective way of showing anger on screen. One could even go out on a limb and call him the original angry young man. This manner of his grew even more effective with the advent of colour. Bulging, bloodshot eyes in a sullen face, and a brooding voice to match – this was quintessential 'angry Dutt', and it held him in good stead in the 1970s, when anger was in vogue. In *Mera Saaya*, this signature grimace was directed towards the supposed imposter.

Raj ensured his audience knew that this animosity sprung from the most tender and sublime love that these two individuals shared. That's what necessitated the flashbacks, bringing out the chemistry between the two actors. Sunil Dutt later referred to the sensitive manner in which Raj Khosla handled the love scenes between them.[6]

On one occasion, the actor had had a long drinking session and appeared quite jaded during the shot. Raj was irked by this and took him to task. The foundations of a long friendship were being laid. Sunil Dutt and Raj Khosla went on to form an association and partnership that extended to at least three movies and one more that the filmmaker ghost-directed at the behest of his friend. More on this later.

Of all the thrillers that Raj gave his name to, *Mera Saaya* could stake the claim to having the most convincing and powerful denouement ever. Despite the seemingly simplistic plot device of twin sisters, the way Raj resolves the various strands of mystery during the climax doesn't feel convenient. Lawyer Rakesh conclusively proves in a courtroom that the woman in the stand is a murderer and a fraud, and has stolen his wife's diary to obtain intimate information about their conjugal life. At this point, the audience doesn't know who to believe, but their sympathy is evenly split between the two leads. In this scene, it is difficult to decide whether to root for Dutt's victory or feel bad for Sadhana, who is at the risk of losing her sanity. Meanwhile, a band of dacoits led by Prem Chopra is in town. They are in disguise and their objective is to meet the good Rakesh, the lawyer, and convince him that the woman he has been keeping at arm's length is indeed his real wife. The woman who died was Nisha, Prem Chopra's companion and the lawyer's wayward sister-in-law. During an encounter with the police, the dying bandit vouches for the truth and the lawyer finally accepts the truth.

This, arguably, is a better ending than *Woh Kaun Thi?*. While the latter had a series of mysteries and red herrings built into the script, in the end it all boiled down to one explanation: that the heroine had a *humshakal*, a twin (Bollywood's favourite buzzword till well into the 1990s). However, in *Mera Saaya*, we already know that there's someone who looks like the heroine. Yet, till the denouement occurs, even seasoned thriller buffs are left scratching their head and wondering what really could have happened. If keeping the audience guessing till the end is a Hitchcockian trait, Raj Khosla was the finest Hitchcockian director India had seen.

With *Mera Saaya*, Raj's affair with Udaipur began. The palaces and fountains of Udaipur are inextricably attached to some of the most memorable songs from the film, 'Mera saaya saath hoga' and 'Nainon mein badra chhaye'. In the years that followed, Raj would keep coming back to Udaipur.

Mera Saaya was also the beginning of a curious trend. Raj Khosla started to stamp some of his films with his distinctive signature in the opening credits. It was a unique, stylized script, which declared that the film was his. But it only appeared in some of his films – not all. Some of his iconic films like *Mera Gaon Mera Desh* didn't have it. From *Mera Saaya* to his swansong *Naqāb*, 13 of his films have this unique 'branding', so to speak.

12

Do Badan Pyar ki Aag mein Jal Gaye

Like many other Urdu poets of his day, Makhdoom Mohiuddin was a card-holding member of the Communist Party. He was known as a radical leftist, taking up arms on occasion. But contrary to this image of violence, some of his most popular creations have emerged as abiding romantic ballads in films. This includes a poem that goes:

Ek chameli ke mandve tale
Mai-kade se zara door uss mod par
Do badan
Pyar ki aag mein jal gaye

(Somewhere, under the jasmine's shade
Not far from the village tavern
There lie the remains of two souls, who by the fire of love did burn)[1]

The words '*Do badan pyar ki aag mein jal gaye*' are more literal than they let on. Makhdoom Mohiuddin had written them when he came across the graves of two ill-fated lovers who were killed because they belonged to different classes of society.

In 1963, the lines were put to lilting music by Iqbal Qureshi for a film called *Cha Cha Cha* (1964). The leads Chandrashekhar and Helen pranced around fountains humming the fateful number, probably unaware of its gruesome origin. The voices belonged to Asha Bhosle and Mohammed Rafi. A year prior, the verse had been used by Jaidev for a fleeting moment in Sunil Dutt's dacoit drama *Mujhe Jeene Do* (1963), voiced this time by Lata Mangeshkar.

The story goes that the lines also inspired Raj Khosla. The lyricist Shamsul Huda Bihari, popularly known as S.H. Bihari, was producing a film via his brother, also credited as Huda Bihari. They had chosen Raj to helm it. Those days, Manoj Kumar spent a lot of time at Khosla Niwas, and was often around during the story discussions on the film. As noted earlier, he was immensely interested in writing and saw these interactions as opportunities to tinker with story ideas.

It was during one of these sessions that Kumar made Raj listen to Makhdoom Mohiuddin's poem. The director, who was puffing away at a cigarette – according to Manoj Kumar, his friend wasn't a habitual smoker; he smoked only when he drank – got really excited. In his excitement, he screamed, 'Panditji Maharaj, *Do Badan* is an excellent title for our film!' In the same breath, Raj suggested that the film should be based on the legend of Heer and Ranjha. It would be a modern-day tale of the star-crossed lovers who were killed because of the social barriers between them, much like the pair that inspired Makhdoom Mohiuddin's poem.

Kumar played another key part in the genesis of *Do Badan* (1966). That night, while lazing around with the day's newspaper in hand, he noticed an ad for a film playing nearby. He immediately rang up Raj and asked him to join him and his wife, Shashi, on an important errand the next day. He asked Raj Khosla to bring his wife, Usha, as well. At a quarter to 10 the next morning, Kumar took them along to Maratha Mandir for the morning show of the Dilip Kumar-starrer *Deedar*, which had originally released 15 years earlier, in 1951. It was rather commonplace those days for old films to have reruns at the theatres (a trend that has resurfaced recently). They were usually morning shows. Both Kumar and Raj had seen *Deedar* earlier, but they loved it even more the second time around.

But why did Manoj Kumar bring him to watch the film? Raj knew something was cooking. It was unlikely that he had been dragged all the way to Khar, where Kumar lived, just for entertainment. There must be more to it. *Deedar* was a definitive film of Dilip Kumar's 'tragedy king' phase; in the story, he is separated from his childhood sweetheart, and eventually goes blind. Manoj Kumar said, 'Ranjha *ko* blind *bana do*. Make Ranjha blind.' Raj jumped at the idea. It rounded off the concept: a modern-day adaptation of Heer–Ranjha where Ranjha turns blind! It seemed like a powerful proposition. And so *Do Badan* was set in motion.

Kumar was working with Raj Khosla for the second time. By then, they were close friends and spent a lot of time together. Raj was, in a manner of speaking, coaching Manoj Kumar for a career in filmmaking. The actor, of course, used to ghostwrite screenplays but filmmaking was still a long way off. In this, his work with Raj proved to be a training ground. They were constantly discussing various projects and the filmmaker encouraged his actor friend to write scenes, scripts and even dialogues. In his interview with me, Kumar said, 'Virendra Sinha *ka naam thha lekin* Raj *mujh se hi likhwate thhe*.' Virendra Sinha was the person credited for the dialogues of *Do Badan*. Evidently, it was Manoj Kumar who wrote those lines. *Do Badan* had some powerful dialogues and scenes. Raj later confirmed that Kumar, who was genuinely interested in writing, wrote almost half the film.[2]

As a plot, *Do Badan* seems fairly simplistic. The nerdy Vikas (Manoj Kumar) and the boisterous Asha (Asha Parekh) clash at college but are eventually drawn towards each other. Asha comes from wealth and poor Vikas is... well, poor. Asha's dad, as all self-respecting rich fathers in the history of Hindi cinema, doesn't see this poor boy as his son-in-law. He announces the wily Ashwini Nath, played by Pran, as his daughter's future husband.

Pran was an interesting choice for Ashwini. For a long while in Hindi cinema, and more so in the 1960s and 1970s, almost everyone was typecast – especially the good guys and the bad guys. Pran had to just make an appearance for the audience to know that something really evil was going to unfold on screen. It became an expectation. Raj seemed to have taken advantage of this sentiment and imbued the character with shades that no one expected. Beyond the fact that the character was being portrayed by Pran, and one desperate and vile act, there was nothing shady about him. The heroine gets married to him early and he promises not to consummate the marriage unless she allows him to. She, of course, despises him. He waits for her to come around. In sum, Pran's character of Ashwini would have been considered as the tragic hero of the piece if not for one dastardly act.

Though Asha doesn't reciprocate Ashwini's feelings, when her father announces their engagement, he feels entitled to her hand. Knowing her feelings for Vikas, Ashwini conspires to get the latter out of the way and orchestrates a road accident. Vikas survives but loses his eyesight. Ashwini, who desperately wants Asha to love him, tries his best to convince Vikas that as a blind lover, he will be of no use to Asha. In fact, he would prove to be an impediment. A frustrated Vikas silently steps away. In all this, no one thinks of checking with Asha what she wants – besides one individual, her uncle, the ever-benign Manmohan Krishna. Her chacha, an artist who lost his love as a young man, is the only one in Asha's life who understands her predicament. He often lends a sympathetic ear, besides a shoulder to cry on. When her father refuses to listen, it is he who takes her side. But in the case of her marriage, nothing works, and she is wedded off to Ashwini, whose joy at having 'won' Asha is short-lived.

Meanwhile, lissome Dr Anjali (Simi Garewal) walks into Vikas's life to mend his broken heart. She tries hard to perk him up, but by then Vikas is on mission self-destruction and no one – not even Asha – can stop him. Asha comes to see him briefly, but he gives her the impression that Dr Anjali is the woman in his life.

Asha's conjugal life is in a shambles. In one poignant scene Asha Parekh and Pran's characters collide. It's one of the best-written scenes of the film. Frustrated with her frigid demeanour, Ashwini confronts Asha. It was a situation rarely seen in mainstream Hindi films. For starters, it was downright unthinkable for a heroine and a villain to get married halfway through the film. Even if it did happen, the villain indulged in every kind of cruelty that a husband could unleash on his wife. But here, Ashwini treats his wife kindly – or that's what he thinks. In their confrontation, he tries to play the domineering husband and reminds her of her *naari dharm,* a woman's 'sacred duty'. What about the man's duty? Asha snaps back. She refuses to kowtow to a man's notions of propriety, especially his opinion on how his wife should behave. Now, much has been said about Raj Khosla being a 'women's director', primarily hinging on his ability to showcase beautiful, glamorous women in all their glory. He definitely deserved that title, but not merely for how beautiful he made women look or even because he had meaty roles for women in his films. It's because in an era when popular Hindi cinema was riddled with misogyny, he turned around and created characters like Asha from *Do Badan* who refuse to take things lying down. Will only her crimes be considered, Asha wonders, because she is Ashwini's wife – a woman? And will he be forgiven merely because he happens to be the husband – a man? Women in Hindi films of the 1960s were often resigned to their fate. Here was one who refused to be, and had the audacity to snap back. It is for creating female characters with agency, with a mind of their own that Raj was a women's director. And he achieved this in the ambit of what was deemed to be 'popular cinema'.

The sub-plot about Dr Anjali and Vikas is well crafted, and Raj managed to portray a platonic friendship between a man and a woman way back when. Simi Garewal's sensitive depiction of this friend who does everything in her power to keep Vikas from imploding won her a Filmfare nod for 'Best Supporting Actress'. Garewal had had a rather enviable beginning to her career, having started off with a Mehboob Khan film (*Son of India*, 1962), followed by a Hollywood spectacle (*Tarzan Goes to India*, 1962) and a Dev Anand-starrer (*Teen Devian*, 1965). For a young actress like her to land a Raj Khosla film was no mean feat either. By this time, the man was being counted amongst the cream of the crop as far as directors were concerned.

Simi Garewal had some good lines, but Manoj Kumar reserved the best ones for himself. Poets were quoted generously. Manoj Kumar as Vikas mouthed truisms like:

Kabhi sher aur naghma ban ke, kabhi ansuon mein dhal ke
Woh miley mujhe toh ai dil, kayi suratein badal kar
– Khumar Barabankvi

(At times as songs and verses, as tears in some cases,
They met me, yes, but with different faces)[3]

Or:

Humko toh gardish-e-halat pe rona aaya
Rone waale tujhe kis baat pe rona aaya?
– *Saifuddin Saif*

(It's the turn of fortunes that makes me cry,
O weeping one, why do you cry?)[4]

Or lamentations of helplessness like: '*Kathputli kare bhi toh kya*? *Dhaaga kisi aur ke haath mein hai... naachna toh padega hi*! (What can a puppet do? The string is in someone else's hands. All it can do is dance!)'

A film based on the legend of Heer–Ranjha can only end one way. But according to Asha Parekh, the original ending of *Do Badan* was supposed to be something else entirely. 'There was a problem with the ending,' she told me, and continued:

> I told Mr Raj Khosla that two people dying at the same time would look very funny. I said I don't think he [Manoj Kumar's character Vikas] should die. I should. I had convinced Mr Raj Khosla. Manoj Kumar came late that day, and he realized what had happened. He was really angry. He said, you take a bet with me and I am going to get it re-shot. If you do it like this, the film will flop. So I said, okay, let's take a bet. I think we took a bet of 100 rupees or so, I don't remember. But finally we had to reshoot the whole thing.

In the final cut, Manoj Kumar's version of the ending was retained. His conviction had worked.

In her book *The Hit Girl*, Asha Parekh talks about how *Do Badan* was a turning point for her as an actress, adding that it was 'directed with a depth of feeling I had never known by Raj Khosla'.[5] Raj Khosla would, she went on, sit and narrate his own experiences to her, and thereby explain the meaning of love and loss. *Do Badan* was an exploration of these themes in inimitable Raj Khosla style. So invested was he in the process that he opened himself up to his lead actress. He egged her on to forget the script and go above and beyond it. Asha tried to dig deep and find resonances of the character in her own life. But it was difficult. She found herself struggling to mine the emotions of Asha Parekh, the actor, in service of Asha, the heroine of *Do Badan*. She shared her predicament with her director. 'You're tying yourself into knots,' Raj told her. 'Your personal life is yours. Still, I would suggest, just attempt to go within yourself, ask yourself questions and you'll find the answers.' Eventually, Asha Parekh says, she drew on her parents' love story to find inspiration for Asha's undying love for Vikas.

With *Do Badan*, a new player stepped into the arc lights – an actor who made his mark as a comedian and would stay relevant for decades on end. When I managed to track down Birbal, aka Satinder Khosla, his fading eyes glimmered as he spoke about his debut and his mentor Raj:

> I bow down before Raj Khosla. I can never forget how he helped me in my career. In fact, when I first got an opportunity to play a major role, it was all because of Raj Khosla. The film *Do Badan* was being shot. The setting was an examination hall. Manoj Kumar, Mohan Choti were there, and others who were preparing for their exams. Raj Khosla said he was trying to find someone

> who looked like a fool. They first tried the lyricist Gulshan Bawra for that role, but he didn't look like a fool. I was sitting there, sporting a butterfly moustache and staring at a big fat book. Manoj pointed at me and asked Khosla, 'How's he?' and Khosla replied, 'He is perfect!' And that's how I got selected for *Do Badan*.

It was a rather simple scene. While Manoj Kumar and Asha Parekh are deep in conversation, Mohan Choti butts in, his forehead laced with *vibhuti*, sacred ash. When they ask him about it, he says that he got it from a priest who said that if he saw four animals while sporting the *vibhuti*, he would surely clear the examination with flying colours. The last animal he mentioned was a donkey. As soon as he says *gadhaa*, donkey, Birbal enters the frame. Seeing him, Mohan goes, '*Ab toh main* exam *mein zaroor pass ho jaoonga*! Now I will definitely pass the exam!'

Birbal looks at him, grins and says, 'Thank you! Thank you!'

Before he knew it, Birbal became a regular fixture in Raj's cinema, though it wasn't until *Anita* that he started getting screen credit. But Birbal wasn't the only one working with Raj Khosla for the first time.

The composer Ravi Shankar Sharma, usually credited by just his first name, went on to earn a Filmfare nomination for *Do Badan*. This was the only time Raj Khosla and Ravi came together, and the soundtrack left a mark. 'Lo aa gayi unki yaad' and 'Raha gardishon mein hardam' were the definitive 'separation songs' and continued to be a part of 'sad song' compilations years after. 'Mat jaiyo naukariya chhod ke' was an evocative ballad by Asha Bhosle. Ravi had originally composed and recorded the ghazal 'Raha gardishon mein hardam' in

The soundtrack of *Do Badan* (1966).

Mukesh's voice for the film *Ghunghat* (1960), but it wasn't used as it didn't fit the narrative. *Ghunghat* was a Gemini Studios production and later when Ravi felt the need for a melancholy track on *Do Badan*, he got in touch with Gemini bigwig S.S. Vasan for the rights of the unused song. Vasan obliged and this time, to fit the leading man, Mohammed Rafi was called in. Rafi voiced three iconic 'sad songs' for the film, including 'Naseeb mein jiske jo likha thha' and 'Bhari duniya mein akhir dil ko samjhane kahan jayein'. Considering that the producer's brother S.H. Bihari was a successful lyricist himself, it might seem odd that he wasn't writing any songs for *Do Badan*. But the lyricist Shakeel Badayuni had formed a prolific partnership with Ravi (though his partnership with Naushad is more well known). Since 1960, Shakeel Badayuni was a regular collaborator on Ravi's compositions. Right from *Chaudhvin ka Chand* (1960) and *Ghunghat*, they had been working together with some regularity. So it was no wonder that Shakeel Badayuni was given the job in *Do Badan* as well.

However, what is more curious about *Do Badan* and its music is Raj Khosla working with the Ravi–Shakeel team. Music was a crucial aspect of Raj's oeuvre, and he believed in forming alliances with music directors. Whether it was S.D. Burman, with whom he made his initial slew of films; O.P. Nayyar, who gave him two musical hits in *C.I.D.* and *Ek Musafir Ek Hasina*; Laxmikant–Pyarelal, with whom he formed a long partnership that was to last till the autumn of his career; or Madan Mohan, who was now scoring most of his films, Raj was more comfortable having long-term collaborators whose consistency he could depend on. Only thrice did he work with composers he never repeated: *Do Badan*, *Daasi* (1981) and on his swansong *Naqāb*.

It was a foregone conclusion that a Raj Khosla film would always find favour with the audiences. Like clockwork, every single film he directed during this period hit the jackpot at the box office (though the first bump in the road was just around the corner) and *Do Badan* was no exception. According to film critic and journalist Ranjan Das Gupta, *Do Badan* beat the behemoth *Guide* (1965) in sheer box office numbers.[6] If Dev Anand had his way, the latter would have also been a Raj Khosla film.

Reams have been written about how Dev Anand set about adapting R.K. Narayan's novel *The Guide* in both English and Hindi, with American novelist Pearl S. Buck for company. The English version was to be directed by Tad Danielewski, a Polish-American filmmaker who was a Royal Academy of Dramatic Art alumnus and taught the likes of actors Martin Sheen and James Earl Jones. The Hindi version was to be helmed by a more illustrious director: Raj Khosla.

Initially, Dev Anand had zeroed in on his brother Chetan to do the honours. Chetan Anand had even started filming, but his constant run-ins with Danielewski threatened to derail the film. Dev chose to complete the English version first. It was completed and released, but the response was lukewarm. It was panned almost universally. Undeterred, Dev plunged into the Hindi production, which was a whole different ball game. Chetan Anand had by then busied himself with directing the war drama *Haqeeqat* (1964). Dev turned to his old friend Raj Khosla to pick up the mantle. Raj had earlier directed *Kala Pani* for Navketan. Not only was it hugely successful, but his film also earned Dev his first award for acting. Outside the umbrella of Navketan, too, Raj had directed Dev Anand in four very successful movies. Moreover, in the early days, certain filmmakers and studios had helped shape the filmmaker's creativity and worldview. Chief among them was Guru Dutt,

Filmalaya and Navketan. *Guide* was a chance for the duo and the film studio to join hands once again. Raj Khosla, always keen to collaborate with friends, was looking forward to it.

But there seemed to be a problem. Waheeda Rehman was Dev Anand's choice for the heroine's role. She was the perfect fit for Rosie, the troubled dancer in a loveless marriage. Waheeda explained to me:

> You see, *jawani mein na insaan ko josh hota hai, gussa hota hai,* ego *hota hai.* In youth, a person has a lot of passion, anger and ego. After the *Solva Saal* incident, we used to meet and interact, there was no problem. But then I thought, this man has said in front of everyone, 'You're finished, you argue too much as a newcomer, you think too much of yourself, etc.' So I decided not to work with him anymore. When *Guide* happened, I told Dev Anand, 'You know Raj and I have history… go ahead and take him [as a director] if you want to. But then I will not work in *Guide*.'

This left Dev in a quandary. He couldn't conceive of another actress as the heroine of *Guide*. Ever since he'd read the novel, it was Waheeda he had imagined in the role. He had even refused Chetan Anand's suggestion of casting Priya Rajvansh, whose English was supposedly better. Since Waheeda was Dev's only choice for the heroine of *Guide*, Raj had to step aside. Vijay Anand stepped in, and the rest is, of course, history.

Raj Khosla and Vijay Anand's career graphs have interesting parallels. Both were known as Navketan protégés. Both had come into their own directing Dev Anand in his prime. Both made some well-received thrillers. If Vijay Anand dabbled with other genres while keeping thrillers as his mainstay, Raj Khosla straddled a wide array of genres.

What would *Guide* look and feel like had Raj Khosla directed it? Worth pondering.

About his choice of heroine in *Do Badan*, Raj later said, 'I cast Asha Parekh in *Do Badan* instead of Sadhana because I wanted a girl with bright, twinkling eyes. Eyes that could also turn into great pools of sorrow. Sadhana's eyes had a natural sadness about them.'[7]

For his next film, Raj Khosla went back to the girl with those 'naturally sad' eyes.

13

The First Bump in the Road

Raj's daughter Anita insists she had nothing to do with the third part of his Sadhana trilogy and it was but a coincidence that her father's 1967 suspense spectacle was called *Anita*. But one is tempted to conjecture. Anita Khosla was seven years old when her father made a film that shared its name with her, one that opens with a worried father consulting an astrologer about what's to become of his daughter. The parallels are uncanny.

Anita, the first release of Raj Khosla Films, the filmmaker's own banner, was dedicated to Guru Dutt, with the first frame carrying a life-sized portrait of the departed legend and the words 'Dedicated to the memory of my Guru'. But the opening sequence is special for several reasons. For one, it has one of the longest pre-credit sequences in a Hindi film, and possibly the only one with an entire song. The title credits of *Anita* appear almost nine minutes into the film. By then, we have witnessed the astrologer scene, the song 'Gore gore chand se mukh par' has played out, and one tiny lovey-dovey bit that became all the rage on Instagram a few years ago. Around September–October 2020, the world lost its marbles over the 'How much *pagal*, very much *pagal*' scene from the movie. Neeraj (Manoj

Kumar), perched atop a tree overlooking a balcony, asks Anita (Sadhana) if she's finally crazy enough to marry him. She replies in the affirmative. The conversation that follows might now be more familiar to the Gen-Z crowd than any other piece of Indian cinema from the 1960s:

> 'How much *pagal*?'
> 'Very much *pagal*.'
> 'How much very much *pagal*?'
> 'Very much, very much *pagal*.'
> 'Very much, very much, very much *pagal*?'
> 'Hm.'
> 'You *pagal*, me *pagal*...'
> 'Me *pagal*, you *pagal*...'
> '*Pagal... pagal*.'

The genesis is unclear, but this innocuous bit from the film was shared on social media and thereupon found new life as a meme. Within a matter of weeks, it was all over Instagram, and several tongue in cheek tributes to it flooded the internet. Musicians remixed it with their own beats. There was a Trump version, and another featuring Mamata Banerjee and Narendra Modi. Madhuri Dixit did her own take on it, so did Janhvi Kapoor.

Anita marked the third instalment of the Sadhana trilogy. Each had been lensed by different cinematographers: K.H. Kapadia in *Woh Kaun Thi?*, V. Babasaheb in *Mera Saaya* and V. Gopikrishna in *Anita*. Despite this, the visual uniformity in these films is clear evidence of Raj Khosla's unwavering consistency as a director. The peering through windows, the tracking shots, the pans, the close-ups, they are all there.

Also with *Anita*, for the third time in a row, Raj Khosla played on the trope of many Sadhanas. In the tradition of grumpy old Bollywood dads, Anita's father (Sajjan) takes umbrage at her falling for Neeraj (Manoj Kumar), a man well beneath her station. But, of course, the father's own choice, Anil Sharma (Kishan Mehta), is a wealthy jerk. Anita encourages Neeraj to enter into a civil marriage with her, but her father convinces her that it might not be a good idea. Anita tries to talk Neeraj into dumping her, but a letter from her raises his suspicions. He tries to meet her and to his utter shock, realizes that she has committed suicide. But something about this doesn't quite feel right. He tries to investigate, and that is when things get a little bizarre. Anita may be dead, but she also seems to be alive and kicking; Neeraj keeps seeing her in different avatars and settings. This confounds both him and the audience. In *Woh Kaun Thi?* the two Sadhanas were revealed to be sisters. Likewise in *Mera Saaya*. But in *Anita*, the denouement was a little different, and the audience didn't deem the revelation in the climax altogether satisfactory.

Anita also marked a significant transition in Raj Khosla's filmography. As noted earlier, he looked for collaborators in music. After having jammed with S.D. Burman and O.P. Nayyar in several films, Raj joined forces with Madan Mohan in *Woh Kaun Thi?* and *Mera Saaya*. Madan Mohan was also supposed to compose for *Anita*, the first film of Raj Khosla's own banner. But legend has it that when Madan Mohan listened to the story the director had in mind, he had issues with the plot. He thought it was a mishmash of *Woh Kaun Thi?* and *Mera Saaya*. He didn't want to do the film. This didn't go down well with Raj. He relied heavily on this partnership, and was looking forward to re-creating the magic of the other two films in *Anita*. In a huff, he hired two young composers who were making waves at this time.

Pyarelal Sharma, all of 27, and Laxmikant Kudalkar, who had just turned 30, had already delivered musical hits in *Parasmani* (1963), *Dosti*, *Mr. X In Bombay* (1964), *Shagird* (1967), *Patthar ke Sanam* (1967) and so on. They were the flavour of the season. When Raj decided to infuse fresh blood into his film, the two talented young men lapped up his offer. This was the foundation for a very long association, one that lasted almost till the frayed edges of Raj Khosla's chequered career. Pyarelal Sharma reminisced, 'It was Laxmikant ji who received a message from Raj Khosla: "Raj Khosla *ne aap ko yaad kiya hai*. Raj Khosla has summoned you." Laxmi ji used to handle the business side of our work. He went and met Raj ji, and that's how we began to work with him. Raj Khosla was soft-hearted, a good human being. He held Lata Mangeshkar in high regard, so some even say that it was Lata Mangeshkar who recommended us to Raj Khosla. This is completely untrue.'[1]

Lata Mangeshkar, on a call with me, agreed: 'This is not true. I did not recommend them to him. I have never even heard this story.'

Laxmikant and Pyarelal may have crossed paths with Raj earlier. As musicians, they had worked with practically every composer of note. A very significant name in that list was S.D. Burman, who, Pyarelal Sharma averred, taught them a lot of what they knew about music. During the 1950s, S.D. Burman was composing music for Raj Khosla's Guru and eventually for Raj Khosla himself.

Regardless of how it came about, the duo were really happy when they got the film. Pyarelal Sharma spoke of the music sittings

The soundtrack of *Anita* (1967).

at Laxmikant Kudalkar's place, a one-room–kitchen on the ground floor of a chawl in Vile Parle, Bombay. The Khoslas, producers of the film, were present throughout the sittings.

The first song they composed for the movie was 'Kareeb aa ye nazar'. The style of the tune owed a debt to Madan Mohan, Pyarelal said, noting, 'We were conscious of the fact that those days he had been working with Madan Mohan ji, and this reflected in the song. Raj ji was very happy with the output.'[2] Another tune influenced by Madan Mohan was 'Gore gore chand se mukh par'. Raj himself is said to have approached the music directors of the film with some tunes for the song. Though his command over music was unquestionable, Laxmikant and Pyarelal had their own ideas about how the song should be composed.

'Gore chand' may have been a romantic tribute. One would not be accused of sensationalism of any sort if one were to state that Raj Khosla had a penchant for falling in love. He fell in love hopelessly, and often. While being deeply respectful of the institution of marriage, Raj was also enamoured with the phenomenon of the 'other woman'. And his interest was hardly academic. In an interview with him in the May 1979 issue of *Filmfare*, Khalid Mohamed writes:

> Women somehow have been the main supports in the director's life. He was always closer to his mother than he was to his father. Got married early. His five children are all daughters. He has fallen in love often, fallen out of love more often, respects the concept of marriage, respects even more the concept of 'the other woman', feels that he understands them and that they understand him.

Raj talks about the other woman in his life too in this interview.[3] In his tell-all memoir, narrated to Sathya Saran, Abrar Alvi also mentions how Raj pursued an actress to a hill station, wooing her all the way. There may be reason to surmise that 'Gore gore chand se mukh par' was brought about to serenade a 'someone else'.

We will examine later how the circumstances of his private life were to influence his creative output in the latter half of Raj's career. But the process may already have started by the time *Anita* was made.

There is another piece of trivia attached to 'Gore gore chand', that dates to 1950. At about this time, director K. Amarnath had cast an emerging young actor named Hamid Ali Khan, who would become known as the iconic 'Ajit', opposite Madhubala for a social drama called *Beqasoor* (1950).[4] The music of *Beqasoor* was composed by Anil Biswas, with lyrics by veteran poet Arzoo Lakhnavi and Ehsan Rizvi. Of the three songs attributed to Arzoo, one goes:

O gore gore chand se mukh par
Kaali kaali aankhen hain
Dekh ke jinko neend ud jaaye
Woh matwali aankhen

The first stanza is identical to the Mukesh version in *Anita*, though the rest of the song deviates. This was an original ghazal by Arzoo Lakhnavi, which was tweaked for the 1950 film. Raj Khosla was as smitten by Urdu poetry as by music. It was a language he was proficient in. In fact, one of his surviving notebooks, where he jotted down details of meetings and tasks, was written almost entirely in Urdu, which demonstrates his level of comfort with the language. Given how excited he was about the song, it is likely he tracked down the ghazal by Lakhnavi and used it in *Anita*. Arzoo Lakhnavi was long dead. He passed away in 1951. In its second coming, the song closely followed the original lyrics. Only one name found mention as a lyricist in *Anita*: Raja Mehdi Ali Khan. Arzoo Lakhnavi was credited for 'Gore gore' in the long-playing (LP) record.

Raja Mehdi Ali Khan came on board for *Anita* because of Madan Mohan. When Madan Mohan had politely declined the offer, Khan had considered doing the same, but it was Madan Mohan who convinced him otherwise. Work is work, after all. Raja Mehdi Ali Khan wrote four songs for the film: 'Saamne mere sawariya', 'Tum bin jeevan kaise beeta', 'Kareeb aa ye nazar' and 'Kaise karoon prem ki main baat'. On 27 July 1966, Raja Mehdi Ali Khan breathed his last. One song was still to be done. Anand Bakshi, a frequent collaborator of Laxmikant–Pyarelal, stepped in and completed the song, 'Hai nazar ka ishara'. Later, when the lyricist's fee was offered to Bakshi, he went to meet the deceased songwriter's wife, Tahira, and handed over the money. A mark of respect from one poet to another.

Besides 'Gore gore', there are two other Madan Mohan-esque songs in *Anita*: 'Saamne mere sanwariya' and 'Karib aa ye nazar'.

Another tune from the movie, 'Kaise karoon prem ki main baat', was an attempt at stirring up the magic of 'Jhumka gira re'. But it was a completely different animal. For one, this time it was Lata Mangeshkar singing. This version is almost as much fun. Almost. Sadhana performed with almost as much verve. Almost. Still, back in the day, it was featured among the top songs of the year on the radio show *Binaca Geetmala*. It's a wonder that today the song is nearly forgotten. It clearly deserves more.

The same can be said of *Anita*, the film. Though not as gripping as its predecessor, *Mera Saaya*, *Anita* is not altogether without merit. There is enough and more for the ardent film buff to feed on. Of the three Sadhana films, the comedy tracks in *Anita* are the most entertaining. Flummoxed by the constant appearances and disappearances of Anita, Neeraj approaches a detective to investigate the case. The detective agency is owned by Razdaan (Dhumal), supported by his able assistant Roshandaan (Birbal). As Neeraj enters the office with his friend, the frenzied noise of typewriters follows them. While Neeraj explains the sightings, deaths and reanimations of his girlfriend to the detectives, the typing noise stops suddenly and there is absolute silence for a moment. Turns out, the pair had been playing the sound of a busy office (which in those days meant simply the noise of a million typewriters) on one of those old tape recorders and the tape had come to an end! Evidently, the agency was out of work and there were not too many employees to speak of, but keeping up impressions was important.

This moment of levity is preceded by another amusing bit. As he steps in, Neeraj looks off the frame and for a few fleeting seconds, Raj shows us a black notice board on the wall that seems to be a motley rogues' gallery showcasing sinister criminals the detectives have been chasing. The notice board is filled with Easter eggs and gags. There's a picture of a white woman missing from 'Maimee Beach' who was last seen in Benaras and whose 'cut-out suit' was found in the Ganga. Alongside is another photo of a woman walking on her hands, with the following scribbled below her: '1) Be aware, 2) She is a killer always walks down-side up.' Beside her is an Indian man with white hair, smoking away. His description reads – '1) A crook called Desh Mukerji, 2) Missing with a minor girl.' This devilish prank was pulled on Dev Mukerji, the art director of *Anita*. Below him we see another woman, labelled simply as Agent - 001. The first Bond film had released five years prior, and attaching numerals to spies was much in vogue. This notice board might remind one of a similar blink-and-miss blackboard in a scene in *C.I.D.* In the scene, CID Inspector Shekhar (Dev Anand) and his colleague Inspector Jagdish (Jagdish Raj) are interrogating a petty trickster called Master (Johnny Walker). If you really squint, you can read the board behind them. It contains the list of police station officers tasked with solving various crimes. While Inspector O.P. Nayyar was in-charge of rape cases, Inspector A. Alvi was supposed to investigate burglaries. Raj Khosla was wont to play these nudge nudge, wink wink inside jokes that were supposed to only be enjoyed by industry insiders in a pre-IMDb, pre-Wikipedia world.

Speaking of hat tips and in-jokes, Raj's admiration for Hitchcock is apparent in *Anita* too. Right from letting the audience peep through 'rear windows' to flashing neon signs through windows, Hitch is everywhere. In *Vertigo* (1958), as Judy (Kim Novak) dresses up as Madeline and walks up to Scottie (James Stewart), looking like an apparition, the hotel room is illuminated with the green glow coming off a neon sign outside the window. In *Anita*, when Neeraj shares his concerns over the conduct of his dead girlfriend with her father, the latter is obviously outraged. As Anita's father expresses his frustration over the way his daughter and her modesty are being violated by Neeraj, who claims to love her, we can see a massive neon X forming outside the window. As it dies down, it is replaced by two smaller Xs in hues of purple, blue and green. Sajjan, who plays Anita's father, looks at them and breaks down.

Anita released on 31 March 1967 at Naaz, Liberty, Chitra, Lotus and other theatres in Bombay. In its release announcement, the *Times of India* said the film provided 'breath-taking suspense'. The audience didn't seem to agree. The suspense, the plot and the music of the film did not work for them. Despite how good the songs were, none of them reached the popularity of the music from any of the other Raj Khosla films so far. Raj later called *Anita* the first major loss in his filmography. This loss hit him hard, and he turned to his mother for some solace. She told him just three words in Punjabi: '*Pehla ghaata changa*. The first loss is okay.'[5] Little did she know that this *ghaata* was to be repeated.

Raj Khosla later revealed, tongue firmly in cheek, how he conceived the opening scene of *Anita*. He would, on occasion, write for film magazines and periodicals. The few pieces that survive today are great reads and an insight into his keen – and mischievous – mind. A snarky side to him would often rear its head in these pieces. Take for example, an article called 'The Mystery of Sex in Indian Films', which he wrote for the April 1967 issue of *Cine Advance* magazine. There are several schools, he said, when it comes to the depiction of love and sex in Indian films. The Bengal school, where the man and woman shoot lovelorn gazes at each other and sigh from a distance. 'Then comes the school which, for want of a more generic term, must be labelled the Bombay school. This incidentally is the school to which I myself belong, though my studies in it, tutored by God, Producer and Censor, have resulted in startlingly tangential results.' In the Bombay school, he says, 'the young man and young woman, or the old man and old woman (pretending to be teenagers) sing lusty duets across trees, rivers, waterfalls, studio-built lotus-ponds, streams, lakes… He snatches her dupatta and she grabs at his shirt. All this is supposed to convey that Cupid is at work!'

And finally, he trains a gun on his own film: 'My latest film *Anita* provides an interesting case in point. The film, before its very titles, was to open with a kiss. The camera was to be in a very tight "close" of the back of the hero's head, and as he pulls back, we were to see the expression of ecstasy on the heroine's face, just after the kiss.' This would be followed by the opening credits, after which our hero would be transferred to Delhi, only to return post-haste on the news of his girlfriend's death. In that opening shot, Raj Khosla goes on to explain, he would have established the expression of love and desire between the two leads in 'about a couple of hundred feet' of celluloid. In addition to delivering aesthetic satisfaction, it would have earned him a pat on the back from the authorities responsible for importing raw stock. 'But then,' he wisecracks, 'the shadow of the scissors fell on me, and I hit upon an original compromise idea! I'd make the hero sit on a tree. I was quite thrilled by my originality and went about in a self-congratulatory trance for a few days until someone reminded me that Raj Kapoor had done the same in the beginning of *Sangam*! Then many others began pointing out either films where [the same thing had been shown]… I stopped counting after two thousand one hundred and eighty films!' This ability to elicit a chuckle or two at the cost of his own work was signature Raj Khosla. Once the film was done, he was able to develop a healthy distance from it, laugh at it, or examine where he went wrong.

Though they actually teamed up for the first time on *Ek Musafir Ek Hasina*, the world knows and celebrates the Sadhana–Raj Khosla partnership mainly through the Sadhana trilogy of *Woh Kaun Thi?*, *Mera Saaya* and *Anita*. But there was another film that could have been celebrated just as much.

For a film-obsessed nation, India has produced shockingly few films about filmmaking or the industry. One of them happens to be *Film Hi Film*, which was released in 1983 and sank without a trace. It had a wafer-thin plot but what was interesting was the inclusion of footage from many shelved or incomplete films. Among them were snatches from a film called *Sajan ki Galiyan* (1966), starring Dev Anand and Sadhana. The film, it turns out, was directed by Raj Khosla. In a letter to a fan dated 31 August 1964 (posted on Twitter by journalist Sam Jawed, said fan's granddaughter), Sadhana listed her forthcoming projects, of which *Sajan ki Galiyan* was a part. The film was also supposed to launch Nargis's niece Zaheeda in a pivotal role.

In the November 1966 issue of *Filmfare*, Raj mentioned that *Sajan ki Galiyan* was still 'in the making'. It had already been two years. The film was being produced by Fali Mistry. Six years before this, Raj had teamed up with Fali's brother, Jal Mistry, to produce *Bombai ka Babu*. Back in the 1960s, Raj had worked with almost all the leading composers who were active at the time: S.D. Burman, O.P. Nayyar, Madan Mohan and Ravi. The one glaring miss in his career was Shankar–Jaikishan, and they were the music directors of *Sajan ki Galiyan*.

The surviving footage of the film includes two songs: 'Hum khoob jaante hain kya dil mein hain tumhare' and 'Humne jinke khwab sajaye'. Going by how throbbing with melody and mirth both tunes are (especially Mohammed Rafi's voice oozing love on 'Humne jinke khwab sajaye'), the album would have been every bit as special as that of other Raj Khosla films till then. The footage also contains an evocative romantic scene between Dev Anand and Sadhana. By all means, Raj seemed to have a winner in his hands. But the film was shelved after shooting a few reels. It is not clear why, and whatever's left of it survives as a glimpse of unfulfilled potential, a Raj Khosla classic that was not to be.

Even as *Sajan ki Galiyan* was being relegated to the cans, Raj Khosla had already moved on to his next. According to him, *Chirag* (1969) was adapted from the plot of a Bengali film. The producer was Premji, who had also produced *Mera Saaya*. Premji had begun as a production controller with Bimal Roy. It was during the making of *Devdas* that he was first acquainted with Dilip Kumar, the hero of the film. This association led to him being invited by Dilip Kumar to handle the production of his ambitious *Gunga Jumna* (1961). Legend has it that it was the actor who encouraged Premji to turn producer with *Mera Saaya*. *Chirag* was his second film as a producer.

In *Chirag*, Raj, once again, cast Sunil Dutt as the hero, owing to the congenial and loving husband that he saw in the actor. In a sense, Thakur Ajay Singh, the hero of *Chirag*, was a spiritual successor to Thakur Rakesh Singh of *Mera Saaya*. Both are obsessively in love with their wives, and would gladly set fire to everything in sight were anything to happen to them. Both mistakenly think that their wives are dead and mourn them in the 'angry Dutt' fashion of contained rage. That, and the fact that both are filthy rich landowners who live in sprawling mansions.

The story of *Chirag* begins when Ajay's sports car bumps into Asha's (Asha Parekh) bike and he just can't stop thinking about her. He tracks her down and finds that all he needs do to woo her is convince her hapless brother, a bumbling country doctor (Om Prakash). Raj Khosla takes his time to set you up for the heart of the plot, which starts unfolding when Ajay and Asha get married. Ajay's mother in the film was played by Lalita Pawar, an antithesis to Nirupa Roy, the quintessential Bollywood mother, if there ever was one. She shone at playing evil, scheming mothers. But in *Chirag*, Raj doesn't paint Pawar in such broad strokes. She does some hateful and deplorable things in the movie but doesn't scream her lines and isn't accompanied by high-pitched music, as in most other films of the period. At the behest of a crafty *munim* (Kanhaiyalal), she starts blaming Asha for 'not bearing children'. She's worried about the continuation of her precious *khandan*, she avers. Asha mopes and Ajay provides solace. But in a freak accident during Diwali, a cracker explodes in Asha's face and renders her blind.

So far, Raj was so good at suspense and thrill that these had begun to be considered the hallmark of his cinema. But, by the end of the 1960s, Raj was a little tired of this genre-centricity. He wanted to explore new vistas and push his boundaries. *Ek Musafir Ek Hasina* and *Do Badan* had given him a taste of romance. With *Chirag* he was trying his hand at a social drama. Here on out, Raj would desist from sticking to one domain.

Till the 1990s, Bollywood socials and family dramas were overflowing with cliches and regressive messaging. A generous amount of those existed in Raj Khosla's films as well. *Chirag* was riddled with cliches, but Raj's superpower was not to make movies that were different, but to handle cliches like nobody else could. He just found a way of making these scenes work. Countless films, Indian and otherwise, have shown characters discovering that they have turned blind. In *Chirag*, the drama Raj Khosla builds in the scene is extremely potent, despite having all the markers of off-putting loud, ludicrous melodrama. On waking up after her accident, Asha is assured by an uppity Ajay that she is absolutely fine. Why is the room so dark? she wonders. Ajay draws the curtains open, whistling all the way. She asks him to turn on the lights. But it's sunny outside, he says. The music kicks in. Asha lets out a shrill, guttural scream and runs away from Ajay, screaming his name. He runs after her. All hell breaks loose. The art of mainstream Hindi cinema hinges on unrestrained cacophony. Everything is writ large. So, to the 'untrained eye' (the unfortunate souls who haven't been raised on Hindi films), some of these outbursts may seem ludicrous and weirdly entertaining. Filmmakers like Raj found ways of containing the chaos.

The reason the character of Asha never becomes irredeemably maudlin is Asha Parekh's spirited performance. For the first hour of *Chirag*, Raj Khosla allows her to turn on her charm. There are at least two dance numbers in the film where Asha Parekh showcases her skills: 'Bhor hote kaaga pukare kaahe Ram' and 'Chhai barkha bahar'. She is a delightful presence in these songs and the romantic scenes. The other half of the film involves an incredible amount of moping, which is also something she excels at. Asha, now blind, thrown out of the house, tries to kill herself and fails, and learns that she is pregnant. What else could go wrong? In this part of the film, she had to mope, weep and pine. Asha Parekh made a fine art of it, one that would hold her in good stead because two years later, in *Kati Patang* (1971), she would be playing another ill-fated woman despairing and pining over a love she could only see but never have.

The soundtrack of *Chirag* (1969).

There is an oft-quoted story about Raj looking to use a line from Faiz Ahmed Faiz's poem for the film. Faiz's poem 'Mujhse pehli si mohabbat mere mehboob na maang' is said to be the marker for his move from conventional poetry to politically conscious outpourings. It had one line that Raj was drawn to: '*Teri aankhon ke siwa duniya mein rakkha kya hai*. The world is useless, without those precious eyes of hers.'

The line serves several functions in the film. When Ajay woos Asha, it works as a love ballad sung by the inimitable Mohammed Rafi: '*Teri aankhon ke siwa duniya mein rakkha kya hai*.' In the latter half of the film, Asha has lost her eyesight and tries to console her anguished husband. She tells him that she will now see the world through his eyes. He starts crying and she breaks into a song, sung by Lata Mangeshkar this time: what else does she have but his eyes ('*Teri aankhon ke siwa duniya mein rakkha kya hai*')? When Raj urged Sultanpuri to use that line from Faiz's poem, he said he could only do so with written permission from the esteemed poet. Now, this was a turbulent time in the subcontinent, and Faiz saab was in Pakistan. It was difficult to get hold of him, especially in that kind of environment. But he was spoken to and permission was obtained. Using Faiz's line as *mukhda*, Sultanpuri wrote two songs, for the two situations described above.

Chirag was supposed to salvage some of the losses incurred on *Anita*. It only did average business when it released. While Raj was somewhat satisfied, the stars were glum. A lot was banking on this project. Neither Asha Parekh nor Sunil Dutt had had major hits since the previous year. Asha Parekh says in her book *Hit Girl*:

> Since we had set our hopes high on *Chirag*, Dutt saab and I were upset, naturally. But Khosla saab kept consoling us with phone calls, saying, 'Come on, it's not the end of the world. Success and failure are two sides of the same coin.' To me he said, 'Asha, the audience did not like seeing you as a blind girl. They love that mischievous sparkle in your eyes.' Khosla saab would never play the blame game which, believe me, is a rare quality.

It is, indeed. But the year 1969, when *Chirag* was released, was a turning point not only for Raj but for the history of entertainment in the subcontinent. A storm was brewing.

14

Two Roads Diverged in a Wood

Raj left Khosla Niwas sometime in the mid-1960s. Depending on which family member's version you believe, it was either after the release of *Woh Kaun Thi?* (1964) or *Anita* (1967). Khosla Niwas was still the centre of the universe for the Khosla clan. Anyone who visited Bombay from Sri Hargobindpur, Gurdaspur or any other part of Punjab could find refuge here. Atmaram Khosla, Raj's father, was 'Bauji' to all, and in the gentle shade of the patriarch, anyone could relax and take a breather.

But by now, both Raj Khosla's family and work were expanding. He had a wife and three daughters, and was by now one of the most respected filmmakers in tinsel town. He was constantly in meetings, and stars would come and go. Raj's brother Lekhraj also had a growing family now. His sons Bolu and Anil Khosla, with Raj's help, were soon going to take a plunge into the film production business. With all this going on, Raj Khosla decided to move out of the house and settle in the sprawling suburb of Pali Hill, which was already gaining a reputation for being home to film stars and filmmakers. Raj and his family settled down on the second floor of a tight-knit apartment complex known as Marina Apartments.

Over the years, Marina has seen several famous residents connected with the film fraternity. One who lived there when Raj moved in was a producer called S.K. Kapoor, who made films like *Night in London* (1967), *Inspector* (1970) and *Dharma* (1973). The first floor was inhabited by Ram Dayal Sabharwal and his family. Ram Dayal had produced over 25 films and directed two, including *Shrimanji* (1968), starring Kishore Kumar and I.S. Johar. His father had produced the first Pakistani film *Teri Yaad* (1948). His brother Darshan Sabharwal was a producer, too. While Ram Dayal lived with his son Dimpy and his daughters at Marina, Darshan lived around the corner at Union Park. His sons eventually became filmmakers, and they adopted their father's name as their last name. One of them, Dharmesh Darshan built a name for himself with films like *Raja Hindustani* (1996) and *Dhadkan* (2000), while his brother Suneel Darshan made a slew of Akshay Kumar films in the early 2000s, including *Ek Rishtaa* (2001) and *Mere Jeevan Saathi* (2006).

Asha Parekh owned two flats in the complex, too, and had rented them to one Mr Sablok. His daughter went on to win a Miss India pageant. As a young girl, she was dating an impish boy who would go on to be a star: Aamir Khan. Aamir's father, Tahir Hussain, lived on the third floor of Marina Apartments with his family. All these children – Raj Khosla's five daughters, Ram Dayal's kids and Aamir Khan – and the other kids of the building were often joined by the Darshan brothers, Dharmesh and Suneel.

Dharmesh Darshan told me in an interview:

> I live in Union Park, Pali Hill. I was born here. Marina Apartments, which is now known as Aamir Khan's residence, was earlier virtually known for being Raj Khosla ji's home. I was in the same neighbourhood, and

> my cousins stayed in Marina. So, I would often go there. Raj ji had these five daughters – Uma, Sunita, Anita, Reena and Sonia. Reena and Sonia were my age. Uma didi, I think, was in boarding school at the time, and I would see Sunita and Anita as my older sisters. They were very sweet to me, and I was very fond of them. They would also visit my home.

Aamir Khan also has fond memories of those days:

> I knew all five daughters, but the ones who were my age were closer to me. Sonia was the youngest. I used to hang out with Reena and Sonia when I was a kid. I remember Anita was very fond of reading, and so was I, even at a young age. So, though Anita was older than me, she and I kind of connected because we used to read a lot. We used to exchange books. The balcony was her room, and it had a lot of books.

Both Khan and Darshan have memories of interacting with Raj Khosla when they were young. He was not like the other grown-ups who never even looked at the kids unless they really needed to. Rather, Raj, on his way to work or when he was back from the studio, made it a point to talk to them. 'Not that he spent a lot of time with us kids, but when he was returning from work and if we were playing hockey, he would make it a point to stop, play with us for a bit, watch us play, talk to us for five minutes and then leave,' Aamir recalled. Aamir Khan later bought Raj Khosla's portion of the house when the Khoslas moved out.

Raj may have left Khosla Niwas but nothing in the world could have kept him away from his family. Every Sunday, he would leave everything to go meet his brother and father. At 11 a.m. on a Sunday, one could find Raj back in Khosla Niwas, spending hours chatting with Lekhraj and playing chess with Atmaram. Familial ties and his roots were always very important to Raj. And that's what moved him to make his next film, *Do Raaste* (1969).

As pointed out earlier, Raj was fond of Marathi theatre and literature and his partner in crime G.R. Kamat would often point him to interesting books and plays in the language. Possibly, this is how he came upon Chandrakant Kakodkar's Marathi novel *Nilambari*. A Goan writer, Kakodkar fought for the liberation of the territory from Portuguese occupation. The author was unbelievably prolific, writing nearly 700 novels in Marathi, most of them about love and relationships. By the time Raj came to him, at least two of his novels had been adapted into Marathi films: *Yanda Kartavya Aahe* (1958) and *Laxmi Aali Ghara* (1965). Unlike traditional Indian novel writers, Kakodkar didn't shy away from depicting physical intimacy, which would often land him into trouble. In 1962, he wrote a short story called 'Shyama' for the Diwali issue of a Marathi magazine called *Rambha*. There were accusations of obscenity, and a suit was filed. Kakodkar fought his own case. He contended that there was nothing obscene about his stories. He introduced certain characters, he said, 'to condemn the worst and glorify the best' and that 'it was never his intention to titillate'.[1] The case went on for years, until Chandrakant Kakodkar was cleared by the Supreme Court of all charges. In a landmark judgment in August 1969, the judges proclaimed that none of the highlighted passages in his story could be considered obscene or vulgar.[2] Raj's adaptation of his novel *Nilambari*, *Do Raaste*, was to be released just four months later.

Besides *Nilambari*, *Do Raaste* owes its origin to another source – Raj's own life. His earliest memories were of Punjab, where Desraj Khosla, the toddler, scampered around among a whole army of relatives and neighbours. He explained later:

> The joint family in *Do Raaste* was my own… I had created the sets exactly like my ancestral home in Punjab. It had 30 bedrooms. We could ride our horses through the house. The stepmother in the film was my own mother in real life. [3]

Do Raaste was the first time Raj would work with a complete newbie as the lead. Even the relatively new Joy Mukerji had done three films before *Ek Musafir Ek Hasina*. But Jatin Khanna, the new kid on the block, was completely untested when he came on board. He had done some theatre, but little else. He had just altered his name to Rajesh to avoid being mixed up with another struggling actor named Jatin Khanna who had played Nanda's boyfriend in *Jab Jab Phool Khile* (1965).

Young Rajesh Khanna had won the United Producers Talent Contest held in association with *Filmfare* and the *Times of India* group, and signed a bucketload of films in quick succession. This included films with members of the United Producers panel, like B.R. Chopra who signed him for *Ittefaq* (1969), G.P. Sippy who roped him in for *Bandhan* (1969), and Shakti Samanta for *Aradhana* (1969).

Contrary to popular perception, Mumtaz and Rajesh Khanna teamed up for the first time not on *Do Raaste*, but for *Bandhan*. Mumtaz was already quite prolific by this time. Even before she signed *Bandhan* or *Do Raaste*, she had worked in more than 50 films, including some significant star vehicles such as *Pyar Kiye Jaa* (1966), *Ram aur Shyam* (1967), *Patthar ke Sanam* and *Brahmachari*. She was also famously working opposite Dara Singh in swashbuckling epics such as *Samson* (1964), *Sikandar-E-Azam* (1965) and *Rustom-E-Hind* (1965). But despite doing these films, she was still seen as a newcomer because none of those roles were author-backed, nor was she mounted in the way a true-blue Bollywood heroine in the 1960s used to be. And that's what she was going to get with *Do Raaste*.

Another relative newcomer who acted in the film was Bindu, the actress Raj chose to play the main role of Nilambari. Bindu began her career playing bit parts in films such as *Santan* (1959) and *Ek Phool Char Kaante*. In *Anpadh* (1962), she had played Mala Sinha's daughter, and even got a Lata Mangeshkar song shot on her: 'Jiya le gayo ji mora sanwariya'. She even had her own leading man, a young actor called Shaminder. But there were no films after that for a while. Falling in love and settling down at 18, she kept movies at an arm's length for a while. But she still had a strong connection with the world of films. Laxmikant Kudalkar – one half of the Laxmikant–Pyarelal duo – was married to Bindu's sister, Jaya. 'We used to live close to where Laxmikant ji usually used to record,' Bindu told me. 'One day, he said, "Why don't you guys come over and watch us record?" So we went there, watched a few recordings and were very happy. Even more so because we got to meet Lata ji!' At this time, Laxmikant and Pyarelal were working with Raj Khosla on the music of *Anita*. One day, they were supposed to join Bindu and the family for dinner. But they were working on the background music that day, and that usually takes a while. It was almost 10 p.m., and since the studio was in the vicinity, Bindu suggested that they should go meet Laxmikant there and nudge him to come home. So, Bindu and her sisters landed up at the studio. How long should they wait for dinner? they asked. Raj was there, watching them. Bindu said, 'Raj ji *ne mujhe dekha aur* Laxmi ji *se poochha*, *ye kaun hai*? *Toh unhone kaha yeh meri saali hai*. Raj ji saw me and asked Laxmi ji, who is this? He told him, she is my sister-in-law.'

'Is she interested in films?' Raj asked.

Laxmi ji said, 'Ask her yourself!'

This was the director of *C.I.D.* and *Woh Kaun Thi?* asking her if she wanted in. Without thinking, she said yes. Raj Khosla gave her a low-down of the new film he was planning to work on soon. Chandrakant Kakodkar's book is, as the title suggests, about a woman called Nilambari. A modern, ambitious woman, Nilambari marries into a family with totally different ideas about life and living. The novel centres around her and how she tackles what she's faced with. Bindu was to play Nilambari. But it was a negative role. Would she still be interested? Bindu took a beat. A negative role? A vamp? People would call her names. Raj studied her expression and smiled. 'You have 15 days to decide,' he told her. She spoke to her husband, and they consulted Laxmikant. 'You should give it a shot,' he said. 'We are the music directors on this film too.'

With *Do Raaste*, Laxmikant–Pyarelal embarked on a new adventure with Raj Khosla. In 1969, they were coming out of wildly popular albums such as *Raja aur Runk*, *Baharon Ki Manzil*, *Izzat* and *Mere Humdum Mere Dost*. *Do Raaste* would surpass them all. In fact, that one film was a milestone for many. Bindu was delighted to run into an old acquaintance on the sets of *Do Raaste*. Right after *Anpadh*, Pyarelal Santoshi had cast her as a lead in a film called *Teen Titliyan*. Opposite her was a strapping new chap called Prem Chopra. It was to be his first Hindi film as a leading man. But the film never took off. She didn't see him again for a while, until they met on the sets of *Do Raaste*. Prem Chopra told her, 'See, Bindu, how it was all destined!' Bindu replied, 'Yes, we were supposed to be hero and heroine. That never happened but now here we are, playing husband and wife!'

A watershed moment in the careers of Raj Khosla, Bindu, Laxmikant–Pyarelal and Mumtaz, *Do Raaste* most of all made a superstar of Rajesh Khanna overnight. *Aradhana* may have successfully projected him as perfect loverboy material, but *Do Raaste* firmly established him as the ideal brother, son, neighbour and boyfriend.

Bindu, Rajesh Khanna and Mumtaz weren't the only ones whose careers were shaped by the movie. A 20-year-old Mahesh Bhatt was in search of himself, as Khosla had been, exactly around the time Mahesh was born two decades ago. One day, Mahesh, young, brash and confident, told the guard of Mehboob Studios, 'Khosla saab *ne bulaya hai*! Khosla saab has called me!' Raj had done nothing of the sort. But one of the things he had acquired from his Guru was an uncanny ability to spot and nurture talent. When this young man walked into his room, he knew the boy would go far. Said Mahesh Bhatt, 'When I went down to his cabin at Mehboob Studios, the first thing he asked me was, "Do you know anything about movies?" "Nothing, sir," I replied. And to that he said, "Good, because zero is a great figure to start!" Thus began my journey in films. I joined him as a production hand.'

Sometime later, another enterprising man joined the ranks of Raj Khosla's burgeoning team. By all accounts, Johnny Bakshi seemed to want to be a producer. He had led a chequered life and washed up on the doorsteps of Filmalaya, Sashadhar Mukherjee's studio, sometime in the mid-1960s. It is unclear whether his path had crossed Raj's, who had also joined hands with Sashadhar Mukherjee at around the same time. But after Filmalaya, Johnny began his career with Khosla and team, as one of the managers at the office of Raj Khosla Films, which was by then quite a landmark at Mehboob Studios. He operated from the office and rarely came on sets. It was only later that he started being actively included in production. But he did have a brush with Rajesh Khanna and Raj Khosla during the success party of *Do Raaste*. Recounting the encounter, Johnny Bakshi said, 'He [Rajesh Khanna] was fond of throwing parties and once he invited me. I attended one such party and found top producers there – J. Om Prakash, B.R. Chopra, Shakti Samanta, Raj Khosla… I told him, "I can't be here. They're my seniors. I respect them. At most I can serve them liquor."'[4] And he did. By the end of the soiree, an inebriated Raj had labelled Johnny the best *saqi* (bartender). Bakshi and Mahesh Bhatt went on to forge a long friendship and association.

The only odd bit is that the movie didn't do much for Balraj Sahni, by far the best performer in the production. It didn't turn the tide for him the way it did for almost everyone else associated with the film.

Chandrakant Kakodkar's *Nilambari* is hard to come by now. It was published in 1962 and while plenty of the author's work is still in circulation, *Nilambari* is not. Conventional online and offline sources don't list the book. A search at well-known Marathi booksellers came out empty. Finally, the Thane branch of Marathi Granth Sangrahalaya extended a helping hand. The place is a veritable museum of Marathi literature, preserving and archiving books, journals and periodicals in the Marathi language. They had a long-worn, tattered but completely legible paperback. It seemed close to the form in which Raj Khosla may have encountered it.

Chandrakant Kakodkar was an ardent admirer of author Sarat Chandra Chatterjee and had a Bengal fixation. Though

Nilambari is written in Marathi, all the characters in the book are Bengalis who live in Calcutta. It is fascinating that the character around whom the book's plot oscillates is called Navendu Ghosh, a possible reference to Nabendu Ghosh, ace screenwriter, who had written Raj Khosla's debut film, *Milap*. Kakodkar's novel centres on the Ghosh family, consisting of Navendu, his step siblings, Dwiju, Satya and Abhaya, and his wife and mother. The book opens with Navendu dragging everyone from their beds because Dwiju is returning from abroad, having completed his studies. The family has struggled for long and it's Navendu who has almost singlehandedly raised his stepbrothers and sisters on his meagre income. Dwiju, with his fancy qualification and even fancier job, is supposed to take over and bring '*achhe din*'. But as they discover at the port, he is already married to Nilambari, of the title. The 'westernized' Nilambari finds it difficult to align with the family's ways. There are confrontations galore, and very soon, a rift occurs. Nilambari and Dwiju move out of the house. As if on cue, Navendu loses his job. The Ghosh family is in dire straits and Satya sells books and vends vegetables to support the family. Help arrives in the form of Kadambini, Satya's childhood sweetheart.

Raj Khosla's film follows the beats of the novel, with some significant changes. It's no longer set in Bengal – though the characters have pretty much the same names, they are North Indians now. Satyendra's (Rajesh Khanna) girlfriend Reena (Mumtaz) happens to be Nilambari's younger sister. There's a do-gooder Pathan stock character called Khan, played by Jayant, created just for the film. In typical Raj Khosla fashion, the film opens with a flourish. Instead of a run-of-the-mill introduction scene, Raj and screenwriter G.R. Kamat devised a unique sequence where the family receives a letter from Birju (Dwiju in the book). Navendu reads it aloud, as each character and their quirks are introduced, and the actors' real names appear on screen. The camera goes around the room, and the opening credits roll. Nilambari's aggression towards her newly acquired family is explained in a scene where her mother, played by the amazing Leela Mishra, sits her down and tells her why she should make her in-laws dance to her tunes.

Bindu remembers that by the time she was on board, the filming had already begun. Raj advised her to come to the sets and observe even before they were to start shooting her scenes. So, she dutifully came to Mehboob Studios each day to watch the stars of *Do Raaste* – now her colleagues – at work. She was introduced to Rajesh Khanna and Mumtaz. They were filming the song 'Bindiya chamkegi', and lyricist Anand Bakshi would joke with Bindu whenever they met at Laxmikant's house, saying 'Bindiya (Bindu) *zaroor chamkegi, dekh lena*. Bindu will definitely shine, wait and watch.'

Bindu was not the only one that Raj asked to be present on set just to observe others and learn. The new star called Rajesh Khanna was also expected to do so. Khanna said in an interview to *Star & Style* in November 1970:

> … this led to a certain amount of tension between us… This is what happened on the first day – (sic) the assistant came, knocked on the door of my make-up room. 'You're wanted on the sets.' 'Why?' I was surprised. 'I'm not in this shot.' 'Yes,' the assistant grinned sheepishly, 'but Raj saab wants you on the sets all the same!'[5]

Rajesh Khanna, fully aware that he was on the threshold of stardom, was irked by this behaviour. Nevertheless, he reached the sets, trying his best to not let the annoyance show on his face. Raj Khosla was frowning at the camera, which was pointed at Mumtaz. Without even turning to him, he instructed Rajesh to sit on a chair. 'I sat,' said Khanna. He explained: 'Wanting to say so many things I ended up saying nothing – just watching him work, and growing more and more interested in what I was watching. In a few months I had understood why Raj Khosla wanted me on the sets all the time, even when I was not required in the shot. He demanded the same of Mumtaz too.'

Khanna goes on to talk about how Raj shot 'Bindiya chamkegi'. According to him, the director kept taking 'fancy shots' of the actress, even as Rajesh Khanna, by his own admission, kept feeling left out and a little affronted. He thought the heroine was getting way too much attention. He kept voicing his concerns, but Raj didn't offer a word in response. He composed Mumtaz's and Khanna's shots separately for the song. A couple of weeks after, Rajesh Khanna was invited to the preview theatre to take a look at the final edited song. The actor, again by his own admission, was stunned by the end result.

In the same issue of *Star & Style*, Mumtaz told journalist Bunny Reuben that she, Rajesh Khanna and Raj Khosla would sit in their separate corners, barely speaking to one another. This was because while Kaka (Rajesh Khanna) thought Mumtaz was getting undue attention, Mumtaz thought Raj was too focused on Khanna. Raj Khosla, however, was completely immersed in the process of song-making and didn't lose any sleep over what his stars were thinking. Just like Kaka, Mumtaz was bowled over when she saw how 'Bindiya chamkegi' had turned out. She waxed eloquent on Raj's approach to his work. 'Many a time I have seen him come on the sets to start the day's work as though he is in a daze,' she said, 'as though he is utterly confused and doesn't know what to do. And gradually, he gets transformed. The moment he looks through the camera's eye he is a different person.'

In a telephonic interview with me, Mumtaz elaborated that Raj was very particular about time, but Khanna would often turn up on the sets almost three hours late, so the filmmaker had to shoot her close-ups first. '*Nau baje ke shift mein* 12 *baje toh woh* [Rajesh Khanna] *aate thhe.* For a 9 o'clock shift, he [Rajesh Khanna] would turn up at 12. So, Raj ji had to take my close-ups first, and I used to find it a little difficult because how could I give the reactions by myself? But Raj ji used to say, "Mumtaz, *main uske dialogues bolunga. Tu pehle apne* close-ups *de de, phir main* Rajesh Khanna *ko pakdunga aur usko late chhodunga.* Mumtaz, I'll say his dialogues. You give your close-ups first, then I'll catch hold of Rajesh Khanna and let him off late."' Although there may have been a choreographer, Mumtaz remembers it was Raj who directed the song.

The way the song is presented, it feels like a mini-movie of its own. Satyendra sits with his book on the terrace. He is reading (or feigning), and Reena, draped in a perilously enticing orange saree, tries to draw his attention. When all else fails, she picks up a pipe lying nearby and peeks at him through it. The camera – followed by the lot of us – peeks in too. It's through the peep hole that the song begins playing. From the pipe, we move to another cavity – the earthen pitcher, the *matka* (destined to be even more ubiquitous in Bollywood songs in about a decade and a half). This is eventually followed by a fishing net and a mirror. Mumtaz dazzles through it all, effortlessly consuming Rajesh Khanna's attention (and ours).

Raj had perfected the art of projecting the heroine ever since Madhubala and Sadhana, and Mumtaz was the apotheosis of this. Over the years, many have dubbed him a 'heroine's director'. Raj himself would have agreed. But Mumtaz presented a different point of view in an interview:

> Many of the directors I have worked with are either 'heroine's' directors or 'hero's' directors… In the case of Raj Khosla I found that he never played any favourites.

> He was strictly the 'film's director'. By this I mean that he did not make the film lop-sided in the favour of either the hero or the heroine, but kept the story strictly on its own graph, and developed his film as the audience would like to see it - not as the hero or the heroine, or any particular actor or actress would like to see it.[6]

One of the highlights of *Do Raaste* was the way in which Khosla dealt with the 'negative' characters. The film actually begins with Birju's (Prem Chopra) love letter to his family. Even when he's back from abroad, he is depicted as a loving, dutiful brother and a doting uncle. This, of course, changes when his bride, Nilambari, brings him over to the dark side, so to speak. But even Nilambari, the instigator, the conspirator, the woman who is seen as driving a wedge through the family, is not depicted merely as an evil schemer, the villain of the piece. Bindu delivers a career-defining performance as the modern woman who's been there and done that and doesn't see the need for a large family to stick together unless there are synergies to be had. Bindu said of her experience, 'Raj ji told me, "You've got beautiful eyes. So, know how to use them. I'll tell you how." He also told me how to look at the camera. "If you are to look at the camera, don't look at it straight. Keep it a little sideways – face *thodi tedhi rakhna*. This improves the framing of the face and makes it look even more beautiful." I've never forgotten that. Whichever films I did after that, the cameramen always applauded me. All credit goes to Raj ji. He is the one who taught me all that.'[7]

Raj Khosla's signature storytelling is also evident in two underrated songs in the movie. The title song, sung by Mukesh, gets the least attention of all, yet it delivers the central idea of *Do Raaste*. We see the family grappling with the stepmother's illness and Navendu taking care of her. In stark contrast, Prem

Chopra is seen living it up at a nightclub as you hear the lines: '*Do rang duniya ke, aur do raaste*'. (This brings to mind a similar situation in Manoj Kumar's *Upkaar* [1967], where one brother toils while the other – Prem Chopra again – parties at a nightclub.)

Just one year before *Do Raaste*, a 12-year-old boy called Naeem Sayyed had shot to almost instant superstardom with his turn as a tiny Mehmood dancing to 'Hum kaale hain toh kya hua dilwaale hain'. The film was *Brahmachari*, directed by Bhappi Sonie, Raj Khosla's former assistant. Naeem was labelled 'Junior Mehmood' and became the most sought-after child star of the 1960s. At the height of his stardom, all his films had to accommodate a song or two that allowed him to showcase his histrionics. In *Do Raaste*, that song was 'Apni apni biwi pe sabko guroor hai'. The song, in spirit, shares similarities with 'Mere angne mein' (*Laawaris*, 1981) in that it extols the 'virtues' of men with wives of 'different' appearances. Lata Mangeshkar is the voice of Junior Mehmood as he prances about the Gateway of India, picking one couple after the other. Raj Khosla cast two of his old colleagues as the husbands: Rashid Khan and Johnny Walker. Johnny Walker and Khosla had been compatriots in the Guru Dutt camp, and the actor had been cast in Khosla's first two films, *Milap* and *C.I.D.* They were thus long-time associates and friends. Johnny Walker's daughter Tasneem Kazi spoke to me on the phone: 'Daddy appeared in the song in a cameo, and he was happy that Raj Khosla saab had thought of him. By the 1970s, work had started to dwindle. He was doing fewer roles now. But when Khosla saab requested him to appear in that song, *woh bade khush huye*.' Incidentally, Johnny Walker also appeared in Khosla's *Meraa Dost Meraa Dushman* (1984).

The songs of *Do Raaste* did manage to achieve a certain degree of immortality, and garner views on YouTube even today. Most of them feature Rajesh Khanna and Mumtaz.

The soundtrack of *Do Raaste* (1969).

Before his stardom had solidified, Khanna had a number of singers singing for him, right from Mohammed Rafi to Mukesh to Mahendra Kapoor. It was only with *Aradhana* that the world began to see Kishore Kumar as his 'voice'. In *Do Raaste*, Rafi sang the solo 'Yeh reshmi zulfen' and 'Chhup gaye saare nazaare' for him, while Kishore Kumar sang the melancholy 'Mere naseeb mein ae dost tera pyaar nahi'. Kumar was about to leave on vacation to tour the US and UK in April–May 1969, and Laxmikant–Pyarelal got hold of him at a day's notice, the evening before he left.[8]

Do Raaste was a film so close to Raj's heart that he even invoked K.L. Saigal, whose song became a recurring motif in the film. 'Ek bangla bane nyara' is an abiding Saigal classic from *President*, which had become the anthem of a generation, symbolizing hope and progress. During the opening credits, as Navendu reads the letter from his brother to the family, the tune plays in the background. Then, as Navendu lounges with his stepmother, the song plays in the background, on an old gramophone record. Khan steps in and says, '*Purana gaana sunta hai aur naya sapna dekhta hai*? Listening to an old song but seeing new dreams?' The song also wafts in when Navendu talks to his departed father's photograph, assuring him that all is now well. The first frame of *Do Raaste* is a declaration of gratitude to Hindustan Musical Product Ltd. of Calcutta for allowing use of the song.

Do Raaste was a behemoth of a hit. Rajesh Khanna and Mumtaz became household names, a pair that would go on a streak of phenomenally successful movies. The movie album was one of Laxmikant–Pyarelal's biggest chartbusters that year, and Raj was already planning a reunion of sorts – in November 1970, *Star & Style* featured interviews with Mumtaz and Rajesh Khanna, in which both spoke about 'starting a new journey together' with Raj Khosla. Both of them mentioned the title: *Prem Kahani*. But this would see the light of day only after six long years.

Seventeen years later, Raj said of *Do Raaste*: 'I'll always cherish the moment when I showed my mother *Do Raaste*, the only film of mine she'd ever seen. My tall, blue-eyed mother was in tears when she saw it and held me like a baby in her arms.'

Within a few months of *Do Raaste*, Saraswati Khosla breathed her last. Raj was beside himself with grief. She was a formidable woman, whose influence had shaped Raj as a person. The folk tunes she hummed to him as a child made it to some of the most memorable songs in the history of Hindi film music, such as 'Jhumka gira re' and 'Bindiya chamkegi'. It was she who exhorted him to move on when *Anita* was a disaster. His life revolved around the women in his life, and she was the one who mattered the most to him. Now, she was gone. Raj was bereft, but as his mother had told him during one of the biggest setbacks in his career, he had to move on.

By some accounts, Raj was also facing some financial pressure because *Anita* had failed, and *Chirag* had underperformed. 'He was going through financial distress,' says Mahesh Bhatt. 'There was a big problem... his films hadn't worked. His office was unable to pay salaries. There were people coming to his door – dressmen, makeup men asking for money and they were being told, "*Haath tang hai, mil jaayega*. The coffers are empty right now. You'll get paid soon enough, don't worry." Those were the dark days.' Everything was hinged on the box office verdict of *Do Raaste*.

On the first day of *Do Raaste*'s release, Bhatt was at the Royal Opera House. Next to him was Waman Bhonsle, the legendary editor who had just begun his journey with Raj Khosla (Bhonsle was to be with him till the very end). It was 5 December 1969 and right across the road at Roxy, *Aradhana* was running to a packed house nearly every day. But the Opera House was almost empty. A manager by the name of Desai, a veteran observer of the trade, came to Bhatt and Bhonsle and said, '*Saamne woh* Shakti *ki* picture *chal rahi hai* Aradhana, *woh advance mein* housefull *hai. Yaha par log nahin aate. Ye* picture *doobegi*. Shakti's picture *Aradhana* is running across the road, it's a full house in advance. No one comes here. This film will sink.'

When he heard this, Bhatt broke down. Bhonsle had seen it all before, but the young Bhatt, all of 20, was emotionally attached to the film. Waman Bhonsle later said in an interview, 'I recall Mahesh Bhatt weeping openly when *Do Raaste* opened poorly at Royal Opera House in Mumbai and the doorkeeper told us on the second or third day that it was a flop, unlike *Aradhana* in the movie-hall across the road. Bhatt had worked a lot on the film. But Raj-ji was confident.'[9] Raj was. He knew the value of his product. Especially this one.

After a week or so, Bhatt and Bhonsle were back at the theatre. This time, the place was bustling with spectators. Evidently, the positive word of mouth had helped. A last-minute tweak might have played a role too. Initially, in the last scene, where the stepmother talks to her stepson, G.R. Kamat had scripted some touching lines about mother–son relationships. When the film was released, Raj found that the audience did not accept what was being said in the film.

Raj was in a fix. The early responses were in, and it was clear that the ending hadn't worked with the people. He reached out to his friend Sadhana for her thoughts. Sadhana and Raj had worked on four films by then (not counting the ill-fated *Sajan ki Galiyan*). Over the years, she had become a confidante and a sounding board. He showed her his films, and she told him what she felt. One fine morning, she landed up at his house, offering a solution. She suggested that he end the film differently. End with that song 'Bindiya chamkegi', she told him. Though this recommendation might have seemed a little off-kilter, Raj went with it – he respected Sadhana's judgement implicitly. The scene with the stepmother was now replaced with the song. The rewards were plentiful. 'I had great respect for her judgement, so I did what she suggested. And it worked and how! At the end of the film the audience gave it a standing ovation. But I was still a disappointed man. I was in love with the lines I had planned for the end,' Khosla said.[10]

Do Raaste was well on its way to success. It ran more than 50 weeks at the same Opera House where the staff had written the film off. At the silver jubilee celebrations, Raj Khosla invited Raj Kapoor to give away trophies. He also announced a bonus for some of his team members, Mahesh Bhatt among them. 'I remember getting a bonus of ₹300, which was my one month's salary. He gave 300 bucks extra to me for shedding tears!' Bhatt chuckles.

Do Raaste had taken care of the financial difficulties and more. At the cusp of a new decade that represented a whole new era of filmmaking in Bollywood, Raj Khosla was about to dive into a genre he hadn't tried before.

Raj in the happiest phase of his life: with his parents Atmaram and Saraswati Khosla, his brother Lekhraj, Lekhraj's wife and their kids, Bolu, Tanny, Premi and Kupi.

Raj Khosla getting wed, just a day before the filming of *Milap* (1959) started. In attendance are friends Dev Anand and Guru Dutt, besides K.N. Singh.

Raj Khosla's wedding. Guru Dutt and Geeta Dutt can be seen overlooking the proceedings.

Raj Khosla with his new bride Usha, flanked by Geeta Dutt.

Moment with a mare.

Astride his favourite animal.

From Raj Khosla's debut as an actor in C.L. Dheer's *Raen Basera* (1948). The film had a release but was later lost.

Courtesy: Lakshmi Priya

Raj Khosla with Dev Anand and Sachin Dev Burman. This is during the shoot of Chetan Anand's *Funtoosh* (1956) at Mehboob Studios. Raj must have dropped in for a chat.

Raj Khosla with O.P. Nayyar while shooting the song 'Yeh hai Bombay meri jaan' for *C.I.D.* (1956), at Marine Drive.

Raj Khosla with actress Minoo Mumtaz and his crew, filming the song 'Boojh mera kya naam re' from *C.I.D.*

Mr and Mrs Raj Khosla with the car that Guru Dutt gifted him after the success of *C.I.D.*

Possibly after a match of cricket. Some recognizable faces here, including Guru Dutt and Sahir Ludhianvi. Raj is sitting on the ground, second from left.

Goofing around on location.

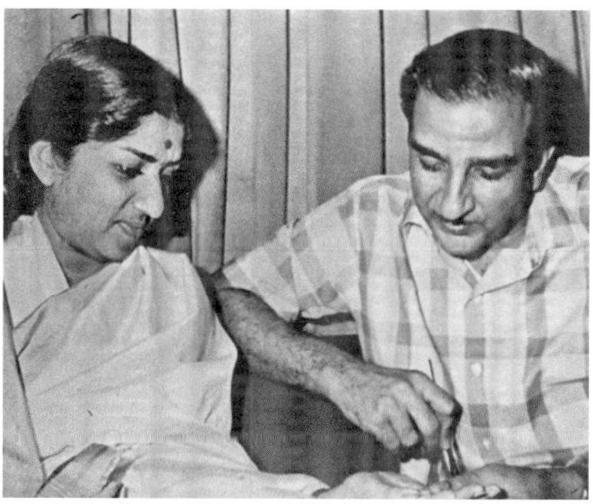

Sharing a moment with the Nightingale, Lata Mangeshkar, with whom he had some precious songs.

With sisters Lata and Usha Mangeshkar.

Raj Khosla with K.N. Singh.

Raj Khosla with actors Waheeda Rehman and Jagdev during the making of *Solva Saal* (1958).

With Rahul Dev Burman.

Raj Khosla and Manoj Kumar while shooting *Woh Kaun Thi?* (1964).

Manoj Kumar and Parveen Choudhary during the shooting of the song 'Shokh nazar ki bijliyan' from *Woh Kaun Thi?*.

With Rahul Dev Burman and N.N. Sippy.

With Lata Mangeshkar and Sadhana.

Raj engaged in an intense conversation with one of his closest friends in the industry: Sadhana.

With Sunil Dutt, a moment of warmth and camaraderie.

With one of his dearest friends and collaborators, Sunil Dutt.

Engaged in yet another conversation with Sadhana.

While shooting *Do Badan* (1966) in Gulmarg.

With N.N. Sippy and Simi Garewal.

Raj Khosla, Manoj Kumar and Asha Parekh engaged in picturizing the song 'Mat jaiyo naukariya chhod ke' from *Do Badan*.

A poster of *Do Raaste* (1969) depicting Raj Khosla's name on the director's chair, an instance of his stardom as a filmmaker at the time.

Directing Johnny Walker while filming the song 'Apni apni biwi' from *Do Raaste*.

Conferring with Tun Tun on the sets of *Do Raaste*.

At the success party of *Do Raaste*, with Raj Kapoor and Asit Sen.

RK with RK, at the success party of *Do Raaste*, sharing a laugh. While one Raj was basking in the success of *Do Raaste*, the other was nursing his wounds from the debacle of *Mera Naam Joker* (1970).

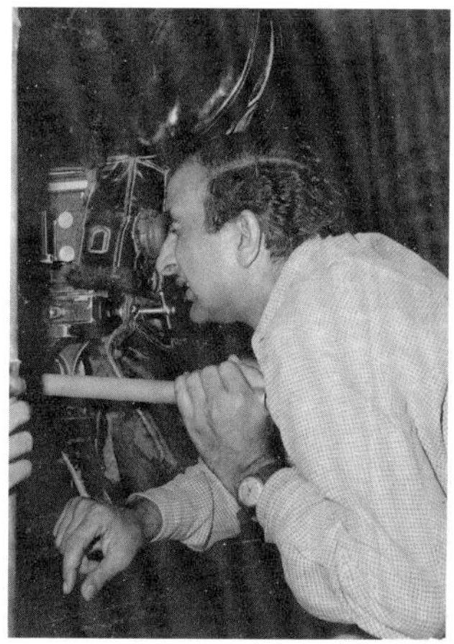

Man at work: Raj Khosla peeking through the camera to make sure his vision is captured right.

Shooting *Mera Gaon Mera Desh* (1971) with Dharmendra at Udaipur.

Raj Khosla and Kabir Bedi right around the time *Kuchhe Dhaage* (1973) came out. The lobby cards of the film can be seen in the background.

During the original *mahurat* of *Prem Kahani* (1975), with Rajesh Khanna and the original choice for the heroine, Moushumi Chatterjee.

With Mumtaz during the shoot of *Prem Kahani*. Rajesh Khanna in the background enjoying a smoke.

Raj Khosla with Nutan, filming a scene from *Main Tulsi Tere Aangan Ki* (1978).

Vijay Anand paying respects to Raj's father, Atmaram Khosla.

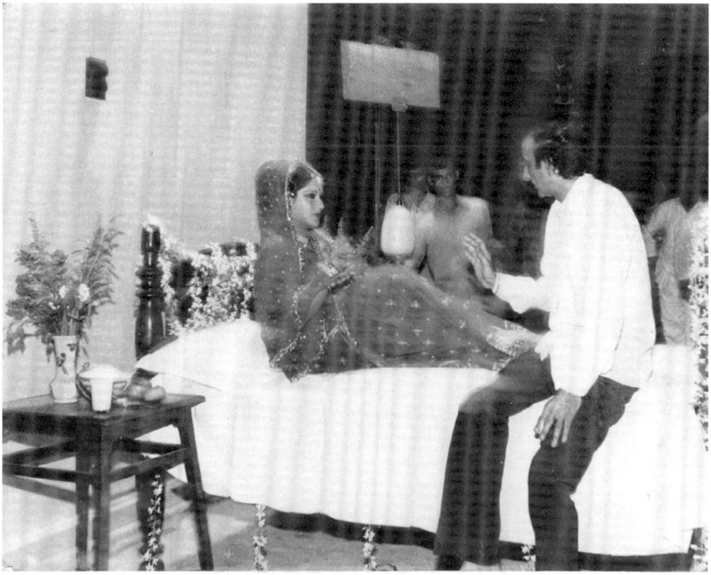

Raj Khosla explaining a scene to Moushumi Chatterjee, possibly on the sets of *Daasi* (1981).

Raj Khosla at an exhibition celebrating his contribution to Hindi cinema.

Raj Khosla directing Padmini Kolhapure and Raj Kiran on location for *Teri Maang Sitaron Se Bhar Doon* (1982).

Raj Khosla directing Rishi Kapoor and Farha for *Naqāb* (1989).

15

What Do You Wish Me to Do With You?

Sometime in the 1960s, journalist Tarun Kumar Bhaduri, Jaya Bachchan's father, wrote a book called *Abhishapta Chambal*. Originally written in Bengali, the book was later translated to English as *Chambal: The Valley of Terror*. It contains a vivid account of Bhaduri's travels through the heart of the Chambal valley, interviewing dreaded bandits and their kin. What emerges is a fascinating tale of violence, bloodshed and generational rivalries. Bhaduri also tries to trace the origins of the Chambal bandits. According to his narrative, in the late twelfth century, when Rajput king Prithviraj Chauhan drove away a band of Tomar Rajputs from Delhi, some of them settled in the Bhind–Morena area of Chambal. Away from home, angry and humiliated, they launched an assault on Prithviraj Chauhan.[1] Thus began an endless, bloody battle to return home. For generations, the Tomars first fought Prithviraj Chauhan and then every subsequent ruler of Delhi. They needed coin to survive, and looting became the only way to replenish the coffers. Long after Prithviraj Chauhan and the Tomar Rajputs were gone, their successors picked up the mantle. It became a ritual: '*Khoon ka badla khoon*. Blood for blood.' The warriors had now become bandits, but the fight had to go on. The natural ravines of the valley allowed them easy cover from the police. Legends about *daaku*s like Maan Singh, Putlibai and Lakhan Singh spread far and wide, and the Chambal valley, once named after the Charmavati river, became synonymous with dacoits.

In the twentieth century, dacoity had become a menace that had existed for well over 700 years. There was something in Chambal's waters, it was said, that made men and women thirst for blood. In the 1960s, Bhaduri's book (through its various translations) stirred public imagination with riveting tales of bloodshed, honour and adventure from the ravines. Around the same time, Acharya Vinoba Bhave, the social reformer, urged the dacoits of Chambal to lay down their arms. Many infamous bandits surrendered subsequently. Moved by this episode and its Gandhian underpinnings, Raj Kapoor made *Jis Desh Men Ganga Behti Hai* (1960), which was helmed by his favourite director of photography Radhu Karmakar. The film was a thundering success, and is often credited with introducing the bandit film to unsuspecting audiences. But at least three years before that came *Mother India* (1957), which featured dacoits in good measure. Sunil Dutt played Birju, the rogue son, who runs away from home and picks up a gun. *Mother India* itself was a remake of *Aurat* (1940), where the wayward dacoit son was played by the magnificent Yakub. Even so, possibly the first time one encountered the true-blue Chambal *daaku* in Hindi cinema was *Mujhe Jeene Do* (1963), with Sunil Dutt playing the outlaw again.

Raj Khosla, having aced a bunch of genres by then (crime films, romance, thrillers, family drama), was now on a quest to make a bandit film. The result was a *daaku* film that would, in many ways, define the template for the genre. The filmmaker had had a brush with dacoity in his youth. In an interview,

Raj said, 'A dacoit gang had once left a note in our home at Sri Gobindpur that they would attack on a certain day. I wasn't there when they came, but I was told the police was summoned and there was a regular gun deal.'[2] But what formed the immediate impetus for his new film was a news item he read in the paper.

In the 1960s, newspapers were rife with episodes of loot and murder by dacoits, punctuated with reports of encounters with the police. But there was one stray incident where the residents of a village decided to fight back. Reportedly, these villagers came together and attacked the dacoits, killing about 13 of them. The number is specific because that is how Raj Khosla remembered it.[3] The news struck him for how bizarre the villagers' action was. And there was the germ of an idea.

The 'Khosla Enterprises Story Department' swung into action. In the early 1970s, this was quickly becoming the norm. Every production house worth its salt had a 'story department'. In most cases, these 'departments' would consist of screenwriters and those who specialized in writing dialogue. Raj's faithful scribes G.R. Kamat and Akhtar Romani were definitely a part of his.

For *Mera Gaon Mera Desh* (1971), Raj didn't want a typical Hindi movie villain, cut out from cardboard. He was looking for someone far more sinister, a character that was pitch black, from beginning to end. A sheer embodiment of evil. And against all conventional wisdom, he went to Vinod Khanna, the resident Adonis of Bollywood. 'When I offered the role to Vinod Khanna,' Raj later said, 'I told him that the role was entirely black with no shades of grey. That he was to be a merciless dacoit who even killed children. He agreed unconditionally.'[4] Khanna, at the time, was playing minor supporting roles, mostly negative. But this was the first time he was being offered something to sink his teeth into and showcase what he could really do. And he did.

To Vinod Khanna's credit, he used his good looks and appearance to accentuate the evil of Jabbar Singh. His frame, his gait, his sharp features, that sculpted jawline – he employed everything that he was gifted with to underscore the cruelty and menace of Jabbar. He was helped in abundant measure by Raj and Kamat, who ensured that the script didn't reveal even one redeeming quality in the character.

For decades, people have drawn parallels between *Sholay* and *Mera Gaon Mera Desh*, if only to point out the uncanny similarities in plot detail. The thakur without a limb hires (a) goon(s) who decide(s) everything by the toss of a coin to fight a bandit called J(G)abbar Singh. Both Gabbar and Jabbar are child murderers. But what makes Jabbar Singh's evil a shade deeper is that you (almost) see him do it. Dharmendra, who famously played the lead in *Mera Gaon Mera Desh* (and also in *Sholay*), had an interesting take on the irredeemable evilness of the character: 'We used to sit together in the evenings, drinking. He would drink and I just sat there… I had quit for a while. I used to tell him – Raj ji, the darker this dacoit character [Jabbar Singh] gets, revenge would be that much sweeter. I had some characters in mind [that he could kill] – Purnima ji's character, the child… Of course, finally it was his job to decide how to bring it to screen. But he used to hear me out attentively.'[5]

Dharmendra had to work on his physique for the film. Till this point, except for thrillers and spy movies such as *Ankhen* (1968), *Yakeen* (1969) and *Baazi* (1968), he was seen as the dashing romantic hero who featured mostly in films with strong female characters. Even those other films didn't see him indulging in a whole lot of action. *Mera Gaon* was the first instance where Dharmendra played the bona fide action hero – recruited to rid his village of dacoits – and he had to look the part. Raj was very clear about the kind of look he wanted from his hero: fit and in peak physical form. The entire cast and crew of the film had stationed themselves in a village called Cheerwa, about four kilometres from Udaipur. Short of shooting in Chambal valley, this was as authentic as they could get. Every morning, the villagers of Cheerwa woke up to scenes of a strapping Dharmendra riding a horse, playing badminton or cycling through the dirt roads.

But that was not enough. One of the things that Dharmendra shared with Raj Khosla was an acute fondness for booze. But Raj had sworn him off alcohol. '*Kya rakkha hai daru-waru mein*? What is the point of alcohol?' he would tell Dharam with a smile, before settling down with a drink himself as darkness fell. With cropped, crew-cut hair and a chiselled face, Dharmendra began to look the part of the tough guy who could take on a band of dacoits. 'One afternoon, we were sitting in the fields,' Dharmendra reminisced, 'when Lekhraj, his [Raj's] brother came to see us. We used to call him "Papa ji". He was a cheerful chap, always smiling. Papa ji left some bottles of wine for us. Raj ji said, "*Kya hai, kaisi hai ye* wine? *Dekh zara*… What is this, how is this wine? Take a look…" That moment, I could see a child in him, craving for it as if it's a toy, and getting a friend to play with it on his behalf. He offered me a swig. I told him wine wasn't my thing and that I was off drinking in any case. But he kept insisting, in a warm, affectionate tone so characteristic of him, and I gave in.' Dharmendra was only providing company, but as the day wore on, Raj brought out his favourite harmonium and sang his Saigal numbers. One thing led to another, and the evening was submerged in drunken revelry.

In an interview, Raj recounted the same episode: 'Dharam had to do a lot of riding. I told him he'd have to stop drinking as I wanted him looking fresh. And he stopped drinking. I'll never forget how he thirsted for a drink. One day I relented and got some bottles of wine for lunch. Dharam really cherished that meal.'[6]

Dharmendra also remembers a riding scene that involved a certain degree of risk. Raj Khosla forbade him from pulling any such stunt. Ravi Khanna, who was composing the action scenes, tried to stop him as well, but Dharmendra had made up his mind. 'I'll do it myself,' he told Ravi Khanna, 'just take care of Raj ji.' After he did it and fell down right in front of the camera, Raj Khosla was in tears. He was sobbing and reprimanding Dharam at the same time. 'Why did you do it, Dharam, why? *Lag jaati toh*? What if you had gotten hurt?'

This aspect of Raj Khosla's personality came up several times during the research for this book. Despite being in an industry where men displaying vulnerability were scoffed at, Raj was known to wear his heart on his sleeve. He didn't hesitate to show emotion. When his heart swelled over, he wept. When a loved one was in pain, he wept. Towards the later years, this tendency became even more acute. Many of his later-day interviewers have mentioned him breaking into tears talking about his Guru or his mother. Sometimes he would hark back to the past and tears would flow. While speaking about how sentimental the director could be, Dharmendra said, 'He used to try to hide his pain. *Lekin dard chhupaye kahan chhupta hai*! But where can you hide pain! It was visible right on his face. Drinking was his escapism… which became a habit later on.'

Opposite Dharmendra's Ajit was Asha Parekh as his love interest, Anju. Asha Parekh's heroine was the ubiquitous village belle, a staple in 1970s and 1980s movies. The '*gaon ki gori*' was one of the dozen stock characters that popular Hindi cinema had groomed over the decades. But this was a Raj Khosla film. So even in an action drama with brawny men sweating and fuming and guns blazing, Parekh had a meaty enough part. When the dacoits swoop down on the village, she is one of the dissenting voices who wants to speak up against them. At the start of the film, when Ajit is found ogling at the women bathing in the river, she smears his face with dung and shoos him away. She knows her way around a gun, and during the final showdown with the bandits, she is not found wanting. For the role of Anju, Parekh had to blend this fiery aspect of her character with being the lissome lass that Ajit falls in love with.

The rest of the cast played their roles with panache too. The part of Ajit's adoptive mother was played by Purnima, who was a popular heroine in the 1940s and 1950s. Raj had crossed paths with her earlier in *Jaal*, where he was an assistant and she had played the part of Lisa. In *Mera Gaon Mera Desh*, she plays a woman with mental health issues who is convinced that she is the mother of Ajit, who is actually an orphan and a stranger to the village.

Jayant was cast as Major Jaswant Singh, the ex-serviceman who hires Ajit to rid his village of the scourge of dacoits led by Jabbar Singh. Jayant played the one-armed *fauji* with aplomb. Both this role and the one in *Do Raaste* had ample scope for caricature. But Jayant infused these characters with a certain kind of wit that was unique to him. In *Mera Gaon*, he looks at Dharmendra's character with warmth and amusement, constantly on the verge of a smile, as if the veritable He-man were nothing but a man-child.

For whole generations of moviegoers, the name *Mera Gaon Mera Desh* conjures up the imagery of one song. Jabbar Singh has Ajit and Anju bound to pillars in his den. Tensions run high as the bandit leader contemplates when and how to kill them. In

The soundtrack of *Mera Gaon Mera Desh* (1971).

these circumstances, Jabbar's moll Munni breaks into song. Raj had major apprehensions about the scene, and he kept putting off shooting it. To him, it was a hackneyed scenario, as old as the hills: the hero and heroine tied up in the villain's den as the 'vamp' presents an elaborate song and dance routine. But it was crucial in the context of the film, and finally he had to get down to it.

But what would the song be? It had to be situational. Munni had been recruited by Jabbar to spy on the villagers, especially Ajit and his friends. But unbeknownst to him, she now empathized with the enemy. The dacoit wanted his prisoners dead. And the song had to reflect this complexity, this being a Raj Khosla film. Like so many songs in his films, it had to flow like a conversation. 'I was narrating the situation to Laxmikant and Anand Bakshi,' Raj Khosla later said. 'Anand immediately came with the dialogue of Sikandar (Alexander) and Porus, and came up with "Maar diya jaaye…" The song was written in two minutes.'[7]

The tune drew on Alexander's question to the Indian king referred to as Puru, whom the Greeks called Porus. Apparently, when the king, defeated in battle, was brought to Alexander in chains, the Greek emperor asked him, 'What do you wish me to do with you?'

The king replied, 'Treat me, o Alexander, like a king.' Alexander was supposedly impressed enough to reinstate Porus to his throne. The song expands on Alexander's query, and beyond the first line, it is all Anand Bakshi:

Maar diya jaaye, ke chhod diya jaaye
Bol tere saath kya sulook kiya jaaye
Zeher diya jaaye, ke jaam diya jaaye

(Kill you or spare you

What do you wish me to do with you?
Make you a drink, or poison you
What do you wish me to do with you?)

Just a while before this song comes on, Ajit has accused Munni of being a traitor and humiliated her. So, one of the strains in the song goes:

Aa rahi hai hansi teri kahaani pe
Aaj tu hai meri meherbaani pe
Tod diya jaaye, ke dil jod diya jaaye
Bol tere saath kya sulook kiya jaaye

(Your story makes me smile
You are at my mercy all the while
Should I break your heart, or pardon you
What do you wish me to do with you?)

The entire song is pictured with Munni swirling through the den, stopping by either Ajit or Anju or Jabbar Singh. The tension between the characters is accentuated as she flings water at Ajit's face and whips out a knife when she's near Anju. By the time the song comes to an end, Munni has poisoned the gang and set the lovers free. Discussing the song, Pyarelal told me that Laxmikant could have very well composed the lines in a simple, rousing tune and it would still work. But the way he ended up setting those lyrics to tune, anyone who understands music would marvel at the creation. 'Even an accomplished musician would touch his feet!' he said. Pyarelal also pointed out to me that the song was picturized so well that it did not matter that Dharmendra and Parekh, the two leads of the film, were tied to pillars, completely out of action! 'We said to Raj Khosla ji, "Raj ji, Dharmendra is the hero of the film, and you've tied him to a pillar. A great dancer like Asha Parekh, and you've tied her down too! Poor Vinod Khanna is sitting in a corner, and you've handed him a bottle. What's gonna happen?" Raj ji laughed.'

Munni, in fact, played by Laxmi Chhaya, is the character in *Mera Gaon* who leaves the maximum impact on you. Unlike others in the film, she is constantly swinging between light and shade. In the beginning, she seems to be the quintessential gangster's moll, dancing to his tunes and spying on his behalf. We discover over the course of the film that her heart is in the right place, and she would like to help the villagers in their fight against her boss.

Laxmi Chhaya's first-known appearance in movies was as a 10-year-old in Mahesh Kaul's *Talaq* (1958). By the time she was in her teens, she was moving in and out of films sets, playing the heroine's friend or one of the dancers. She was light-footed, danced like a dream and had incredible screen presence. In 1965, she appeared alongside Ted Lyon and the Cubs – an Anglo-Indian band seen in a string of Hindi films in the 1960s and 1970s – in a livewire of a song called 'Jaan pehchan ho' from *Gumnaam* (1965). Laxmi Chhaya was front and centre, sashaying as if she were made of sheer electricity. The song attained global popularity in 2001 when it was featured in the opening credits of Terry Zwigoff's *Ghost World* (2001). Who was this woman, dancing like mad? By the late 1960s, she was so popular that a film called *Duniya* (1968) had a whole song dedicated to her: 'Tu hi meri Laxmi, tu hi meri Chhaya', sung by Mohammed Rafi, picturized on her and Johnny Walker. The cult of Laxmi Chhaya was furthered with the coming of the internet and the blogosphere buzzed with her exploits. But till *Ghost World* – and

'Jaan pehchan ho' from *Gumnaam* (1965), featured in *Ghost World* (2001).

the internet – came about, the most widely seen and celebrated turn of Laxmi Chhaya was in *Mera Gaon Mera Desh*.

So far, she had only appeared in bit roles and dance numbers. This was the first time someone – a filmmaker like Raj Khosla, no less – had trusted her with a full-fledged role. And as many have pointed out over the years, her performance as Munni, the dancing girl, became one of the highlights of the film. She had three songs devoted almost entirely to her. Besides 'Maar diya jaaye', there were 'Aaya aaya atariya pe koi chor' and 'Apni prem kahaniyan'. The last was another 'conversation' song. In the garb of a love song, it conveys certain specific messages meant to help the cops identify Jabbar Singh, who seems to have turned up in a disguise. Sample these lines:

Kurta hai neela
Rang pagdi ka peela
…
Aankhon ko meeche
Dekho sanson ko kheeche
Wahan peepal ke neeche
Mele mein sabke peechhe
Khada hai…

(In a kurta blue
And a turban yellow too
…
Eyes half-shut, stands he
His breath held, under the peepal tree
Behind the crowds, there's he)

Laxmi Chhaya later told radio presenter Ameen Sayani about her experience making the film with Raj Khosla: 'He gave me the lengthiest and most important role of my career in *Mera Gaon Mera Desh*.' When Sayani complimented her on her performance, she said, 'It was all due to him,' adding, 'he respects actors a lot. He would explain a complex scene as if he had just told us something very trivial. At the time, even we didn't feel that what he explained to us was a big deal. Only when we see it on screen do we realize what a great scene we have pulled off. It is all due to Raj ji.'[8] In the same interview, she narrated a story that highlighted Khosla's indelible wit and charm. Laxmi was supposed to join the crew of *Mera Gaon* in Udaipur a few days after the shoot began. The day she arrived, they were unable to get any sunlight – it was all cloudy. As she made her entry, Raj joked that Laxmi had indeed brought *chhaya*, shade, with her!

Some claim that Laxmi Chhaya was initially signed on to simply play the vamp, Jabbar Singh's spy. But her work was so impressive that the role kept expanding. Munni falls for the man she's been asked to spy on. She follows her heart and switches sides, gets accused of spying by the man she loves, sets him and his partner free at great personal risk, only to meet a gory end at the hands of her employer.

Laxmi's performance as Munni struck such a chord that a year later, she was starring as a heroine opposite Shatrughan Sinha in a film called *Kundan* (1972). The film tanked and Laxmi Chhaya was back to her dances. She left a trail of brilliant – and often underrated, even overlooked – dance numbers.

Asha Parekh points out Raj Khosla's use of the round trolley (a device used to move the camera around the subject in a circular motion) in the song 'Sona lai jaa re': 'The whole song was on the round trolley. There were a few close-ups in between, but otherwise it was the round trolley. So he experimented a lot at times, when he was in the mood. Sometimes, he was not in the mood to shoot. Then later he would say, "*Achha… karte hain…* Alright, let's do it.'"

And here is another aspect of Raj's filmmaking and work ethic. One moment he'd be hard at work, with his entire focus concentrated on how to get a great shot. Another time, he would be seen smiling, telling everyone to pack up. Sometimes it was even hard to get him to the sets. Mahesh Bhatt, the controller of production and assistant director on *Mera Gaon Mera Desh*, recalls, 'Waking him up and taking him to the shoot was one hell of a task, which we were doing in Udaipur, where we were outdoors, at the mercy of the clouds.'

Raj used to say, as Johnny Bakshi wrote about him a few years after his death, that if a child went to school everyday, studied diligently and passed with flying colours, it didn't impress him at all. What he did find impressive would resonate with a lot of us. 'The real thing is to bunk school as much as possible, don't study at all throughout the year, just put in a few weeks of study before the examination and then stand first in class. That's an achievement,' he used to say. And that, as Bakshi illustrated, informed his approach to work. 'He always tried his best to cancel his own shooting, even involved his artistes to help him postpone shooting, and while he was on the set, he would delay work by disapproving a scene and trying to rewrite it with the help of the artiste.'[9]

In fact, according to Mahesh Bhatt, Raj Khosla was working on the screenplay of *Mera Gaon* as he shot the film. Bound screenplays were largely unheard of around this time. There was a story or a story idea, and a vague arc. The scenes and dialogues were written on the fly, right before that specific scene was filmed. In some instances, the writer would sit and feverishly scribble the lines on a piece of paper while the actors were being called to the set. But Raj liked to be an integral part of the writing process. Bhatt recalls, 'Once, he was on the set, sitting with his writers. Jayant Dharmadhikari was his assistant writer, and there was G.R. Kamat as well. It was almost lunchtime and we had not taken any shot. I asked him where to place the camera and he gave me a dirty look. "Can you please give me some time to be? I am incidentally also writing my screenplay!" He used to keep his scripts very fluid. He had the courage to shoot something, and then go back and reshoot.'

The rewriting was not happening only on paper. If Raj thought something had to be corrected, he would go back and shoot that particular scene all over again. 'He was a maverick,' says Bhatt.

The climax of the film brought the whole village together, both on camera and off it. In the film, Ajit, after a spectacular face-off with the bandits through the deserted lanes, manages to inspire the villagers to pick up whatever weapons they can get their hands on and confront the dacoits, eventually defeating them. This was not too far from what happened in real life, as Raj Khosla and team shot the climactic battle. The entire village of Cheerwa assembled, and they brought weapons. Some of them brought antique guns, including one from 1595, and some swords. They were so charged up to fight, that Raj had to explain to them that Vinod Khanna and Dharmendra were actors, and had nothing against each other. The residents of Cheerwa treated the crew well, pampering them with buttermilk and makke ki roti. And the production team of *Mera Gaon Mera Desh* responded in kind by building a high school for the villagers.[10]

Mera Gaon Mera Desh continued Raj Khosla's rampage through the box office. The brilliantly mounted action scenes, the dialogues, the performances and the songs endeared the film to the masses.

Dharmendra consolidated his career as an action star, but it was Vinod Khanna who walked away with the most adulation. His performance proved that he wasn't just a pretty face.

What also strikes one about *Mera Gaon Mera Desh* are the visuals, and how the epic canvas was captured. During a 1973 interview, a journalist described Raj's approach to the film in a way that sums up his larger filmmaking style too: 'a jazzy, slick style of filmmaking, innovations, shooting from quick and startling angles, the camera perpetually in motion, sudden and unexpected zooms, fast cutting, jump cuts.'[11] All of this was in full display in *Mera Gaon Mera Desh*. The fact that he was collaborating with a brand new cinematographer didn't hurt either.

With *Mera Gaon*, a new cameraman had joined Raj Khosla's fold. Pratap Sinha, like Raj himself, was a Navketan alumnus. He had assisted Fali Mistry on *Nagin*, and was the second unit/operative cameraman on *Guide*. He started his career as a cinematographer with Ram Mukherjee's *Hum Hindustani* and Dev Anand's *Teen Devian*. Raj scooped him up and ever since *Mera Gaon*, they were inseparable.

A new idea was brewing. A whole new generation of actors had appeared on the horizon, and Raj was making new friends. Raj Khosla Films had an office at Mehboob Studios – gifted by the studio owners, and which later went to Johnny Bakshi. Over the years, it became a sort of a pilgrimage for actors and technicians working at Mehboob to drop in to pay their regards to the great Raj Khosla. At this point, in the early 1970s, two young actors named Amitabh Bachchan and Jaya Bhaduri also came visiting. Among these 'pilgrims' had been Vinod Khanna and Kabir Bedi. Raj Khosla would cast Vinod in several films. Following the great success of *Mera Gaon Mera Desh*, he wanted to cast him as a dacoit once again, but this time not as the antagonist. At least, not in the conventional sense.

16

Of Threads, Thieves and Guns

I met Kabir Bedi at a posh but relaxed Bandra eatery. Looking as dapper as ever, the septuagenarian recounted his first encounter with Raj Khosla:

> I had just done a play in Bombay called *Tughlaq*, which was the talk of the town. It was a brilliant play by Girish Karnad – the opening act had me standing with my back to the audience, completely nude, under a top light. It drew gasps from the audience and the play got me very well known in Bombay. Raj ji had heard of the play, and he sent Johnny Bakshi to track me down, and I met him in Shivaji Park. We chatted for a while, and he took me home. That was Raj Khosla for you. He'd take you home, and he'd play chess. He was an avid chess player and when he played with me, I knew that instead of looking at the board, he was studying me. And that was when he told me he had a role for me. Me and Vinod [Khanna] were to play leads in this film. I knew Vinod from before. And after the grand success of *Mera Gaon Mera Desh*, Raj Khosla was a force to reckon with.

What also made Kabir Bedi a good fit for the role was his expertise in horse-riding. Raj's passion for horses had taken a new dimension. Now that he was a fairly successful filmmaker, he could indulge in his childhood love of riding. He had a farm, and he used to frequent Mahalaxmi Racecourse. Lorna Desouza, one of his trusted aides at Raj Khosla Films and his secretary from 1971 until the late 1980s, told me that he had a horse called Sweet Sally, which he used to ride at Mahalaxmi. On one of his birthdays, Lorna recalled, she gifted him a painting of horses, and he was overjoyed.

Now, after *Mera Gaon Mera Desh*, this love had seeped into his work. Though real-life Chambal dacoits were too busy running through the ravines to afford horses, Bollywood dacoits have always been seen astride the animal. No dacoit movie was complete without shots of *daaku*s storming into the village on their horses, leaving clouds of dust in their wake. It may have something to do with the fact that Indian dacoit films were at some level inspired by the Hollywood westerns, which couldn't be conceived without horses. Now that Raj had tasted success in this genre, he wanted to make more so that he could spend more and more time around horses. Ketan Anand, filmmaker and an ardent admirer of Khosla, says, 'He was a damn good horse-rider. He used to ride the bloody horse while shooting!'

Kuchhe Dhaage (1973), Raj Khosla's fifteenth film as a director, hinged on a key phenomenon that was rampant among Indian dacoits, especially the ones from the Bhind–Morena area of Chambal: revenge. '*Khoon ka badla khoon*' was a philosophy passed down through generations and blood feuds were a way of life. As recorded in Tarun Bhaduri's books *Abhishapta Chambal* and *Behar Baaghi Bandook*, mothers raised their children to avenge their fathers, and it was an unbroken chain that went back hundreds of years. If his father were killed by a dacoit, it was the son's sacred duty to inflict revenge on the perpetrator. This was not murder. It was duty – 'dharm'.

This cold-blooded tradition forms the central conceit of *Kuchhe Dhaage*. Based on the testimony of Pandit Tulsiram (Kabir Bedi), Thakur Bahadur Singh (Dev Kumar), a bandit, is sentenced to death. Bahadur's wife, the *thakurain* (Nirupa Roy) lets out a wail and swears that her soon-to-be-born son will slaughter Pandit. Over the next 20 years, *thakurain* raises her son as a killing machine, with no desire stronger than that to avenge his father. Her son grows up to be the dreaded dacoit Lakhan Singh (Vinod Khanna) who guns Tulsiram down one fateful morning. With his dying breath, Tulsiram vows that his son Roopa (Kabir Bedi) will settle the score.

Lakhan and Roopa begin their cat-and-mouse game through the valleys of Chambal as they bay for each other's blood. Bang in the middle of this bloodlust stands the innocent Sona (Moushumi Chatterjee).

'*Kuchhe Dhaage* was the first Hindi film that I started shooting for, but *Anuraag* (1972) released first. My first Bengali film *Balika Bodhu* (1967) was a platinum jubilee hit, and I was famous in Calcutta. The film's music director, Hemant Kumar, aka Hemanta Mukherjee, was soon going to be my father-in-law,' Moushumi said while telling me about her beginnings, one evening in June 2021. Hemant Kumar didn't want his little *bouma* (daughter-in-law) to leave her career after marriage. She was already a star in Bengal, and she had a long way to go. So, when Raj Khosla visited him to see if Moushumi could be cast in his new film, he agreed instantly. Said Moushumi, 'They came home. They were all my father-in-law's friends. He told me I should do it – it was like a home production.' Hemant Kumar had sung for Guru Dutt's *Jaal* and *Pyaasa* and for Raj Khosla's *Solva Saal*. It was an old association.

Shakti Samanta's offer for *Anuraag* came around the same time, but Raj began shooting first and according to Moushumi, he wanted to release his film before Samanta's, to be the first one to introduce her to Hindi film audiences. Also, she was soon getting married, which was believed to be a death-knell for heroines (in Moushumi's case, though, it turned out to be the exact opposite).

The film's first schedule was in Mahabaleshwar. 'He had five daughters. He used to tell me I was his sixth,' said Moushumi Chatterjee about Raj Khosla's affection for her. And this wasn't just some director sweet-talking his heroine. On 8 July 1973, Raj gushed about her in an interview: '…she is fantastic. In all my years, I have never experienced or known anything quite like her, ever. It is my considered opinion and you can quote me on this in headlines! I think if ever any artiste can replace Meena Kumari on the Indian screen, it will be Moushumi Chatterjee…'[1]

But the day he called Moushumi to Mehboob Studios to try on the costumes, she was on tenterhooks. She reached the studio with her in-laws in tow. Raj had made a few sketches. He used to draw quite well, she recalled. 'So, they took me to a room and made me wear ghaghra-choli. The designer Manu Rabadi was there. Here I was, a Bengali girl from an orthodox family who had been wearing sarees from the age of 13 and 14, and now I was wearing a costume that would reveal my legs. The choli had threads behind… my back would be visible! I panicked.' There were, of course, no mobile phones at the time and a scared Moushumi called her husband, Babu (Jayanta Mukherjee, Hemant Kumar's son), from the corridor of Mehboob Studios. 'Please come over and have a look,' she told him. He pacified her gently, put her worries to rest. She donned the costumes and walked about the room. This 'Bangalan' had transformed into Sona, and Raj Khosla was pleased. Moushumi said, 'The actor who was supposed to play my on-screen husband failed to turn up – or something else didn't work out. In the end, they asked my real-life husband Babu to do it, because he was visiting the sets to see me. Babu was running from it, but they insisted.' Babu, or Jayanta Mukherjee, had just been launched under the name of 'Ritesh' as a leading man in the film *Bees Saal Pehle* (1972). That name was retained in *Kuchhe Dhaage*. His character in the latter was called Bhola, whom Sona was in love with.

Roopa and Lakhan Singh were named after real dacoits who roamed the ravines of Chambal. One was a brahmin and the other a thakur. They were sworn enemies. The fight of Chambal dacoits was, at its core, a fight between classes – especially the thakurs and the brahmins. This was just one of the several real-life phenomena that Raj brought into the film. In *Kuchhe Dhaage*, Lakhan is entertained by a pair of nautch girls, and he abducts one of them, Ramkatori (played by Sona Mastan Mirza, the future wife of mafia kingpin Haji Mastan. She bore an uncanny resemblance to Madhubala). In real life, some three decades earlier, Sultana Singh, a dacoit whose exploits had informed legends, abducted a dancer called Gauhar Bano – also known as Putlibai – from a village soiree. She became his lover, his consort, and in time, after Sultana's demise, turned into a dreaded bandit herself.

Back to the story then. On the run from Lakhan Singh's gang, Roopa bumps into Sona, who shelters him. Soon, Lakhan comes looking for Roopa but Sona lies to him, to save Roopa's life. Somehow, both men start liking the innocence of this girl. Roopa becomes the leader of a competing gang, and the feud with Lakhan intensifies. Lakhan gives in to the dark side of his nature and ends up raping a woman. She runs, crying, to his mother. The *thakurain* wanted her son to take up arms for vengeance. The fact that it made him a murderer didn't matter to her. But she hadn't thought that it would make him a rapist, too. She decides to confront Lakhan, and this leads to one of the most intense scenes in the film.

One of Lakhan's men delivers a message that his mother doesn't want to see his face ever again. Lakhan rushes to his mother, and she unleashes her rage. This rapist cannot be her son, she screams. How dare he? I AM your son, Lakhan snaps back. Isn't it she who fed him the poison of hatred since he was a toddler? Instead of giving him education, wasn't it she who taught him to fire a gun? The darkness that is consuming him now is her gift to him. What can he do now for the rest of his life but grope around in it? '*Tumne ek bhole bhaale masoom bachche ko daaku banaya, aur maine us daaku ko pashu banaya. Aur aaj tum mujhko dosh deti ho*? You made an innocent child a dacoit and I made that dacoit an animal. And today you curse me?' The mother is dumbfounded. It was one of the most powerful scenes in the film, and in Vinod Khanna's repertoire of work. It was a spectacular piece of acting, and he had aced it.

The confrontation between Lakhan and the *thakurain*, a powerful scene in *Kuchhe Dhaage*.

The two brutes Lakhan and Roopa are both smitten by Sona. She is the only one who doesn't judge them for who they are or what they do. Her innocence brings out their vulnerabilities. In her presence, their guards slide down and they want to tell her all their secrets. Lakhan, the dreaded bandit, finds excuses to see her. Roopa sheds tears and wonders why he didn't meet her sooner. It breaks their hearts to discover that Sona is in love with Bhola, a boy from the village. They make peace with it. However, Lakhan's mentor, an old-timer he calls Kaka (Trilok Kapoor), doesn't like it one bit that the young toughie gets all weak-kneed around a simple village girl, so he kidnaps her. Lakhan is beside himself with rage at this stupidity. He brings her back to her parents, but both her birth parents and her betrothed Bhola believe being in the dacoit's lair has sullied her reputation. To allay their fears, Lakhan gets her to tie a rakhi on his wrist, thereby making him her brother. This incident makes Roopa see his enemy in a different light.

The above is a somewhat tame description of this cracker of a film. *Kuchhe Dhaage* ends up being a comment on the futility of vengeance and the pointlessness of animosity. The climax of the film stands out in the realm of dacoit dramas for how differently it is handled. Raj Khosla, unlike most mainstream Hindi filmmakers of the time, worked on the tiny details that made up the principal characters. Lakhan, who grew up in the shadow of violence and didn't have time for an education, speaks with a rustic affectation, mispronouncing most Hindi words. But his nemesis, the brahmin Roopa, who was being groomed for the army before his father's death put him on the violent path, speaks almost flawlessly. Kabir Bedi didn't sport a beard back then. In all the films leading to *Kuchhe Dhaage*, he was clean shaven, like most Indian actors at the time. The only exceptions were films such as *Anokha Daan* (1972) where he flaunted a moustache. While making *Kuchhe Dhaage*, it was Bedi who suggested that he should play Tulsiram, the father of his character Roopa. A greying Tulsiram had to wear a beard. Raj later said, 'I found Kabir's face too small for his frame. I suddenly suggested to him, "Why don't you grow a beard?"'[2] Bedi followed Raj Khosla's instructions, and not only did this new look have a remarkable impact on his performance, it also opened doors to international name and fame. In the Western world, Kabir Bedi is known for playing the lead in an Italian TV series named *Sandokan* (1976), where the titular Sandokan – you guessed it – had a beard. Said Bedi:

> Raj ji said to me, 'I think a beard would look great on you for this role.' I said, 'Yes, Raj ji,' and I grew a beard. *Kuchhe Dhaage* turned out to be a big hit, and then every other producer that came to me told me to keep the beard. They said it was lucky for me. In fact, it helped me get the role in *Sandokan* because I looked the part!

The *Sandokan* books, tremendously popular in Italy, were written by novelist Emilio Salgari, with illustrations done by Alberto Della Valle. Alberto had drawn Sandokan as if he knew that 80 years later, an Indian actor called Kabir Bedi would play the role. In his picturization, the pirate is tall, broad shouldered, long haired and his angular face adorns a long, flowing beard.

Bedi also had an anecdote to share about Raj Khosla's propensity to postpone or cancel his shoots.

> He was always clear about what he wanted to shoot. Unless he was sure he had that clarity, Raj ji would find excuses to delay his own shooting… his own shooting, imagine! But once he was on the set, he was absolutely clear. At one point, there was a long gap in the shooting. I always wanted to see America – I didn't have money, but I borrowed some and took off. I went to New York, and to Washington. One day, I got a message, which said Raj ji wants to resume his shooting, and that I must go back. I said, 'What the hell… I want to see America!' But I was needed at work, so I returned, and I went to see Raj ji. But when I asked him about the shooting, he said, 'Shooting *toh* cancel *ho gaya si*! The shooting is cancelled!' I was shocked! When I told him I was in America and I came back just for the shooting, he said, 'Really? I didn't know. If I knew you were in America, I would have made that

> an excuse to cancel my shooting! I would have said, Kabir is in America, and we can't shoot.'

Kuchhe Dhaage was a nuanced and polished cinematic achievement, despite not having A-listers attached to it. Raj Khosla's personal favourite,[3] the film was a success, though not as big as its predecessor. Nevertheless, it happened to be the first film in his career where none of the songs attained cult status. Raj utilized his usual signature camera angles and shot the songs with as much care as his other films. All the songs were Lata Mangeshkar solos, except the *mujra* 'Kaam lete nahi bandook se', which was a duet with Hemlata. Sona Mirza featured in another exquisite *mujra* 'Zara se agar bewafa hum na hote', where the dancing girl tries to get her abductor Lakhan Singh killed. There is a shot where Lakhan trains his gun on her and peeps at her through the barrel, and the audience joins in. This brings to mind a similar shot from *Do Raaste's* 'Bindiya chamkegi'. Nearly all other songs featured Moushumi Chatterjee. There was no trace of the middle-class Bengali heroine from Calcutta in the vivacity and charm with which she performed in 'Kachche dhaage ke saath' and 'Mere bachpan tu jaa'.

The soundtrack of *Kuchhe Dhaage* (1973).

Thus far, Raj Khosla had only produced films that he was planning to direct. *Do Chor* (1972) was the first time he was making an exception. One of the things that Raj had inherited from his Guru was the inclination to work with a stable team. He liked working with the same set of people, whether it was his actors, composers, technicians and crew. Even so, by now, he had been making films for almost two decades, so the core team he liked working with had undergone several changes. With one exception. Since his very first film way back in 1955, *Milap*, one person had been by his side. B. Padmanabham had assisted Raj Khosla since then, and had seen him through thick and thin.

Padmanabham Bandodkar hailed from the Bhilgaon area of Maharashtra. It was during his years with Guru Dutt that Raj Khosla had recruited him as an assistant. With *Do Chor*, Raj offered his long-time lieutenant an opportunity to direct a film under his banner. It was the third project of Raj Khosla Films after *Anita* and *Do Raaste*. (*Kuchhe Dhaage* was the fourth.)

Dharmendra and Tanuja were cast in the lead roles. Tanuja had developed a fascination for numerology. In many films during this period, she was credited as 'Tanujaa'. That extra 'a' could be attributed to numerology. Her interest was shared by her producer – Raj was once asked about the curious spelling of *Kuchhe Dhaage*. 'Numerology!' he replied.

Do Chor is, as the title would suggest, the tale of two burglars. One of them, Tony (Dharmendra), is flabbergasted because someone else has been beating him to his 'targets' and bleeding them dry. This copycat leaves a swastika at the scene of the crime. Tony must track down this thief, partly because the cops are breathing down his neck and partly because he has a reputation to protect. To his surprise, the thief turns out to be a woman, Sandhya (Tanuja), who has been stealing back her own inheritance from the men who robbed her father. Tony and Sandhya fall in love, and go on the run from the police, looting the remaining names on her list.

Although Padmanabham was given a free hand to make the film, Raj did monitor closely. He would often drop in to talk to the cast and crew. In fact, just like on his own films, he would keep urging them to pack up and take it easy. Dharmendra said, 'He used to come to the shooting and tell everyone, "Pack up *karo yaar*! *Kitna kaam karoge*? Pack up, guys! How much will you work?" He was like a king, but also very, very innocent in his own way.'

Dharmendra also recalled that once, Mahesh Bhatt, who was an assistant director in the film, had forgotten to bring his costume for a scene:

> *Ye meri* costume *bhool aaye*. He forgot my constume. I was supposed to change into a driver's clothes and escape. He told me, 'Dharam ji, I forgot your clothes, and it's too far back to the hotel. *Kya karein*? What do we do?' Raj ji was supposed to come that day. We were shooting on the Goa highway, and I noticed some truckers had stopped to watch the shoot. I borrowed the clothes of one of the drivers and put them on.

Dharmendra also remembers going to Jet, S.D. Burman's iconic home, for the movie's music sittings. This was the first time S.D.'s son, Rahul, was composing for Raj Khosla. Work on *Kuchhe Dhaage* was progressing simultaneously and Laxmikant–Pyarelal were busy, so Pancham had to be brought in. All the songs are liquid gold, and retain their popularity even now, especially 'Kali palak teri gori' and 'Chahe raho door, chahe raho paas', where Dharmendra and Tanuja look like a million dollars. Laxmi Chhaya was back in *Do Chor* and in the *mujra* 'Mora chhota sa balamwa', she tries to entice Tanuja, who, disguised as a young man in a French-cut, is supposed to be the *balamwa* (beloved).

The soundtrack of *Do Chor* (1972).

The movies have always been volatile business, and they were more so back in the 1970s. The transient nature of success is nowhere as evident as in the movies. You can be at the top of your game and just one Friday could wash it all away. And so, stars and filmmakers have always tried to devise other ways to stay afloat.

In 1973, Dharmendra and Raj partnered with some others to build a movie theatre in Jaipur. It was called Amber Theatre and was the first of its kind to have a lift. Dharmendra told me:

> During the shoot [of Do Chor], we had this idea of making a theatre. We got a plot in Jaipur and built it there. We installed a lift as well. But one of the partners refused to pay up. When I discussed this with Raj ji, he said, '*Humne kaun se apne liye banaya hai*? *Bachchon ke kaam aayega*. Where have we made it for ourselves? It will come in use for the kids.'
>
> I said, '*Humein nahi de rahe hain, bachchon ko kya denge*! He isn't giving it to us, what will we give the kids!' So then we sold it.

Raj Khosla had been in films for over two decades by then, if one were to account for his stint as an actor in *Raen Basera*. Along the way, he had done playback songs, assisted Guru Dutt, made some highly successful films, a few flops, and seen the pinnacle of success as a filmmaker. All this while, he had his family around him. His brother Lekhraj had already wet his toes in production with *Anita*, with Raj as co-producer. It didn't quite shape up the way they had expected, but with *Do Raaste,* Raj tasted blood. It was a humongous success and with it, he had seen the kind of prosperity he had never experienced before.

It was time to take it to the next level. Lekhraj and his son Bolu Khosla joined hands with Raj to form Khosla Enterprises.

The banner was supposed to produce collaborations between Raj, Lekhraj, and Lekhraj's sons, Bolu and Anil Khosla, two young men raring to participate in the 'family' business.

Raj had been grooming his nephews for the film business. Bolu Khosla had been assisting Raj since *Mera Saaya*, while Anil, also known as Tanny Khosla, joined the business from *Mera Gaon Mera Desh*. After *Mera Gaon*, there were two more films made under the banner of Khosla Enterprises: *Raaste kaa Patthar* (1972), which was directed by Mukul Dutt, and *Kabeela* (1976), directed by Bolu himself. *Raaste kaa Patthar* had Amitabh Bachchan and Shatrughan Sinha in principal roles. Raj Khosla was aware – and immensely appreciative – of these emerging talents in the industry. Right after Amitabh Bachchan won his first Filmfare Award for *Anand* (1971), Raj threw a bash to celebrate the win. Amitabh was in attendance along with his parents, Harivansh Rai Bachchan and Teji Bachchan. As for Shatrughan Sinha, Raj cast him alongside Dev Anand in a film called *Shareef Budmaash* (1973).

17

Gentlemen Crooks and Poets in Love

Shatrughan Sinha explained over a phone call:

> I went to meet him at Mehboob Studios. I think the casting of *Mera Gaon Mera Desh* had just concluded, but I was still hopeful of bagging one of the main roles. It was a very intriguing role, and I wanted to do it, but I realized that it had already been given to Vinod Khanna. The person who took me to meet Raj ji couldn't introduce me properly – he didn't even mention that I was from FTII and was looking for a major role. Raj ji took a cursory glance at me, and then said, 'Okay. See if he can ride horses, he can be cast as one of the riders.'

It was not what Sinha was expecting. He was a trained actor, and was already being considered for several other roles. He wasn't there merely to play a horse rider. 'That's how I thought initially,' he said. 'I came home and didn't go back. But Raj ji was a sharp observer and had incredible memory. Much later, when I was gradually making a name for myself, Raj Khosla ji summoned me. I went to see him, and he told me about a part in *Shareef Budmaash*. "It's a small role, so decide if you want to do it. But I can promise you one thing. Regardless of how big this role is, mark my words – the moment you appear on screen and speak your dialogues, you'll get the kind of applause you've never got before."' Even when he was performing negative roles, Sinha had already earned a reputation of attracting more claps and whistles than – in most cases – the hero of the film. Raj Khosla knew this and was predicting an even better response to his role in *Shareef Budmaash*.

It was with Dev Anand that Raj Khosla's story had really begun. It was he who had facilitated Raj's alliance with Guru, and then when Raj started making films, it was Dev who starred in all his early films. Right from the mid-1950s until the end of the decade, every single Raj Khosla film had had Dev Anand as the lead star. They worked on five films together until *Bombai ka Babu*. Raj was for a time also an integral part of Navketan – he had directed *Kala Pani* for them and was supposed to do *Guide*. Later, in 1966, they began work on *Sajan ki Galiyan* but it never saw the light of day. For the next seven years, their paths didn't cross. And them in 1973, Raj Khosla was back in Navketan again, calling the shots on *Shareef Budmaash*. For Raj, it was homecoming on two fronts: he was back at Navketan and he was making a crime thriller again.

Amit Khanna, media maven who has worn several hats over the years, was barely 20 when Dev Anand saw the talent in the youngster and offered him a job at Navketan. At 21, Khanna was the executive producer on *Shareef Budmaash*. He told me over the phone, 'It was during the shooting of *Mera Gaon Mera*

Desh that Dev saab asked Raj Khosla to make another film for Navketan. He immediately agreed because he had great regard for Dev saab. I only got involved when the film went on the floors. Somehow, Raj ji took a liking to me. As I was handling production on behalf of Navketan, I would meet him quite regularly.' Raj, much like Dev, had developed a fondness for this young man who was intelligent beyond his years. Once, Raj was in a sitting with the writers of *Shareef Budmaash* – screenwriter K.A. Narayan and Prakash Raj, who wrote the dialogues. Some situations in one of the schedules were being discussed. They were at Khosla's Marina Apartments, and Amit Khanna was also present. Khanna, listening intently, thought that the sequence didn't make any sense, and he said as much. The veteran K.A. Narayan got a little offended at what he perceived to be a brash youth's impertinence. But Raj really liked his suggestion and said, 'Why don't you work out the sequence?'

Amit Khanna was also the only one who could handle Raj's idiosyncrasies. Raj Khosla, like so many creative spirits throughout history, couldn't be tied down. He wasn't fond of convention, of rules. This defiance and refusal to toe the line often irked people. In an industry where time was, quite literally, money, he would only shoot when he wanted to. By his own admission, he had a troubled personal life and there were occasions where he would indulge in the pain, or just submerge it in alcohol.[1] 'He wasn't an easy person to handle,' Amit Khanna averred. 'Often, he would disappear and not be accessible for two–three days. Sometimes, he cancelled shoots and went on drinking binges. But I had developed such an equation with him that I always knew. I could always reach out. And he never rebuffed me.'

It was during the making of *Shareef Budmaash* that Dev and Raj, who had a longstanding relationship and shared immense respect and admiration for each other, had their biggest fight. Says Amit Khanna, 'He [Raj Khosla] got busy with *Kuchhe*

Dhaage, *Shareef Budmaash* got a little delayed. There was a bit of misunderstanding between Dev saab and him, and I ultimately had to pacify them both and the film got made.' Speaking of the incident, Raj told Sheila Vesuna in July 1986:

> We were on location at Srinagar. I am a late riser whereas Dev is up and about early in the morning. From my hotel room I lifted the curtain and could see Dev pacing the lawns. It was 8:30 am. I got up, was ready in 45 minutes and went down and apologized to Dev. But he was furious. We had the first quarrel of our lives. He said, 'What sorry? It's all your boozing that keeps you from waking early. It was to be a 25-day schedule.' I was quite angry. I told Dev I'll finish your shooting in 19 days. Dev laughed sarcastically. But I stopped drinking at night and on the seventeenth day, the work was done. What then happened was the bookings for the return journey could not be had and the unit stayed on. Dev then joked, 'You better foot the bills now.'[2]

Shareef Budmaash didn't find Raj Khosla in his element, many said. It was considered to have a poor script and an average story. Though it performed decently at the box office, it wasn't in the league of some of Raj Khosla's – or Dev Anand's – recent hits. One would imagine that contemporary critics had a field day, but history has been kinder to the film. Today, many see it for what it really was – an enjoyable and entertaining romp. Director Sriram Raghavan swears by it. An avowed Raj Khosla fan, Raghavan lists *Shareef Budmaash* as one of his most favourite thrillers from the 1970s. 'It's one of the silliest of movies, but it's also great fun. I watched it after I'd seen *Johny Mera Naam* [1970], and I thought it was too good. I keep showing it to people, because it's mad fun!'[3]

Shareef Budmaash also happens to be among the more successful collaborations between Raj and R.D. Burman. Pancham and Raj ended up working together in five films, among which the songs of *Do Chor*, *Sunny* and *Shareef Budmaash* travelled the most. 'Neend chura ke raaton mein' stands tall among Dev Anand's 1970s songs. 'Tere sau diwane' is a quintessential Pancham–Kishore track. 'Mohabbat baazi jeetegi' kind of foreshadows 'Jab tak hai jaan' from *Sholay*, where Hema Malini sings around the hero tied to a pole, desperate to save his life. Typically, the cabaret/'item number' in a film was reserved for Asha Bhosle, while Lata Mangeshkar would sing the romantic numbers and the duets. The soundtrack of *Shareef Budmaash* turned this notion on its head, with Asha Bhosle essaying all the romantic ballads and duets with Kishore, while the only 'item number', 'Meri mohabbat mein har ek badnaam hai', was voiced by Lata. The filming of the song brings to mind 'Kareeb aa ye nazar' from *Anita* (1967), although the songs themselves are apples and oranges. In both the songs, the camera glides along as the heroine sashays along a bar counter, weaving mysteries along the way.

The soundtrack of *Shareef Budmaash* (1973).

Shareef Budmaash had as stellar a cast as you could have in the 1970s. Dev Anand and Hema Malini were joined by Ajit, Jeevan, Helen, Sudhir, Bhagwan Dada, Jankidas, Rashid Khan, Manmohan, D.K. Sapru, Trilok Kapoor and Mac Mohan. Trilok, Bhagwan and Sudhir were ubiquitous in Raj Khosla films of the period, whether in a home production or otherwise. Sudhir, aka, Bhagwandas Luthria, much before emerging as the flamboyant 'handlebar' Sudhir, had played the well-meaning but bumbling, clean-shaven police officer sandwiched between the villagers and the bandits in *Mera Gaon Mera Desh*. In *Shareef Budmaash*, he still has a bald top lip but is one step closer to his nefarious self as he plays the spoilt kid who steals from his mentor. Dev plays a crook who turns out to be a cop. The days of playing dark, edgy, conflicted characters were behind him – Raj and Dev had brought to life some of the best examples of this archetype. This was also the only instance when Raj Khosla and Hema Malini collaborated on a film.

Shareef Budmaash also turned out to be the last film in which Dev Anand and Raj Khosla worked together. There can be a perception that this was because of their falling out on the sets of *Shareef Budmaash*. But this couldn't have been true, because soon after, somewhere in the mid-1970s, there were at least two films announced with Raj as director and Dev as actor. One of them was an idea by Amit Khanna where he modelled two characters on Karna and Arjun from Mahabharat, and placed them in a Muslim social. The two characters were to be played by Sanjeev Kumar and Dev, and the film was initially called *Nawab aur Sharab*. Evidently, the censors took umbrage at '*Sharab*', this being during the Emergency, and so the title was altered to *Nawab aur Shabaab*. Sunil Dutt and Zeenat Aman were to co-star in it. There was a *mahurat*, a few reels were shot, but the film was eventually shelved. A picture of the *mahurat* has been doing the rounds of Instagram and Facebook the past few years.

In the same vein, a film called *Tijori* was announced, to be directed by Raj Khosla, starring Dev and produced by Mushir–Riyaz. The poster of the film screamed 'Dev Anand unlocks Mushir & Riyaz's "Tijori"', and this was followed by an announcement: 'Going on the floors 29th June, Filmistan.' But this was not to be.

By this time, Raj's office at Mehboob Studios was getting too cramped for his burgeoning team. Raj Khosla's secretary Lorna Desouza told me:

> It [the Mehboob Studios office] was too small for us. We just had one room and one out-room. So, there was no place for anything else. Or anyone. The peon had to sit outside. Raj ji was a well-known name, not just in the movies but in the outside world as well. So, when he started looking for a bigger office, he got one. It was a 2,500-square-feet office space at Jain Chambers, near Bandra station. It housed all of us. It had a beautiful main sitting room, and we had cabins for the assistants and executives. Raj saab also had a big… a giant cabin. We were pleased to shift to a bigger place.

As she went on to describe, there was a long corridor that flaunted posters of his films, including *Woh Kaun Thi?*, *Do Badan* and *Kala Pani*. The office also prominently displayed life size portraits of the two pole stars in Raj's life K.L. Saigal and Guru Dutt. Lorna was the only woman in the office, and she was treated with the utmost respect – so much so that for 18 years, the thought of looking for a more 'secure' job didn't cross her mind. So it was for everyone else working there. Even in months when no films were on the floor, every employee was paid their salary. There were no exceptions to this. None.

Around this time, Lekhraj Khosla launched yet another banner, which was called Khosla Combine. Raj floated a new film under it, one that he had announced six years earlier, after the grand success of *Do Raaste*. With *Prem Kahani* (1975), he wanted to replicate the success of *Do Raaste*. The premise of the two films, however, is as different as chalk and cheese.

The ill-fated love story of renowned Urdu poet Majaz Lakhnavi formed the genesis of *Prem Kahani*. Lakhnavi was in love with the daughter of a man who was a close compatriot of Mahatma Gandhi and Pandit Nehru. But the woman in question was betrothed to another man, and there is one version of the story which says that Lakhnavi continued to pine for her even after she got married. Unrequited love got the better of him, and he sought refuge in the bottle. This aspect (of romance with a married woman) was also depicted in *Kahkashaan*, a Doordarshan show on Urdu poets.

The story of Lakhnavi moved Raj enough to conceive *Prem Kahani* (he was officially credited for story). It also struck a chord with the filmmaker at a much deeper level. He was in the same boat as Lakhnavi. While talking to an interviewer about the conception of the film, Raj conceded that there is an autobiographical element in the film. 'Makers do reveal themselves in their films,' he said. 'It's no secret anyway…' He implied that everyone knew about him and his relationships, his weaknesses. 'Anyway, call it a weakness if you like… I can only take solace in wine. Will you have some?' he offered the interviewer.[4] This was going to be a significant aspect of his work here on: much like his mentor Guru Dutt and his protégé Mahesh Bhatt, he was trying to find himself in his films. In fact, these three men had curious parallels. All three had (or have had), in varying degrees, autobiographical elements in their films, found love outside marriage, and sought comfort in alcohol.

The year is 1942. Rajesh (Rajesh Khanna) is the resident poet of the college, ever ready to drop couplets at a moment's notice. One day, he breaks into a ghazal on the college lawns, surrounded by gushing classmates. The song sounds a little unusual for the 1970s, with what seems to be Saigal's disembodied voice emanating from Rajesh Khanna's lips. It takes a beat to realize that it is Raj Khosla's voice.

Raj had clandestinely placed here a song in his own voice, a repeat of what he had done with 'Hum bekhudi mein' in *Kala Pani*. This time it was a cappella, a song without any musical accompaniment.

One of the rare, little-known instances of Raj Khosla singing for a movie.

Yun toh humne dil ke safar mein
Dekhein hain dildaar bahut
Jaane kya hai dekh ke tujhko
Aajata hai pyar bahut
Teri gali se uthkar hum bhi
Jaanib-e-sehra jaate hai
Lekin humko yaad aayegi
Ye teri deewar bahut
In aankhon ki baat pe mat ja
Unka koi theek nahin
Biknewaale, jaldi kya hai
Aur bhi hain bazaar bahut

(In the journey of the heart
Lovers I've seen aplenty
But there's something about you
That fills me with love mighty
I leave your doorstep
And walk to the wilderness
But your walls I'll never forget.
Don't listen to these eyes
They can't be trusted

O dear seller, what's the haste?
Other markets exist)

This song, hiding in plain sight, was never included in any cassette or LP, and isn't available on YouTube (except as a part of the movie itself) or any music streaming platform. Raj ensured that nobody knew about it, and he didn't credit himself for either the song in *Kala Pani* or *Prem Kahani*. Even the music directors didn't know about them. But while 'Hum bekhudi mein' from *Kala Pani* was written by Majrooh Sultanpuri, 'Yun toh humne' is yet to be claimed. It couldn't have been Anand Bakshi, because the music director duo would have been made aware of it. Could it be Faruk Kaiser, who, in addition to being a poet and lyricist himself, was also the chief assistant director? Or, more interestingly, could it have been Raj Khosla himself? We will probably never know.

Rajesh, in the film, has no interest in the freedom movement and prefers to instead indulge in courting Kamini (Mumtaz), the love of his life. In fact, his friend Dheeraj (Shashi Kapoor), someone he has deep regard and affection for, is a police officer.

Rajesh and Kamini are almost convinced of a future together and have no reason to suspect otherwise. But Kamini's father, Rai Bahadur Sinha (K.N. Singh), resolves to marry her off to a qualified officer of the law. She refuses to comply, and her father dares her to go propose to her lover. Meanwhile, a personal tragedy forces Rajesh to introspect, and he decides to plunge headlong into the freedom struggle. But before that he has to kill the poet and the lover in him. So, when Kamini arrives to seek his hand in marriage, he lets her think that he was just having fun, with no real intention of getting married. 'Good riddance!' she says, goes back to her mother and demands to be wed to the man her father has chosen for her.

Unlike generations of heroines before her, Kamini refuses to be stepped on. She had come to Rajesh as his lover, his equal. When he turns her down, she doesn't wallow in misery or cry over her fate. She says, 'I won't beg of you to accept me. Nor would I kill myself over this. If you expect me to remain unwed, you are mistaken. I will be married soon, and to a good man too. You're going to regret this, I promise you.' The dialogues, written by Rahi Masoom Raza, convey the fury of a woman scorned. Almost around the same time as *Prem Kahani*'s release, screenwriting duo Salim–Javed were redefining how women were portrayed in mainstream Hindi cinema, with the inclusion of characters such as Parveen Babi's in *Deewaar* (1975), where she didn't need to justify her way of life or her profession as a sex worker. But most of the women portrayed were still like the sacrificing mother in *Deewaar* or the poor widow in *Sholay* who needed rescuing. In that realm, Kamini walked tall.

In the new alliance with Rahi Masoom Raza, Raj also found a lifelong friend. Raza, who was from Ghazipur (Rajesh, the hero of *Prem Kahani*, is also from Ghazipur) and had already made a name for himself in literary circles, had always been a keen movie buff (they say he watched the same films in successive shows, armed with a pen and a notebook), but had to struggle quite a bit to find work when he landed in Bombay in 1967. Dharmvir Bharti and Kamleshwar, literary giants themselves, extended a helping hand, and Raza was soon writing the dialogues for Khosla Enterprises's *Raaste kaa Patthar*, followed by Hrishikesh Mukherjee's *Mili* (1975). Raza found new friends in both directors. Besides their love for poetry and literature, the three of them shared another passion: chess. Hrishikesh Mukherjee was known to spend hours between shots playing the game. Raj Khosla had inherited the love for the game from his father. Visitors to Khosla Niwas, who often included actors, would be invited to play with Atmaram Khosla, whom everyone called 'Bauji' in reverence. For Raj Khosla, Rahi Masoom Raza was one of the few industrywallahs he could call a friend. Raza would visit him at home and they would plunge into the world of pawns and rooks.

The original cast of *Prem Kahani* was slightly different from what it ended up as. In a 2022 *Firstpost* article, journalist Subhash K. Jha wrote, 'So impressed was Khosla with Moushumi's potent mix of impishness and oomph that he signed her again for *Prem Kahani* with Rajesh Khanna. But the hero wanted his favourite heroine, Mumtaz, and Moushumi was out.'[5] There is a photograph of Moushumi Chatterjee at the *mahurat* of *Prem Kahani*. About this, Moushumi said to me:

> I was cast for *Prem Kahani*. I even did the *mahurat* shot. Raj ji's nephew, Bolu Khosla, had a flat in the building where I used to stay. He was the executive producer of the film. One fine day he came down and asked why I was not compromising with Rajesh Khanna. All the big heroes those days wanted the heroines to listen to them. But I was in the industry only to work, not to oblige anyone. I told as much to Bolu Khosla. About a week later, I was shooting at Mehboob Studios when Mumtaz came to me and told me, 'I know you were doing the picture, but now they have approached me. I hope you don't mind.' I said, of course not. At least she had the decency to let me know.

But there is another aspect to this story. In the 1970 issue of *Star & Style* (a good five years before all of this happened),

Mumtaz said in an interview that she was really looking forward to recreating the magic of *Do Raaste* in *Prem Kahani*, which was her next film with Raj Khosla.

Vinod Khanna's cameo as a Pathan named Sher Khan can seem quite startling for anyone who has followed Vinod's career in the 1970s. Despite playing several bold and aggressive characters, Vinod often gave off a calm, cool-as-a-cucumber vibe. It is difficult to imagine him as a slightly buffoonish, loud, stereotypical Bollywood Pathan. But Vinod pulled off the role with aplomb. In fact, his performance is one of the dramatic highlights of the film. In one scene, Vinod breaks into a rendition of 'Ae mere pyaare watan' in his own voice, as Rajesh, whom he is transporting secretly, gets teary-eyed thinking of the family he has left behind. Rajesh, now a revolutionary and fugitive from the law, plans to hide out in his friend Dheeraj's bungalow. He reaches on the day of Dheeraj's wedding, and finds that the bride is none other than Kamini. At this point, twin drama ensues. While Dheeraj must protect his friend, he also has to interrogate Sher Khan, whom the cops have booked for transporting a rebel. Sher Khan knows that his inquisitor is Rajesh's friend, but he plays along. Matters are further complicated by a greedy constable (Yunus Parvez) who is hell-bent on breaking the Pathan. Meanwhile, Kamini must contend with her ex living in her husband's house. One scene unfolds like a *mushaira* when the lights go off and Rajesh is egged on by his friend to recite a few lines. In candlelight, a soft war erupts, with Rajesh and Kamini exchanging couplets, a thinly veiled debate about love, loyalty and betrayal.

In another scene, Dheeraj orchestrates a mock trial, asking his wife to judge whether Rajesh was justified in sacrificing his girlfriend at the altar of nationalism. Kamini wonders if the girlfriend would have preferred being a rebel's widow rather than settle for marrying someone else. Cut to a close-up of a

The Noor Jehan track from *Azra* (1962), featured in *Prem Kahani.*

massive radio phonograph that plays an old Noor Jehan track:

Kuchh bhi na kaha aur keh bhi gaye
Kuchh kehte kehte reh bhi gaye

(Nothing was said and yet said it all
While saying something, couldn't speak at all)

The camera zooms in through a window frame as Kamini stares into the distance. A light drizzle washes her face as she starts weeping, with the song playing in the background. All drenched, she turns her gaze inside and finds Rajesh looking at her from across the room. Their eyes lock and a fleeting moment is shared between the two. It almost starts to seem like she might just give in to her desire. The radio keeps blaring Noor Jehan's velvet voice:

Baatein jo zabaan tak aa na saki
Aankhon ne kahi, aankhon ne suni
Kuchh hothon par, kuchh aankhon mein
Ankahe fasaane reh bhi gaye

(Words the tongue left unsaid
Eyes spoke, eyes listened
On the lips, and in the eyes
Untold stories did often rise)

They keep looking at each other for a beat or two more. She sees fragments of herself reflected in a tri-fold mirror. Not a word is exchanged as Rajesh walks across the room to shut the window.

Of course, Dheeraj walks in and breaks the spell, managing to be charming and annoying in equal measure. The entire sequence unfolds without the two actors sharing a single line of dialogue. The Noor Jehan song was from a 1962 Pakistani film called *Azra*, composed by Master Inayat and written by Tanveer Naqvi.

When I asked Mumtaz about this scene, which includes a phenomenal piece of acting by her, she couldn't remember it. Understandable, considering the plethora of roles and films she did over the years. But what she did recall was Vinod Khanna's stellar work, even in a cameo. 'What the audience will always remember about that film is that role of Vinod Khanna as the truck driver, protecting the hero. I also liked his performance in that role. He was excellent in it,' she said. Sher Khan had to lay down his life trying to protect Rajesh. But he really shouldn't have bothered, because Rajesh, too, met with the same fate.

Prem Kahani was the only time Shashi Kapoor collaborated with Raj Khosla. Kapoor, while being a very competent actor, had made a career of playing second fiddle in mainstream films. In *Prem Kahani*, he does the job well, and with oodles of charm and charisma, often threatening to steal the show from Rajesh Khanna. The very next year, he was to play another husband running into his wife's ex-lover, and embrace it again with panache: *Kabhi Kabhie* (1976).

Despite the drama and some credible performances, *Prem Kahani* fell short. The pieces didn't just come together. It had great dialogues, but felt disjointed. There were many far-fetched and unintentionally funny moments, but one of its weakest aspects was a lack of detailing. It was set in the early 1940s, and yet everyone was clad in 1970s attire, including the policemen. Even a train shown in the movie was from the 1970s. Speaking of trains, in a scene where Rajesh and Dheeraj meet at the station, the latter is supposed to be leaving for Ghazipur. But as the train starts sliding out of the platform, you can read the label on it that announces that it runs between Panvel and Diva.

By 1975, Rajesh Khanna's luck as a star was fast running out. *Prem Kahani* was his only major release that year and it had everything going for him. There was the winning combination of Raj Khosla – Rajesh Khanna, Mumtaz, Laxmikant–Pyarelal and Anand Bakshi – that had earlier delivered a historic success like *Do Raaste* that had helped consolidate Khanna's stardom. Khanna's famously held superstition, that his on-screen death would guarantee box office gold, was also complied with. But regardless of all this being in place, the film didn't perform nearly as well as he would have hoped. Raj later recounted a story about Kaka's famous tardiness. Apparently, the star would sit around in the gardens of Mehboob Studios, make everyone wait and only report much later in the day. One day, Raj came and sat at the other end of the garden. Even after taking his time, when there was no call for the shot, Kaka demanded to know what was wrong. He was told that Raj Khosla was in the garden this time and the shoot hadn't started. Rajesh Khanna understood. There was no problem after that.[6]

Like any Raj Khosla film ever made, *Prem Kahani*'s soundtrack doesn't disappoint. It was peak Laxmikant–Pyarelal, and the music was memorable. Two of the songs are still strongly recognizable: 'Prem Kahani mein ek ladka hota hai, ek ladki hoti hai' and 'Chal dariya mein doob jaayein'. The latter even made it to *Binaca Geetmala*'s top 10 songs for 1975. Shooting that song was no cakewalk though, as Mumtaz explained:

The soundtrack of *Prem Kahani* (1975).

> When you do so many films with the same actor, you invariably develop a certain kind of chemistry. But Rajesh Khanna was not very good where dance and music were concerned. So, I used to support him as much as I can, with difficult songs. In 'Chal dariya mein doob jayein', there was a portion that went:
>
> *Teri zulf udegi toh ghata chha jaayegi*
> *Ghata chha jayegi toh pani barsega*
> *Pani barsega toh mann tarsega*
> *Mann tarsega toh…toh…toh…*
>
> This type of singing he found difficult for lip movement, you know. So, then I used to tap him gently with a finger, and he used to start. With a little squeeze on his shoulder, he knew that he must sing now!

That was also the last song Mumtaz shot before she got married. She had decided to quit acting. 'The whole staff was crying. Everybody. Raj ji *ke bhi aankhon me aansoon aa gaye thhe*. Raj ji also had tears in his eyes.' Another really impressive song in the film is 'Kya meri prem kahani', which, in many ways, sums up the persona of Kamini, who lies at the heart of the film.

Prem Kahani, Raj Khosla hoped, would replicate the magic of *Do Raaste* and empower him to work on one of his pet projects: an adaptation of the Mahabharata. He wanted to shoot part of it in Rome because, according to him, the city had expert charioteers. He wasn't sure of the casting yet, except one. 'I definitely want Rajesh Khanna to play Krishna. He has the smile and the natural diplomatic behaviour,' Raj Khosla said to K.N. Subramaniam for the 7 March 1975 issue of *Filmfare*. But the commercial fate of *Prem Kahani* robbed the audiences of the chance to witness Rajesh Khanna in yet another avatar.

Post *Prem Kahani*, Raj was planning to make another film for his brother. A banner called Lekhraj Khosla Films was floated. Under the new banner, a film called *Angoor* was announced. Dharmendra and Hema Malini were in the lead and Raj was set to direct the film. But when *Kabeela*, a home production under Khosla Enterprises, turned out to be a flop, this other project also fizzled out.

18

Tulsi and a Biker Gang

Despite all his years in the film industry and his notable work with major Hindi movie stars, the number of friends Raj Khosla had in the industry could be counted on the fingers of one hand.

Rahi Masoom Raza was among them, and so was Sunil Dutt. Raj and Dutt could have run into each other at various points throughout their early lives. Elphinstone College, where Raj studied, and Jai Hind College, Dutt's alma mater, are little more than a kilometre apart, and both were active in theatre during college. Sunil, still going by his birth name Balraj Dutt, was associated with Radio Ceylon in the early 1950s, around the same time that Raj dabbled with radio. While Balraj hosted a show called *Lipton Ke Sitare*, Raj was featured by Ceylon on *Rang Tarang*. While interviewing Dilip Kumar on the sets of *Shikast* (1953), director Ramesh Saigal asked Balraj to appear for a screen test, which led to him being offered the lead in *Railway Platform* (1955). Raj Khosla debuted as a director with *Milap* in the same year. They worked together for the first time on *Mera Saaya* and then followed it up with *Chirag* three years later.

The two were not only friends; they also had family relations. Their daughters went to the same schools, and the families used to visit each other often. Priya Dutt, Sunil Dutt's daughter, said, 'For me, Raj uncle was dad's friend. I had no connection with him being a filmmaker. He used to be working with dad. I have these fragmented memories of him coming home.'[1]

This friendship led Dutt to turn to Raj Khosla during two critical junctures of his filmmaking life. One of them occurred in the early 1970s. From acting, Dutt had taken the leap to producing films through his own banner, Ajanta Arts. In the initial years, Dutt focused his energies on making films that, according to him, pushed the boundaries of cinema: *Mujhe Jeene Do*, *Yaadein* (1964) and *Reshma aur Shera* (1971). '*Reshma aur Shera* bombed really badly,' said Priya Dutt. 'My dad realized that to really make money in this film industry, you need to go very commercial.'

The disastrous response to *Reshma aur Shera* cut deep. It was a pet project for Dutt and its failure to draw in audiences left him distraught. Creditors lined up outside his door for their pound of flesh. Even credible acting offers seemed to have stopped coming his way. One day, Dutt called his team to the office and told them that he had no alternative but to let them go. He may have to close Ajanta Arts. But his team took up the cudgels and decided to put together a project that would hopefully reverse the fortunes of the banner. Screenwriter K.K. Shukla was roped in. He would soon find great success writing Manmohan Desai blockbusters such as *Amar Akbar Anthony* (1977), *Parvarish* (1977) and *Suhaag* (1979), but at this point, he was mostly known for writing Narendra Bedi's *Rafoo Chakkar* (1975). Shukla had a revenge story in mind, which became *Nehle peh Dehlaa* (1976).

At this juncture, Sunil Dutt turned to his old friend Raj Khosla. Raj, who had always maintained that Dutt was like a younger brother to him, instantly agreed to direct his new venture. The film was shot near Sunil Dutt's bungalow – sometimes on his terrace – and at Mahabaleshwar. Raj Khosla's daughter Sunita reminisced, during a conversation with me, that the family had been part of the schedules at Mahabaleshwar.

Of all the films he had directed for others, Raj had the most liberating experience with *Nehle peh Dehlaa*. Compared to what Raj had experienced before, Dutt was a dream producer to work with. He spared no expense and allowed Raj Khosla every indulgence. Raj later said, 'It was the only film in my life where the producer gave me everything I wanted. The sky was my limit.'[2] But as a director and storyteller, Raj was once again venturing into untested waters. Though it had existed as early as *Kismet* (1943), the lost-and-found variety of storytelling became an unbeatable box office magnet in the 1970s, with everyone from Prakash Mehra to Nasir Hussain and Vijay Anand having their go at it, even as Manmohan Desai remained the uncrowned king of this dominion. Raj Khosla, though, hadn't really hopped on to this bandwagon just yet. Thrillers, dacoit dramas, suspense and noirs he had done, but this was new territory.

The story of two long-lost brothers (Sunil Dutt and Vinod Khanna) and their friend (Saira Banu) who were separated as children because of the actions of a smuggler (Prem Nath) who killed the boys' father and framed the girl's father for the murder, *Nehle peh Dehlaa* makes no bones about being a typical kitschy 1970s potboiler, warts and all. It is garish, over the top and great fun to watch with one's tongue firmly in cheek. Khanna, Dutt and Banu were projected as a trio of baddies, all clad in leather, astride motorcycles. Bollywood never quite had biker movies, but this one came the closest – so much so that in several of her interviews, Saira Banu called it the *Dhoom* of its times.[3]

Nehle peh Dehlaa has little to do with the Raj Khosla brand of filmmaking. It was one of those films that he did for a friend – it just wasn't his style. Saira Banu's Beena wasn't really a Raj Khosla heroine. She wasn't mounted like any of the other actresses in the Raj Khosla pantheon. But Banu had lately acquired the image of an attractive and sensual heroine, which was utilized in the film. Moreover, the thing about Raj Khosla songs is that they don't just become hits – they go down in history. But none of the songs in this film fit that description. Despite the presence of the great R.D. Burman and Anand Bakshi, who wrote all the songs here, the songs of *Nehle peh Dehlaa* didn't leave a mark.

The soundtrack of *Nehle peh Dehlaa* (1976).

There is one track, though, that merits special mention: 'Mashooq apne shabaab mein'. Bindu and Saira Banu are at the villain's lair, and a pool party is in progress. Everyone is wearing masks, including General, Prem Nath's character. The song goes:

Mashooq apne shabaab mein
Karte hain parda hijab mein
Kaisa zamana aaya dekho
Ke dekho aashiq khade hain naqaab mein

(Lovers, in their prime
Find veils to hide behind
It's a strange time
When lovers stand in masks)

The two ladies shimmer around the pool, mocking the men in masks. As both Banu and Bindu lip through the lines, you could swear that it's a duet. But it is Lata Mangeshkar singing for both women. Much like Raj, R.D. Burman was no stranger to experimentation.

Sunil Dutt, after the debacle of all the serious films he had made, left no stone unturned to ensure that this new film of his would serve popular entertainment in droves. And that's just what was achieved. While it didn't exactly break any record, the film was able to get a good run at the box office. Raj Khosla had delivered. He had stood up for a friend. It was now time to make a movie for himself. And this time, he turned inward.

Mahesh Bhatt once quoted his mentor Raj Khosla to Anupam Kher in an interview, 'Filmmaker *apne* fictional stories *mein nanga ho jaata hai. Jaisa woh hota hai woh nazar aata hai*. A filmmaker is stripped naked in his stories. He can be seen as he is.'[4]

In the realm of filmmaking, loneliness is an epidemic. Orson Wells suffered from it, Ritwik Ghatak was plagued by it and Raj Khosla's own Guru was burdened by it. In India, in particular, although everyone begrudgingly concedes cinema to be a director's medium, it is essentially seen as a viewer's medium. The director's urge for self-expression has to often go up against – and comply with – what the 'market' needs and wants. Thus, the process of filmmaking itself is a solitary exercise. This loneliness has led many an auteur to seek refuge in the bottle or the arms of a lover. In the case of Raj, it was possibly both. The truth was, as he admitted in an interview,[5] he was leading a double life. 'I am a Gemini,' he said, 'I've just got to have a double life – one is my work, the other is my love life.' Despite the finger pointing and aspersions it might lead to, he didn't try to hide this aspect of his personal life. And yet, he was a husband and the father of five daughters he loved to a fault – and they loved him back. It invariably led to complications that affected him deeply at an emotional level.

At this point in his filmmaking life, Raj was probably asking himself the same questions that he had seen Guru Dutt grapple with once he had done his share of crowd-pleasers and was at the cusp of self-exploration in his films. Raj Khosla had, for the first time, allowed his life to seep into his work with *Do Raaste*, for which he sought inspiration from Chandrakant Kakodkar's novel *Nilambari*. Coincidentally, it was with his second adaptation of a Kakodkar novel that he delved a little deeper into his life.

Raj had read Kakodkar's new book *Ashi Tujhi Preet*, and set it aside. He didn't think much of it then. But sometime later, a conversation with G.R. Kamat made him sit up and see the contours of a film in the story. 'One day my writer G.R. Kamat narrated to me the concept of the Tulsi plant, of how Vrinda fell in love with Lord Krishna who reciprocated with a condition that there would be no entry for her into the house,' Raj said wistfully to interviewer Sheila Vesuna.[6] This became the basis for *Main Tulsi Tere Aangan Ki* (1978), which starred Vijay Anand.

It was probably during Chetan Anand's soirees at 41, Pali Hill, that Raj had noticed a bright, sprightly teenager hanging around and smiling a million watts. The Anands called him Goldie because of the colour of his hair. The world would soon come to know him as Vijay Anand. He was next in line after his brother Chetan to wield the director's baton. Vijay was almost a decade younger to Raj Khosla, but they debuted as filmmakers at around the same time – Raj Khosla with *Milap* and Vijay with *Nau Do Gyarah*. Over the years, the two built filmmaking reputations that ran parallel to each other. Both started off with crime thrillers ('noirs') and then transitioned into dramas. Both were known for their brilliant sense of music and great song picturizations.

Ketan Anand, Chetan Anand's son after whom Navketan was named, spoke to me at length, juxtaposing Goldie and Raj:

> When you look at the pantheon of films this man [Raj Khosla] has done, it is incredible. There are only two people I consider masters in filming songs: Mr Raj Khosla and Mr Vijay Anand. The way they shot their songs… and they did it without dance directors. The dance directors were only there to choreograph the movements. All camera movements, shot taking, imagery and imagining was done by these two directors. And the camera was never static. It was always on the move. Goldie's songs moved the story forward. And I think Raj Khosla started that.

He added:

> I feel that Raj Khosla was very much a pioneer of modern Indian cinema. Maybe he was a little ahead of Goldie there. Because he ventures into romanticism, he does mystery films, he makes suspense, he brings in that carefree lover image of Dev Anand, and then he moves on to the dacoit films…

According to Ketan Anand, it was Johnny Bakshi who suggested that Raj Khosla cast Goldie as the husband-lover at the centre of *Main Tulsi Tere Aangan Ki*. Raj was looking for someone who would fit the role, someone without a distinctive star image. And here was his old friend Goldie, who, though more of a star director, had a good deal of acting experience. His first film as an actor had been *Joru ka Bhai* (1955) and he was featured as a lead opposite Shakila in *Agra Road* in 1957, the same year that he debuted as a director. Alongside a plethora of cameos in Navketan films, he had featured in Chetan Anand's *Haqeeqat*, and played leads in *Double Cross* (1972), *Chor Chor* and *Kora Kagaz* (both 1974).

Instances of noted filmmakers featuring in the works of their colleagues are more plentiful than one would imagine. Around the same time that Raj would have called Vijay Anand with the offer, Steven Spielberg's *Close Encounters of the Third Kind* (1977) would have released. Among the cast was acclaimed French filmmaker and one of the founding fathers of the French New Wave, Francois Truffaut. And it wasn't a cameo. Truffaut was even nominated for an award! More recently and closer home, Anurag Kashyap has featured as an actor in films by Vikramaditya Motwane, Tigmanshu Dhulia, A.R. Murugadoss and Lokesh Kanagaraj. But it is an object of endless curiosity – what does such a process look like? How does a filmmaker relinquish control to someone of his own tribe? Do they collide, or share notes?

In the case of *Main Tulsi*, we had two talented and self-assured – if a little maverick – directors who were secure in their own skin. Raj Khosla, especially, regardless of his talent, never allowed the craft to consume him enough to lose sleep over who walked away with the credit. 'I'm not an ambitious person,' he once said. He continued:

> I don't want to make the best film ever made, the film that will be a landmark… I don't have the meticulous sense of design and purpose which many others have. Maybe this lack of ambition of mine makes my actors realise I'm not making the film for myself. They tell themselves, 'He's not going to take away everything, all the credit, he's going to share with us.' I project my actors to their very best. To design a film so that I, the director, stand out is easy. Very easy. There are techniques to it.

> And there is another way: narrate your story and the actors are all that are to be seen on the screen. That's what movies are about.[7]

The above statement begins with a line that indicates a lack of interest, and then ends with one that implies deep thought and conviction about the craft. Unlike several 'serious' filmmakers of his generation, Raj wasn't interested in making self-indulgent films to satiate his creative ego. To him, that kind of flex was just too easy. It was his job to make the film and make it well. He was more than happy to let the others hog all the limelight. This quality of his is what endeared him to every artiste he ever worked with. So, when Johnny Bakshi suggested Vijay Anand for the role, Raj jumped at it. He knew the value that he would bring to the role and the film. He gave Goldie a wide berth to try out his own ideas, just like he gave a free hand to Manoj Kumar while making *Woh Kaun Thi?* and *Do Badan*.

The role of Tulsi went to Asha Parekh. Raj had first offered it to Rakhee Gulzar, but she turned it down; Tulsi dies less than one thirds into the film. Raj then met Parekh and narrated the role to her. She was so taken in that she said she would love to do the role, on one condition. 'He came to me and said that I want you to work in this film. And he sat and narrated the whole thing. I said, "You promise me that you will not change any scene. You'll do exactly as you're saying. Then I'm ready to do the film,"' Parekh remembered, in a conversation with me. Her role was the beating heart of the film, irrespective of the length of footage allocated to her.

Thakur Rajnath Chauhan (Vijay Anand) rescues Tulsi (Asha Parekh) from a brothel and puts her up at his *kothi*. The two get intimate, but Rajnath's mother (Purnima) is in no mood to approve his relationship with a 'fallen woman'. (The radio phonograph from *Prem Kahani* reappears along the way, blaring a Noor Jehan song once again. This time, Tulsi wistfully listens to 'Aaja meri barbaad mohabbat ke sahaare' from *Anmol Ghadi* [1946], composed by Naushad and written by Tanveer Naqvi.) The mother exerts pressure on Rajnath to marry a woman of high birth. He resists but the noble Tulsi urges him to go through with it. Enter Sanjukta (Nutan), the new *thakurain*, who, understandably, resents Tulsi's presence in their lives. It is then, after the wedding, that Tulsi reveals to Rajnath that she is pregnant. Rajnath feels helpless. The two women have a showdown where Sanjukta gives Tulsi a piece of her mind. Tulsi promises to leave. That evening, tending to the little plant of tulsi in her courtyard, she sings:

Main tulsi tere aangan ki
Koi nahi main tere saajan ki

(I am but the tulsi plant in your porch
Nothing do I mean to that lover of yours)

That night, Tulsi commits suicide. With her dying breath, she makes her lover swear undying love for his wife. Sanjukta breaks down at the news and swears to make it her business to raise Tulsi's son in the best way possible. Sanjukta gives birth to a son, too, and during a horse-riding incident soon after, Rajnath sustains an injury that proves to be fatal. At this point, the plot jumps about a decade and almost becomes a whole new film.

Asha Parekh, in the tradition of the great Raj Khosla heroines, managed to deliver an appropriate performance for the role. By this time, the team was four films old, and had developed a certain rhythm of its own, which shows in the film. During the making of *Do Badan*, Parekh had shown some trepidation trying to understand what being in that kind of undying love truly felt like. In *Main Tulsi*, in which she was playing the title role, she had to once again essay an intense kind of romance. Raj joked, 'By now I am sure your definition of love must have changed from those *Do Badan* days.'[8]

During her death scene, Parekh told me, Raj Khosla and his director of photography Pratap Sinha were so affected that they kept the camera running and left the set while the rest of the scene was executed. If that seems a little exaggerated, it should be considered that – as we have seen earlier with the incident involving Dharmendra's stunt during *Mera Gaon Mera Desh* – Raj Khosla was an overtly emotional, almost maudlin person. He just needed an opportunity to sob and let it all out. Most of the crew that he had assembled were also of this nature, Pratap Sinha included.

The other pivotal role in the film, almost a counterpoint to Asha Parekh's role, was that of Nutan. Nutan's work in the 1950s and 1960s had fetched her both awards and credibility as a serious actor. She had done some memorable films in this period but what instantly comes to mind when one thinks of her are the two films she did with Bimal Roy: *Sujata* (1959) and *Bandini* (1963). Both were exceptional movies and her performances in these will go down in history. In 1978, she gave an interview to Subhash Vohra of BBC. During the conversation, Vohra advanced the opinion that films in the 'good old days' were so much better and good films were not being made any more. While she didn't disagree entirely, Nutan added that serious films were still being made, and that the film she had just done, Raj Khosla's *Main Tulsi Tere Aangan Ki*, was comparable to *Sujata* and *Bandini*.[9]

In an industry defined by allure and star power, Nutan sought out roles that were considered risky and unconventional. In one of the Bimal Roy films mentioned earlier, she played a woman serving time for murder; in the other, she was an '*achhut*' ('untouchable') girl in love with a brahmin boy. In *Main Tulsi*, her character goes through stages. She starts as a bride furiously protecting her turf, delivering vicious salvoes at Tulsi, whom she sees as a rival. Then, when Tulsi dies, Sanjukta – distraught and consumed with guilt – decides to see to it that Tulsi's son, Ajay, gets the best education and career that she can provide. She soon has a son of her own, Pratap, whom she almost ignores in a bid to ensure this. When Ajay returns from boarding school, she quickly gives him the top job in the family business. Once again, her own progeny Pratap is left in the lurch. She does care for her son, but not as much as she cares about making up for the injustice committed all those years ago. In her zeal, she overcompensates, making even Ajay a little uncomfortable.

The soundtrack of *Main Tulsi Tere Aangan Ki* (1978).

There are all the Raj Khosla hallmarks here. The horses, the fluid camera, the windows (this time, they even get a song of their own: 'Ye khidki jo band rahti hai'). But most of all, it's how he lets the film soak his understanding of human relationships in every carefully crafted scene, dialogue and song.

A standout track from the film is 'Chhap tilak sab chheeni re', originally a poem composed by fourteenth-century Sufi mystic Amir Khusro, which was adapted by Laxmikant–Pyarelal and Anand Bakshi. Bakshi took the main refrain 'Chhap tilak' and four lines from the middle, weaving a tapestry around them.

Khusro wasn't mentioned in the opening credits, though he was duly credited in the LP record. Curiously, the same was the fate of Asha Bhosle, one of the playback singers, performing with none other than her sister. No one can say with absolute certainty how many songs the sisters Lata Mangeshkar and

Asha Bhosle have sung together, but by all accounts, the number should be well under a 100 – less than 1 per cent of their vast repertoire. According to Dr Mandar V. Bichu, music enthusiast and connoisseur, their very first song together was 'Ye ruki ruki hawayein' from *Daman* (1951). Since then, a handful of composers have made the two sisters sing in unison. Laxmikant–Pyarelal made them sing the soulful 'Ae kaash kisi diwane ko' for *Aaye Din Bahaar Ke* (1966). They came together with the composer duo for *Main Tulsi* more than a decade later. According to Asha Bhosle, the song was important to Raj, and he kept dropping in at the recording booth where the sisters were singing. 'Maybe this song was close to his heart. Maybe he had learned it too. *Hum dono behne gaa rahi thhi*, we sisters were singing, and he appreciated that a lot. He kept coming to the recording booth and saying to us, "*Yeh jagah bahut achhi li hai tumne*. That movement you took right there, it was really good!"' she said.

Khusro's composition was an ode to his guru. Written entirely in Braj Bhasha, the lines encapsulate both physical and divine love, showing the love between a devotee and their god. The poem depicts a lover having their identity eroded with just a glance of the beloved. It is this last aspect that Raj Khosla wished to examine. A divine hymn for the almighty became a love song for mortals. Village girl Geeta (Geeta Behl) has fallen for bad boy Pratap (Deb Mukherjee), and on this particular morning, she is a little inebriated. She swirls around, consumed and utterly drunk in his love as a group of minstrels start singing Amir Khusro's love ballad.

Raj wasn't new to staging *mujra*s and the film features two beautiful ones. As the opening credits roll, we are in Tulsi's *kotha*. She dances to the thumri 'Saiyan rooth gaye', performed by famed classical vocalist Shobha Gurtu. This composition was Shobha's own. Shobha's mother, Menaka Shirodkar, had learned music from the same Ustad Vilayat Hussain Khan who had also taught Jagannathbuwa Purohit, Raj Khosla's music guru. Right from his debut *Milap* to *Kala Pani* and *Kuchhe Dhaage*, Raj had often employed *mujras*, but never had he combined an actual thumri with it.

Another *mujra*, sung by Anuradha Paudwal and Hemlata, 'Nathaniya jo daali', is a vivacious number and both singers shine. As usual, it is incredibly well choreographed. Pratap, Sanjukta and Rajnath's son, indulges in debauchery at the *kotha* where two dancers entertain him. One of the dancers happens to be played by actress Heena Kausar, the daughter of the legendary director K. Asif. And the other one, matching Kausar in her charm and exuberance step for step, is the singer we know as Poornima. Born Sushma Shrestha, Poornima shot to fame in the early 1970s, singing R.D. Burman compositions such as 'Tera mujhse hai pehle ka naata koi' (*Aa Gale Lag Jaa*, 1973) and 'Kya hua tera waada' (*Hum Kisise Kum Naheen*, 1977). Later, she adopted the name Poornima and sang several chartbusters in the 1990s, especially in films directed by David Dhawan. In *Main Tulsi*, she was credited as 'Purnima'.

The title song of *Main Tulsi Tere Aangan Ki* revolves around the germ of the story. About it, Pyarelal told me, 'I felt very strongly about the song, so I told Lata ji, "I'll sit with you on this." So, while the song itself was composed by Laxmikant, it was me who taught it to her.' There is another anecdote about the first line of the song that Laxmikant narrated to journalist and critic Rajiv Vijayakar. Apparently, Raj had just these five words stuck in his head, but he had no idea how the rest of the song should flow. Vijayakar writes in his book *Music by Laxmikant Pyarelal: The Incredible Melodious Journey*:

> Khosla had told Laxmikant about his new film and the title, and Laxmikant had made the basic tune that we

> all know now for the mukhda. They went to Anand Bakshi's home, where he was lying in bed with a foot raised and in plaster, because he had suffered a fracture. After giving him a narration, Raj Khosla told him, 'We need a second line to complete the mukhda.' And instantly, Bakshi said, "That is simple. It should be 'Koi nahin main tere saajan ki'!" The filmmaker broke down as he told me, 'In six everyday words, Anand Bakshi had encapsulated the entire story of my film!'[10]

It's evident that Raj Khosla was emotionally invested in the film. Though autobiographical, none of the characters were from his life; it was the theme, the premise, that had a certain resonance with what he was going through at the time. Telling the story of Tulsi, the 'other' woman, and her sacrifice meant the world to him. But he was also a conservative, and held immense respect for the institution of marriage. Said Raj in an interview:

> I could have stretched the first half and ended the film with Tulsi's death. The point was that her sacrifice isn't enough. Her son has to keep up and add to what she did. If I hadn't made Tulsi die, she would have lived away from her man but they would meet regularly. The wife, the husband and the woman would all be living a double life. Living under torture continuously.

To which, the interviewer asked if that was what was happening to him. Raj replied in the affirmative.[11]

This pathos of Tulsi was carried throughout the film and summarized in the title song. Tulsi sings, directing her entreaties as the other woman, to the wife:

Main tulsi tere aangan ki
Koi nahin main tere saajan ki
Maang teri sindoor bhi tera
Sab kuchh tera kuchh nahin mera
Mohe saugndh tere ansuan ki

(I am but the tulsi plant in your porch
Nothing do I mean to that lover of yours
It's all yours, the thread and the sindoor
By your tears do I swear)

Later, as Tulsi is being taken away, Rajnath asks the funeral procession to stop outside his mansion so Tulsi can have one last look at the home that could never be hers. At this point, the song wafts in again, with her last words to Sanjukta:

Kaahe ko tu mujhase jalati hai
E ri mohe to tu lagati hai
Koi saheli bachapan ki

(Why do you envy me?
I think of you
As a long-lost friend from childhood)

Instead of being relieved, Sanjukta is inconsolable at the death of Tulsi, the woman she accused of stealing her husband from her. And this, in effect, is the whole film.

Raj Khosla shot *Main Tulsi Tere Aangan Ki* in two of his favourite locations: Mehboob Studios and Udaipur. He had earlier shot *Mera Saaya, Mera Gaon Mera Desh* and parts of *Kuchhe Dhaage* at Udaipur. He had an emotional connection with the city and the soil of Rajasthan. But in his films, Rajasthan is never depicted with the stereotypes of the deserts, sand dunes, camels and caravans. His Rajasthan was full of ponds, lakes, palaces, fountains and horses. Lots and lots of horses. His assistant and integral team member Inder Khosla says:

> *Uss dharti se pyar thha unko.* He was in love with that land. He was so in love with that place that we used to head straight to Udaipur, and then once there, we used to decide where to go and shoot – maybe 20 or 25 kilometres from there. Raj saab made *Mera Gaon Mera Desh* in Cheerwa village, and then went back there to make *Meraa Dost Meraa Dushman*. They used to love him dearly, and it was their love that sort of pulled him there. The villagers used to send us food every morning, and along with that, pitchers full of lassi for all of us.

Inder Khosla, who hails from the same village as Raj, remembers being given a small role where he was supposed to engage in banter with Vinod Khanna, right before the song 'Ye khidki jo band rahti hai' began. The song features Khanna, smeared in *gulaal* and astride a horse, trying to persuade Nita Mehta (who played his love interest, the daughter of another thakur who owns a stud farm) to come down and play Holi. For the duration of the song, Vinod never gets off the horse, and struts around Naini's mansion as she peeks from windows and *jharokhas*. In a soundtrack otherwise dominated by the women, and rightfully so, this was the only Mohammed Rafi song, and he hit it right out of the park.

At the Filmfare Awards next year (1979), *Main Tulsi Tere Aangan Ki* managed to secure three nods: Best Film, Best Actress (Nutan), and Best Dialogue (Rahi Masoom Reza). It was exactly 20 years ago that a Raj Khosla film had been recognized at Filmfare for the first time. At the sixth Filmfare Awards held in 1959, Dev Anand had won the award for 'Best Actor', while Nalini Jaywant won the award for 'Best Actress in a Supporting Role'. Four of Raj Khosla's films had won awards so far:

1959
Kala Pani
Best Actor – Dev Anand
Best Actress in a Supporting Role – Nalini Jaywant

1965
Woh Kaun Thi?
Best Cinematographer B&W– K.H. Kapadia

1967
Do Badan
Best Actress in a Supporting Role – Simi Garewal
Mera Saaya
Best Sound Recordist – Manohar Amberkar

But Raj himself had never been recognized for his filmmaking. With *Main Tulsi*, he finally won an award for Best Film. But the 'Best Director' award eluded him till the end of his days.

Maverick American filmmaker Terry Gilliam said about Federico Fellini and the female-centricity in his work: 'They terrify him. He loves them, he hates them. They're mothers, they're virgins, they're daughters, they're whores. They're everything. It's the worship of the female in all of its glory.' And though Raj Khosla and Fellini, while being contemporaries, were from entirely disparate galaxies, and any comparison would otherwise be ludicrous, this singular obsession somehow binds them. Raj was immensely affected by the women in his life. Whether it was his mother, his wife, his five daughters or all the women he ever claimed to love, they all impacted him deeply and thereby shaped his work. It was the reality of the times and the ecosystem Raj was working in that he had to have hyper-masculine men as protagonists, but even there, the women came out winners. And this is even more true of *Main Tulsi Tere Aangan Ki* than most other Raj Khosla films.

Main Tulsi Tere Aangan Ki was released in August 1978. On 15 and 16 October that year, Raj Khosla married off his two eldest daughters, Uma and Sunita. His daughters were little slices of his heart. A young Dharmesh Darshan was witness to a distressed Raj Khosla breaking down in the dead of night. 'Raj Khosla ji had kept the wedding at the Marina compound. At around 2.30 a.m., after the *bidaai* had happened, I saw him sitting in the corner and bawling. I didn't understand how this senior man was crying like a child. This is the man who shot and created that cult *bidaai* song of *Bombai ka Babu*: "Chal ri sajni ab kya soche"... what picturization!' Darshan recalled. The song, he said, might have been one of the influences for his own very popular *bidaai* song, 'Dulhe ka sehra suhana lagta hai', from *Dhadkan*.

There may have been more than just the sad father of the bride Darshan saw in Raj Khosla that night. His two eldest daughters, Raj explained in an interview to *Filmfare* in 1980, missed out on a lot of his parental love when they were growing up.[12] He was determined to ensure that the three younger girls, Anita, Reena and Sonia, got every bit of the love and attention they deserved.

19

Salamat Rahe Dostana Hamara

Of Raj Khosla's five daughters, Uma and Sunita, the eldest ones, were born less than a year apart in the late 1950s. In an interview to me, Sunita reminisced about the weekends spent at Khosla Niwas. Their grandfather Atmaram Khosla – Bauji – would arrange delectable meals and snacks for the kids. The kids interacted more with Atmaram than with their grandmother. She didn't talk much. But she used to get dresses stitched for the girls from the nearby Gandhi Market. Whenever there was a birthday or a similar celebration, she would get them frocks. There were in fact so many that they rarely had to buy dresses.

Come Sunday, Raj would join them. It didn't matter how busy his schedule was, or where the outdoor shoot had been scheduled. Raj always made it a point to be there. The bouts of chess would then begin. Sunday afternoons were extra special, because that's when they went downstairs, where Lekhraj and his family lived. In addition to all kinds of mouth-watering food, this is also when the girls got to hang out with the youngsters, and the *mehfil* would begin. All the cousins and Tanny's (Anil Khosla) friends would arrive. They would have dinner together and biryani was served. They were also joined by Das, the house help, and Junior, the dog. There was unending chatter, fun, laughter and singing. Sometimes, the sounds of singing would draw the girls' father downstairs. Raj would call for his harmonium and throw caution to the wind. Some film folks who lived in and around Matunga, like Manoj Kumar, would drop in too.

Manoj Kumar revealed an interesting titbit about Das, the help. Like everyone else in the household, he, too, was from Punjab. Always clad in a lungi and kurta, Das was quite the character. Whenever Raj opened a bottle, he would be right behind the door, only half of his lean frame visible, and cough loudly. Raj would look in his direction, and the 'master' and the 'servant' would break into a quarrel. '*Nahi doonga tere ko*! I won't give you any!' Raj would say, and Das would snap back, '*Aage se laake nahin doonga*! *Akela peeyega, mar jaayega*! I won't fetch any for you in the future! If you drink alone, you'll die!' Kumar would witness this exchange with amusement.

Even when Raj's mother, Saraswati, passed away, the visits continued. Raj Khosla was always a dutiful son to his father. But now, they became even closer. During one of the conversations between Raj and Manoj Kumar over lunch, Kumar spoke excitedly. Raj was listening but not responding. Kumar, obviously irked at this, asked him why. Raj took a beat and then said, 'Bauji says, never speak when you are eating.' Atmaram was everything for him. Whenever life threw a problem at him that he felt he couldn't quite tackle, he'd place it before Bauji, and was provided an answer. He would tell his daughters, satisfied, '*Mera* problem solve *ho gaya*. My problem has been solved.'

While he shunned the typical industry parties and didn't throw any himself either, Raj Khosla did have star guests dropping in. At his prime, some of the biggest stars have found their way to his doors. With the stars in the hall, the kids were crammed inside in another room. Obviously, they wanted a peek.

When they asked, 'Daddy, why won't you let us meet these people?' he'd just rebuff them with, 'What do you want to do meeting these people? *Koi zaroorat nahi*! There's no need!'

But when people from his inner circle – which included Dev Anand, Sadhana, Sunil Dutt and Rahi Masoom Raza – paid a visit, Raj Khosla was a little lenient. With them, the girls could mingle.

Despite everything, once Uma and Sunita had been married off, Raj started to feel that he hadn't spent enough time with his eldest daughters. He felt he had to make up for it with the younger three. Anita, Reena and Sonia have fond memories of being around him in his later years. Anita recalls one instance where a Parsi gentleman kept calling incessantly. Raj, tired of answering repeatedly and explaining that he had got the wrong number, decided to have some fun. He changed his voice, said his name was Dinshaw and addressed the caller as 'Dikra'. The girls were rolling on the floor.

He enjoyed a unique relationship with each of his daughters. Sonia, for instance, recalled that her father didn't take any interest in her studies till she was in the ninth standard. She was not a particularly good student till then. But when she got to her tenth, Raj Khosla got more involved and started insisting on better grades for her boards. Consequently, she worked hard and managed to score a First Class, which, by her own admission, seemed quite impossible earlier.

Reena had a singing voice and whenever he was feeling low, Raj would ask her to sing. Her voice would cheer him up. She'll be a great singer one day, her father predicted. 'Dad had a soft spot for Reena,' said Anita later in an interview to *Filmfare*, 'But *mujhe bas daantte hi rehte thhe*. He kept scolding me. I was the rebellious one. I wanted my way. It was always "you can't do this" and "you can't do that" with me.'[1] Anita had a degree in mass media and wanted to make her foray into the world of filmmaking. But Raj Khosla would have none of it. For all his work celebrating such glorious women on screen, he had his own notions about what women in his family should and shouldn't do. He didn't want his daughter within miles of the film industry. So, when Anita showed an interest in joining the industry, he refused. Despite the restrictions and refusals, she did end up writing about films and filmmakers (including her father) for several publications.

It was Yash Johar who pursued Raj Khosla with the idea of his next film *Dostana* (1980). Johar is one of those figures in the annals of Indian cinema who have often been spoken about but rarely chronicled. According to his son Karan Johar's account in *An Unsuitable Boy*, Johar apprenticed under a Mr Dubey, a *Times of India* photographer. When Mr Dubey called in sick, it was up to Yash Johar to show up on the sets of *Mughal-E-Azam* (1960) and take pictures on his behalf. He took some photos of Madhubala that day, which got him more work at *Times of India*. Following this incident, which occurred in the 1940s, Karan Johar writes, Yash Johar joined films.[2]

But according to Rajkumar Keswani's *Dastan-E-Mughal-E-Azam*, Madhubala wasn't cast until at least February 1952, when Sterling Investment Corporation, the producers, put up an ad in the papers, inviting young women to send in their pictures for the role of Anarkali ('THAT GIRL MIGHT BE YOU!' screamed the ad).[3] Much before that, in May 1951, Amiya Chakravarty's *Badal* had been released, in which Yash Johar was credited for 'publicity'. It was produced by Varma Films, a renowned banner with which Yash did another film called *Aurat* (1953), and was credited as 'publicity-in-charge'. This was followed by a stint as production executive at Filmalaya, and with Nasir Hussain, and then, in the early 1960s, an opportunity to work with Sunil Dutt. Yash Johar was a witness to the inauguration of the latter's production house Ajanta Arts around 1962, and worked with Sunil Dutt on the production of the first two projects under the banner, *Mujhe Jeene Do* and *Yeh Rastey Hain Pyar Ke* (both 1963). While he was still there, Dev Anand, whom he had earlier worked with in *Jab Pyar Kisise Hota Hai* (1961), asked him to come to Navketan for three months. He could go back to Ajanta Arts after that. They were making *Guide*, and those three months turned into nine years, and Yash Johar ended up handling the production of several Navketan films. Raj was associated with Navketan and briefly on-board to direct *Guide*. One could surmise that this was when Raj met Johar. Both were Navketan protégés, in their own ways.

During the late 1960s and early 1970s, Eastern exoticism was hotter than ever. International filmmakers were lining up to shoot in India. Yash Johar's reputation as a consummate production manager attracted offers from Hollywood projects that wanted help with location hunting. It was decent money, and Dev Anand encouraged Johar to take them up. As early as 1967, actor Amrish Puri reminisces in his memoirs, Johar came to him about a role in *Maya*, the NBC adventure series. In 1969, Bruce Lee wrote a story called 'The Silent Flute', based on which writer Stirling Silliphant wrote a screenplay, and they envisioned shooting in India. They roped in Yash Johar for scouting locations, but the project was later shelved. Johar also worked with American director John Frankenheimer, who was in India to explore locations (possibly for *The Horsemen* [1971], a film set in Afghanistan; it was finally shot on location in Afghanistan). As luck would have it, John Frankenheimer walked in on the shoot of *Mera Gaon Mera Desh* at Chandivali studio. The song 'Apni prem kahaniyan' was being filmed. Raj Khosla had instructed his team to carry on and stepped away for a moment. Mahesh Bhatt remembers it, because he was right there when it happened. Frankenheimer came in, had a look-see and departed. The maker of *The Manchurian Candidate* (1962) missed meeting the maker of *Woh Kaun Thi?* by a whisker.

After his Hollywood sojourn, when Johar returned to Navketan headquarters, he found his assistant Yash Kohli occupying the chair that was once his. If he resumed duties, the boy would be relegated to an assistant again, and he didn't want to discourage a youngster. If there was one thing that Yash Johar had acquired over his two-decades-long experience in the film industry, it was goodwill. Everyone loved and respected him. Now, where could he go from Navketan? The only logical next step was to start a banner of his own. And thus, Dharma Productions was born. The year was 1979. And for Dharma's maiden film, he turned to his Navketan comrade Raj Khosla.

By his own admission, Raj had lost interest in films after *Main Tulsi Tere Aangan Ki*. 'Scotch became my favourite companion,' he would say of this period later.[4] Offers still came, but Raj didn't have the same zeal as before. Anita remembers Yash Johar persistently convincing Raj to do his film. 'Dad did that movie due to the sheer perseverance of Yash Johar,' she says. Though Raj also regretted in one of his interviews that he had become 'complacent and careless' after *Main Tulsi Tere Aangan Ki*,[5] his daughter Sunita remembers his attitude differently. 'It was all fine during *Dostana* because I was there with him for the whole outdoor shoot. He was in complete command of his faculties. We had gone to Ooty. *Ek maheene hamaari* shooting *thhi wahan pe*. We shot there for a month,' she said.

It was a Salim–Javed film that Raj Khosla had agreed to direct. Salim Khan and Javed Akhtar, both superstar screenwriters, narrated the story of *Dostana* to Raj Khosla.[6] He was the only director ever considered for the project. And yet *Dostana* wasn't what you'd call a typical Raj Khosla film (Even Salim Khan agreed during our interview: '*Unke* type *ki* script *nahi thhi*. It wasn't his type of a script.'). The only comparable film Raj had done earlier was *Nehle peh Dehlaa* (in the sense that both were urban action dramas typical of the 1970s and 1980s).

Salim Khan recalled his interactions with Raj with utter fondness:

> It was a pleasure working with him. *Bahut* soft *kism ke aadmi thhe*. He was of a soft demeanour. But more importantly, he was a good man. *Aaram se kaam karte thhe*. He made it all seem effortless. He had great sense of music and script. In my opinion, besides Raj Kapoor, if there was one director who understood music and used it well in his films, it was Raj Khosla.
>
> *Shaam ko unke saath baithne mein, baat karne mein mazaa ata thha*. It was fun to sit with him, chat with him in the evenings. He was a pleasant drinker. Drinking is also an art. Sometimes you have one drink with someone and never want to be around them again.

They would often meet at Raj's favourite haunt: the Otters Club in Bandra. But even before that, they ran into each other at Rahi Masoom Reza's place, because Salim's partner-in-crime Javed Akhtar used to frequent that house. Salim also pointed out that when you have stars like Shatrughan Sinha and Amitabh Bachchan in your film, it's easy to get weighed down. 'But he [Raj Khosla] managed them rather well,' Salim observed.

Raj Khosla, too, was impressed by the talent and professionalism of Salim–Javed. It was the first time in his life that he had encountered a script that was complete in the truest sense. It even had dialogues. The pair left nothing unsaid and rarely allowed directors to meddle with their work. 'Not even a comma or full stop was changed in *Deewaar*,' Salim said to illustrate. But he also pointed out that Raj had a great sense of script, saying, '*Ye nahi thha jo de diya wohi kar liya*. It wasn't that he did whatever he was given. *Achhe* suggestions *dete thhe*, *unka* contribution *hota thha*. He gave good suggestions, had his own contributions.' While the writer duo, who were probably the only star writers in the history of Bollywood, didn't allow the minutest of alteration in their scripts when they worked with the likes of Prakash Mehra, Yash Chopra and Ramesh Sippy, they were willing to accommodate the suggestions of Raj Khosla. But how extensive were these suggestions? In his 1981 interview, speaking about *Dostana* and Salim–Javed, Raj explained:

> When I first got their script and read it – incidentally they were the first ever writers to give me a complete script including dialogue, which is remarkable in itself – and found it was a middling job. There was no snobbishness involved in this, just the plain truth being spoken. I told them about this. I told them there were certain weaknesses which had to be punched out, things put in, otherwise we would collapse. They agreed, and we worked it out. Every problem I put across, they found the alternatives, worked out things and gave the script back to me.[7]

Raj Khosla was still top of the food chain, and fresh from a major box office success. After he came on board as director, Amitabh Bachchan was cast. Just about eight years prior, when he was a nondescript young actor, Raj had cast him in *Raaste kaa Patthar*. The other cast members finalized were Zeenat Aman and Vinod Khanna. Khanna had had productive collaborations with both Bachchan and Raj. With Raj, he'd done five films, including their recent triumph *Main Tulsi Tere Aangan Ki*. Raj Khosla was easily one of the few who contributed to Vinod Khanna's success and ascendancy as a star. They shared a warm friendship, and this camaraderie with Raj Khosla was one of the reasons Khanna had done that cameo in *Prem Kahani*.

Khanna and Bachchan had been pitted together in six films, the latest one being *Muqaddar ka Sikandar* (1978). The media was abuzz with stories of their rivalry. *Dostana* would have been Vinod Khanna's last work with both Raj and Bachchan. But it was Raj, if one of his assistants is to be believed, who decided that Vinod Khanna might not fit the role. There was a point in the film where Zeenat's character had to choose between Amitabh Bachchan and his friend. Raj Behl, who assisted Khosla on *Dostana*, remembers a statement by the director that was relayed to him by Pravesh Sagar, the chief assistant director on *Dostana*. Raj apparently said, 'Vinod Khanna is such a handsome man… why would she leave him?' It didn't seem plausible to him that she would choose Amitabh over Vinod. And in came Shatrughan Sinha with his own bag of charms.

'He had so much confidence in me, that even if it seemed that other stars were a little bothered by my presence, Raj Khosla didn't care about it at all. He never bothered about such things. He used to say with pride, "*Hamaara* hero Shatrughan Sinha *hai*! So what if he's a little late? He finishes work early and leaves early." He had a lot of affection for me. I have great memories,' Sinha reminisced.

Depending on who you talk to, there are equally fascinating stories about Amitabh Bachchan's punctuality and Shatrughan Sinha's tardiness on the sets of *Dostana*. 'Despite coming in late sometimes, he would mug up 10 pages worth of dialogues in minutes!' said Inder Khosla, visibly impressed by Sinha's skills. Meanwhile, Raj Behl remembers arriving on the set just five minutes late and being greeted by the sight of Bachchan sitting there and having a shave, as he'd pull him up for being late.

About working with Sinha and Bachchan, Raj explained in an interview to *Filmfare*:

> You give Shatrughan Sinha 40 lines and he's ready within five minutes – he won't take six minutes. Amitabh is ready the minute you give him his dialogue, as many lines as you want… Also, when I know that time is short, I won't break up my scene into many shots. I take it in one shot… I want all kinds of movements within the single shot – the kind of results you normally achieve by intercutting, but I don't have time for intercutting shots – these actors give me all I want, in one continuous shot of two or three hundred feet. In *Dostana*, there were occasions when we were stuck for maybe an hour because some actor wasn't available, then we got ready for the take in ten minutes and did the scene in half an hour.[8]

While filming the song 'Mere dost kissa ye kya ho gaya', Shatrughan Sinha was available on only one of the four days it took to shoot the song. Raj left out the shots for Shatru, while shooting the rest of the song with Bachchan and Zeenat. On the day that he was present, Shatru's shots were filmed and added in the right places. Raj Behl recalls shooting another scene with both Amitabh and Shatrughan. 'Shatru ji used to arrive at 12, while Amit ji was there at seven. Raj ji (what a craftsman he was!) did the scene without Shatru ji and later, when Shatru ji used to come, he used to add his close-ups and shots,' Behl said.[9]

The film had a major action scene in the climax for which no expense was spared. Literally and figuratively. The team went to London, and foreign technicians like Jim Allen and Gerry Crampton were employed. For 1980, it was quite the spectacle. Ravi (Sinha) and Vijay (Bachchan) are in hot pursuit of Daaga (Prem Chopra) and Balwant (Amrish Puri), who try to sneak away in a two-seater mini plane. Ravi, who is shown as a flying enthusiast early on in the film, gets on a chopper to tail them, with Vijay hanging on to it by the landing gear. As the copter takes off, you can clearly see that it is indeed Bachchan who's dangling precariously by the belly of the craft. Once it's in the sky, a double replaces him. Moments later, Vijay hops down on a runway and gets into a truck. Now it's the truck and the chopper chasing the baddies. That's a fancy chase sequence for a 1980s Bollywood actioner and one would assume it was because of the scale of the stunts and the need for the right professionals that Raj Khosla and Yash Johar chose to shoot this bit in London. There was no attempt to show off the London skyline because in the movie's timeline, all this was supposed to be happening at a 'flying club on Goa Road'.

Shatrughan Sinha remembers 'Raj ji' telling him about the London schedule: '*Tum aaram se aao*. Come whenever you want, whether in the afternoon or after lunch. Take your time. There's no hurry. It's an action scene. You don't even have to get into the helicopter. Let Amitabh do his thing. You'll be down there enjoying the view. I'll manage everything. *Koi baat nahi. Main hoon na*! No worries. I'm there!'

No discussion on *Dostana* can be adequately concluded without mentioning Zeenat Aman. She was an incredible presence. Despite it being a film about two men and their friendship, *Dostana* conjures up images of three people. She brought the right measure of appeal and sophistication to the role. Helen's character is also unforgettable. Her big reveal in the end was one of the highlights of the film. Her role was reminiscent of Laxmi Chhaya's in *Mera Gaon Mera Desh*, although that was a more nuanced and extensive part.

Like every other film of Raj Khosla at his prime, the soundtrack of *Dostana* included several memorable songs. Laxmikant–Pyarelal had delivered once again. The crowning glory was 'Salamat rahe dostana hamara', which had Shatru and Amitabh on screen, with Kishore Kumar and Mohammed Rafi voicing them. In a pantheon of about 65- or 70-odd songs, this could very well be the definitive Kishore–Rafi duet.

The soundtrack of *Dostana* (1980).

Rafi's 'Mere dost kissa ye kya ho gaya' also has great recall value, and was written with panache by Anand Bakshi. 'Bahut khubsoorat jawan ek ladki', while being incredibly peppy, with Kishore Kumar employing his baritone to suit Bachchan's, would raise eyebrows today because of its lyrics, which essentially put down women for wearing skimpy clothes and urge the listener to decide whether the stalker is at fault.

Na dekhe koi toh sharafat hai uski
Jo dekhe toh kuchh bhi chhupe na nazar se
Koi diljala muft maara gaya
Mere doston tum karo faisala
Khata kiski hai kisko de hum sazaa

(If they don't look, it's their virtue
If they do, nothing is hidden from view
Poor lovesick boys get pulled up
My friends, think up:

Whose fault is it, who must take the rap?)

... And then, typical of this argument, hark back to the women of the past, and blame it all on ever-changing 'fashion':

Haseen toh hamesha haseen thhe magar
Kabhi raaston pe nikalte na thhe
Badalte thhe woh bhi kai roop lekin
Naye roz fashion badalte na thhe

(The pretty were always so
But never to the streets did they go
Their styles did change, their looks did play
But fashions didn't change day by day)

This otherwise brilliant song is also somewhat symptomatic of Raj Khosla's own conflicted worldview when it came to women. He put women on a pedestal, preferred them to be educated, erudite, well read and well spoken, but at the same time, remained tied to the idea of a traditional Indian woman. This was seen in *Do Raaste*, where Nilambari (Bindu), with her ideas of a nuclear family, was portrayed as the home-breaker. Rajesh Khanna asks Mumtaz to abandon her modern (by 1960s standards) attire and don a saree, which leads to 'Bindiya chamkegi'. In *Dostana*, Zeenat Aman bravely drags her stalker (Paintal) to the police station and files a report. Vijay (Bachchan), the officer, locks the goon up but doesn't forget to deliver a sermon to the lady he's just met, and the following exchange ensues:

'*Zara dekhiye apne aap ko. Iss tarah ke kapde pehen kar agar aap bahar sadak par niklengi, toh gundon ki seetiyan nahi bajengi toh kya mandir ki ghantiyan bajengi*? Just

> look at yourself. If you venture out wearing those kind of clothes, what do you think you are more likely to hear: catcalls or temple bells?'
>
> 'What do you mean? *Kya kharaabi hai in kapdo mein*? What's wrong with these clothes?'
>
> '*Bahut kam hain*! *Suna thha ek zamaane mein ladkiyon ko kapdon ka bahut shauk hua karta thha. Ye aajkal aap log kapdon ke maamle mein itni kanjoos kyon hoti jaa rahi hain*? They are too less! I was told that there was a time when girls took plenty of interest in clothes. Why have the lot of you become so miserly in the matter of clothes?'

Later, when he bumps into her at a party, Vijay unleashes 'Bahut khubsoorat jawan ek ladki' on her, elaborating on his rant.

As usual, Raj was involved in every little detail when it came to filming his songs. 'Never once has he called the choreographer and left him to shoot the song. The dance director was there just to show the dance movements. The shot taking, the angles, everything from the *mukhda* to the *antara*… he used to shoot all of it himself,' recalled Raj Behl.

Speaking of the song 'Dillagi ne di hawa', Inder Khosla said that the whole song was shot in Ooty, in a single day. Amitabh Bachchan's availability had to be accounted for, and Yash Johar couldn't manage any other location for the given date. So they had to pack off the entire crew to Ooty, and Raj Khosla shot the song with almost superhuman efficiency. Filming began at around noon and was wrapped up by a quarter to four, without breaking for lunch.

Dostana was a major blockbuster, one of the biggest box office draws of 1980, alongside the behemoth *Qurbani* and Vijay Anand's *Ram Balram*. It laid the foundations of an empire, and until Karan Johar's *Kuch Kuch Hota Hai* (1998) came along 18 years later and ushered in a new era of bling, *Dostana* continued to be Dharma Productions's biggest – and only – success. It was also the last time that Raj Khosla saw that level of box office euphoria.

Raj Khosla later conceded that he should have taken a breather after *Main Tulsi Tere Aangan Ki*, with which he believed he had 'fulfilled' himself. He wished he had taken a break. But offers kept coming his way. If not Yash Johar who came to him with *Dostana*, it was the Thadanis who approached him with an offer to direct *Do Premee* (1980). Kundan and U.A. Thadani were distributors, and this was their first foray into film production. The film had Rishi Kapoor and Moushumi Chatterjee slated for the lead. It was a regular young romance, of the type that had become ubiquitous in Rishi Kapoor's filmography in that first decade of his career. Moushumi had already done *Kuchhe Dhaage* (and was even considered for *Prem Kahani*) with Raj Khosla, but this was the first time Kapoor was working with him. Kapoor writes in his book *Khullam Khulla* that it was a privilege to work with Raj even when his career was floundering.[10]

Neither of the two Raj Khosla films (*Do Premee* and *Naqāb*) Kapoor appeared in found favour with the audiences. *Do Premee* was an unmitigated disaster, but Kapoor came away suitably impressed by Raj Khosla. He writes, 'Raj Khosla was perhaps the suavest of directors I worked with. He was very British in how he spoke and dressed, and was a true gentleman. Impeccable style, fine manners and exceptionally articulate – everything about him was top drawer.'[11] He goes on to recount a discussion about acting with the director. Raj emphasized that acting for him was about style, bringing up his old friend Dev Anand as an example. Every actor must have their distinctive style, he said.

Do Premee was a long time in the making. It began in the mid-1970s, when Moushumi had just given birth to her elder daughter, Payal. Raj named Moushumi's character after her firstborn. Moushumi and Rishi Kapoor had just worked together in *Phool Khile Hain Gulshan Gulshan* (1978). Neither of these two films did particularly well, but Rishi and Moushumi shared an impeccable chemistry, a lot of which spilled over in real life when they had a public banter on social media back in 2015. In an interview given to *Times of India*, Moushumi named Rishi her favourite actor, even calling herself a fan. But she qualified this by saying that Rishi was also a spoilt brat and arrogant at times. In response, Rishi thanked her on Twitter, calling her a crackpot but complimenting her on her ability to 'cry without external help.'[12]

One aspect of *Do Premee* might tie back to Raj Khosla's friendship with Vinod Khanna. It was under the influence and encouragement of Khanna that he started taking an interest in the teachings of Osho Rajneesh. He even went to the Pune ashram and met Rajneesh, but never became a disciple or wore any robes for him. His cousin Arun Bhalla remembers Raj sending him a series of cassettes (along with a tape recorder) of Osho's speeches. He insisted that he listen to them. Bhalla became a lifelong admirer of Osho. But Raj himself remained a sceptic.

This is evident in *Do Premee*. Young lovers Chetan (Rishi) and Payal (Moushumi) face parental disapproval and elope. But a court marriage requires them to tender notice for a month, so they start looking for ways to earn their living. Chetan finds a job as a chauffeur to a rich businesswoman (Geeta Behl) who's seeking peace and spiritual contentment in Prem Ashram and the leader of its cult, a New Age guru known as Mahayogi. Besides spouting psychobabble he clearly doesn't believe in, Mahayogi seems to encourage free love, drugs and superstition. In the song 'Pyar kar pyar kar', Rishi tries to call out the bullshit in Prem Ashram's philosophy and we see censor-approved depictions of substance abuse (smoking cigarettes) and promiscuity (two disciples kissing) among the followers, ostensibly to draw parallels with the Rajneesh ashram.

But Raj goes many steps further, and *Do Premee* ends up being one of his weirdest and (unintentionally) funniest films. Ever so often, a wall in Mahayogi's chamber slides open and he transforms into The Dragon, an evil mastermind who smuggles diamonds concealed in the prayer beads of ashramites. And who plays Mahayogi, aka The Dragon? It's Colonel Raj Kapoor (no relation of his namesake), an illustrious actor–director–writer who is credited for introducing Shah Rukh Khan in *Fauji*. But around this time, Col Kapoor, a decorated Indian Army veteran, was known by another name, with which he was 'introduced' in *Do Premee*: Raj Bharti. You see, he was an ardent disciple of Osho Rajneesh and that was the name he had been christened with at the ashram (he was close to another disciple called Vinod Bharti, whom the world knew as Vinod Khanna). Bharti studied in Khalsa College, Matunga. He was fascinated by the movies and often prowled Hollywood Street, aka Punjabi Galli, at Matunga, once home to Prithviraj Kapoor, K.L. Saigal, Jagdish Sethi and many others. Raj Khosla, of course, was in the same neighbourhood, and they would have struck up a friendship at some point. They remained friends and when Col Kapoor returned from his stint in the armed forces and sought work in films, the two began collaborating on various projects.

Bharti was credited alongside G.R. Kamat and Suraj Sanim for the screenplay of *Main Tulsi Tere Aangan Ki*, and as the only screenwriter for *Do Premee*.

Raj Khosla gives in to his goofy side in *Do Premee*. His love for Easter eggs and in-jokes was evident from the days of *Solva Saal* and *Anita*. In *Do Premee*, when Geeta Behl is asked where she lives, she says '42, Pali Hill', which is the official address for Navketan Films. When Moushumi is engaged to someone else and all seems lost, Rishi sits and listens to K.L. Saigal's 'Karoon kya aas niraas bhayi' from *Dushman* (1939). Mahayogi/Dharam has two minions who are referred to as 'Dharam' and 'Karam'. In the climactic fight sequence, I.S. Johar prays to Lord Hanuman and is given super-strength as a blessing. Mahayogi places his prisoners in a glass enclosure and 'tortures' them with red and blue laser beams. The Dragon's lair brims with gadgets and blinking lights, ubiquitous in 1960s spy movies.

Raj also had his daughters as part of the cast during a party scene. His girls were fascinated by the movies and while he was against them pursuing an acting career with any seriousness, he relented this once for them to show their face in a crowd. He also encouraged them to bring their friends along. So, Uma, Anita, a cousin of theirs and her friends were present in the scene. They are the first ones to walk into the party and Om Prakash is seen welcoming the girls. 'You girls are so natural!' Anita Khosla recalls her father telling her after the shot.

Do Premee can be fun in parts, and it could have well gained some cult following or at least featured in 'so bad it's good' lists if it had some redeeming qualities. It doesn't. Even the music doesn't allow much fodder for conversation. 'Mausam pe jawani hai' and 'Payalia chhanki ke na' are decent tracks, 'Pyar kar pyar kar' resonates more for the storytelling and the visuals than the song itself, and one could argue that 'Allah meri payal bole chhan chhan' is a fairly underrated song, but that's about it. When it was released, the film sank without a trace. The downward spiral had begun for Raj Khosla, and there was no looking back.

The advent of the new decade didn't augur well for him. The 1980s would prove to be a traumatic, disappointing era for Raj and his brand of filmmaking. Video piracy had reared its ugly head, the middle class had stopped thronging theatres and every filmmaker worth their salt had started catering to the only audience that did visit the theatres – the working class. Every single film was a replica of the other, and revenge and love seemed to be the only two themes worth exploring.

On the personal front, Raj faced another debilitating tragedy in 1980: the loss of his father. Atmaram was the light of his life. His worldview – which informed much of his work – was shaped by his father. They spent hours on the chess board, and Atmaram took an active interest in his films. He interacted with the actors, spent time with the crew members and spread general cheer all around. He was the universal 'Babu ji' to everyone. For Raj, it was a tragedy he never quite recovered from.

20

And Then There Were Six

As a filmmaker, Raj Khosla was the least confident from around the 1980s and, in all probability, losing interest in the craft. His work wasn't seeing the kind of success he was so used to. He had on various occasions told his assistants that he loved films but detested the film industry. Mahesh Bhatt recalls an instance after the failure of *Chirag* when Raj asked him to summon his car as he was leaving the studio. He usually boarded his car from the main door of Mehboob Studios near Stage No. 1, but that day Chetan Anand's film was being shot and the place was packed with people. Raj refused to exit from there. 'Are you out of your mind? I've made a flop!' he told Bhatt. 'You want me to pass through all those people, after delivering a flop?' He insisted on being picked up at the other door.

Well, he was only going to make flops for a good while. But right around this time, he also worked on one of the biggest hits of the early 1980s, though it had little impact on his own career.

Decades before the N-word (nepotism, for the uninitiated) made its foray into Bollywood, there was a lot of excitement around the film debut of star kids. Audiences were eager to see how the progeny of their favourite stars would fare on the screen. In the early 1980s, a bevy of stars were launching their children. Raj Khosla was associated with the launches of at least two of them. When Sunil Dutt was pulling out all the stops to ensure a grand debut for his son, Sanjay, the Dutt family was faced with its first great crisis: Nargis Dutt's cancer, which took them to the Sloan Kittering Hospital in New York for treatment. The shooting of Sanjay Dutt's debut film, *Rocky* (1981), which was being directed by Sunil Dutt, was halted. When Sunil realized that it was going to be a while before they could think of returning, he made some tough decisions. *Rocky* couldn't be postponed any further, and Nargis herself was eager to see her son join the family trade. Sunil called up the same old friend he had summoned when his banner Ajanta Arts was facing a crisis: Raj Khosla. He called up Raj from New York and explained his vision with as much detail and precision as possible. Raj Khosla had to complete the film that Sunil Dutt had begun. And in this, no compromise was possible.

Raj was known to defer work in his own films, take ages to conclude a script, cancel shoots, and keep reshooting and changing things. But with friends, especially ones as close as Sunil Dutt, there was no question of being lax or indulgent. The thorough professional that he was, and knowing full well that he could not possibly be credited for the film, Raj did his job. He directed a section of the film and made sure that it integrated into the rest so well that it is near-impossible to distinguish those specific parts. He got to work with some of his regular partners in crime: assistant Faruk Kaiser, dialogue-writer Rahi Masoom Reza and editor Waman Bhonsle. *Rocky* didn't exactly make Sanjay Dutt an overnight sensation. But he was definitely in the reckoning because the debut did so well. 'It was a big thing both for Raj ji to accept that kind of responsibility and for my father to give it to him,' Sanjay Dutt later said in an interview.[1]

Something happened during this period that was quite uncharacteristic of Raj and his approach to filmmaking. He liked to take his time with his films and preferred focusing on one project at a time. It wasn't unusual for him to take two or more years to work on a single project. This would grant him breathing space and allow him to work at the leisurely pace that he so enjoyed. The industry knew and appreciated this because it, after all, gave birth to films such as *Woh Kaun Thi?*, *Do Raaste* and *Mera Gaon Mera Desh*. But in the 1970s, Raj Khosla somehow ended up lending his name to four films at one go: *Do Premee* was conceived as *Balyogi* in the mid-1970s; he launched a film called *Sangeet Sajani* (which later became *Daasi*) in 1976; *Meraa Dost Meraa Dushman* went on the floor in 1978; and in 1979, Shatrughan Sinha's manager Pawan Kumar approached Raj to direct a film starring Sinha, called *Maati Maangey Khoon*. All these films spilled over to the next decade. While *Do Premee* came out in 1980, *Daasi* was released in 1981, *Maati Maangey Khoon* was in the making for years and finally saw the light of day in 1984, the same year that *Meraa Dost Meraa Dushman* was released. Needless to add, all these films fell flat, one after the other. Here's a look at each one of them.

***Daasi/ Sangeet Sajani* (1981)**

For *Sangeet Sajani*, Raj Khosla was once again adapting a book. This time, it was a Hindi novel called *Mangala* by Anant Gopal Shevde. While doing a profile of Raj, journalist Mobin Ansari wrote about the book in April 1976: 'A blind man refuses to succumb to the forces of darkness around him and creates his own bright world of love and success. This novel has been hailed as the "Geeta of the Blind" which has become a source of inspiration and hope for many a blind reader.'[2]

Mangala, published in 1958, was possibly the first Indian novel to also be published in the Braille script. In it, a girl called Mangala is married off to a blind man because of an astrologer's prediction that any healthy man she marries won't survive. Mangala detests this arrangement and finds a way to avenge the humiliation when she sets her eyes on her husband's best friend. She begins a torrid affair with him and runs away. Eventually, she realizes how unfair she has been to her husband and returns.

The element of Mangala's extramarital meanderings in the source material was toned down for the film. As opposed to the book, where she has an affair with the husband's best friend, in the film, the friend (Rakesh Roshan) happens to be an ex-lover who had turned her down initially and is now trying to force an entry into her life. The husband's alcoholism, his relationship with the 'other woman' character (Rekha) could well be another attempt by the director at introducing autobiographical aspects.

Moushumi was cast as the heroine and both she and Raj were convinced that they had a winner on their hands. She had an author-backed role and did justice to it. Sanjeev Kumar was cast as the blind protagonist. There is a very interesting story behind how he was cast for the role:

> Once, when Sanjeev Kumar was returning from Madras by the afternoon flight, he met Amitabh Bachchan, Zeenat Aman and Yash Johar at Bombay airport with camera, lights and equipment, all ready for shooting. When Sanjeev inquired about the delay, Yash Johar replied, 'We are waiting for Raj Khosla.' Sanjeev Kumar, who was notorious for his lack of punctuality, proceeded to plead with Amitabh. 'Please get me a director like

> him.' When Raj Khosla heard it, he promptly cast Sanjeev Kumar in his next film.[3]

One would imagine that the teaming up of Raj Khosla and an actor like Sanjeev Kumar would translate to sheer magic on screen. But the film, which went on to be called *Daasi*, was burdened by too many alterations to the script, star rivalries, cast modifications and an unsure Raj Khosla. Rekha, the 'other woman', was a last-minute addition to the film, possibly to bolster commercial prospects. She remains the prominent face on the poster. Again, the combination of Rekha and Raj sounds brilliant on paper. Sparks should have flown, but no such luck – though the way she was projected in the film might remind one of Raj Khosla's highlighting the beauty of a Madhubala or a Sadhana.

For the first time, Raj worked with two different music directors – Rajesh Roshan and Ravindra Jain. The Kishore–Lata duet in the film, 'Premi sabhi hote hain deewane', composed by Rajesh Roshan, remains popular even after four decades. Asha Bhosle's 'Purani chilmane utha' is one of the few unforgettable ghazals in the film that were completely overlooked. Raj Khosla's handling of the song, his use of props – a harmonium, a sitar, a glass of whiskey – and how the camera comes alive makes it difficult to believe that he was past his prime. The film had other ghazals, such as the evocative 'Piya bin jiya nahi laage', voiced by Bhupinder Singh.

The soundtrack of *Daasi* (1981).

Teri Maang Sitaron Se Bhar Doon/ Shrimati Ji (1982)

Raj Khosla was a big fan of Frank Capra, who had adapted the same short story on two different occasions. Damon Runyon's short story 'Madame La Gimp' was the basis for both his 1933 film *Lady for a Day* and his 1961 outing *Pocketful of Miracles* (in turn, *Pocketful of Miracles* was remade by Jackie Chan as *Miracles* [1989], which became the 'inspiration' for Anees Bazmee's *Singh is Kinng* [2008]).

This story was picked up for the next production of Raj Khosla Films. G.R. Kamat and Jyotin Goel (veteran director Devendra Goel's son) worked on an adaptation initially called *Shrimati Ji*. It is the story of a mother who, despite her limited means, tries to keep up the impression of being wealthy for her daughter's sake. With Nutan in the title role, there was a hope to replicate the magic of *Main Tulsi Tere Aangan Ki*. The final title, *Teri Maang Sitaron Se Bhar Doon*, also seemed to draw a parallel.

The film, the very first production of Raj Khosla Films after the demise of Raj's father, was dedicated to Atmaram. Padmini Kolhapure was cast as the daughter and Raj Kiran played her young suitor. It was one of Padmini's earliest films and she delivered a spirited act. The choice of Raj Kiran as the hero was interesting. A fairly new entrant to the industry, Raj Kiran had only been in moderate successes such as *Patita* (1953) and *Manokaamnaa* (1981), besides cameos in Subhash Ghai's *Karz* (1980) and Raaj Kumar-starrer *Bulundi* (1981). In *Teri Maang*, he turned on his charm like never before.

While Raj Khosla's filmmaking had seen better days, *Teri Maang Sitaron Se Bhar Doon* is not a bad product. One may even call it a tad underrated. Raj Khosla's impeccable song picturization skills come into play in 'Aap ka aashiq hoon main'. He pushes his fascination with windows and mirrors to the limit in how he mounts the song. Our hero places mirrors strategically on each roof and wall leading to his beloved's window, opposite which she has her own vanity mirror. So, when Raj Kiran sings to her from his own terrace far away, she can look at him right in her room. Laxmikant–Pyarelal were back on the saddle as composers and recruited Young Turks Suresh Wadkar and Amit Kumar to sing for Raj Kiran. Wadkar got two songs, 'Aap ka aashiq hoon main' and 'Lo mera naam', while Amit Kumar got the boisterous 'Pehli nazar mein ho gaya hai pyaar', employing youthful buzzwords of the day such as 'what yaar' and 'yes yaar' in a Bollywood song. Another young singer called Alka Yagnik got to be the voice of Padmini Kolhapure.

The soundtrack of *Teri Maang Sitaron Se Bhar Doon* (1982).

Raj extricated earnest performances from Nutan and Amjad Khan. There are some great moments, and the melee during the climax could have been an entertaining farce. But it just doesn't come together. The film didn't set the cash registers ringing, but it recovered the investment by Raj Khosla Films.

Maati Maangey Khoon (1984)

Pawan Kumar, who was manager to both Shatrughan Sinha and Amitabh Bachchan, had turned producer with Hrishikesh Mukherjee's *Abhimaan* (1973). He followed it up with three films starring Shatrughan Sinha – *Khaan Dost* (1976), *Kotwal Saab* (1977) and *Vishwanath* (1978). After the great success of *Vishwanath*, Kumar was looking for a suitable subject for yet another film with Sinha when he happened to watch *Main Tulsi Tere Aangan Ki*. 'I loved the film. Here was Raj Khosla managing to balance commercial success with critical acclaim. It was an act almost impossible to achieve. Of course, I had worked with Hrishi da before. He only made a certain kind of film and couldn't be bothered with the box office. But with *Main Tulsi Tere Aangan Ki*, Khosla had made a good film which was also a superhit,' Pawan Kumar said.[4] This is what drew him to try and collaborate with Raj Khosla.

It was 1979 when Pawan Kumar approached Raj with the idea of directing *Maati Maangey Khoon*. The film was being produced by Kumar and Lakhan Sinha, Shatrughan's brother. Besides Shatrughan Sinha, Reena Roy and Rekha were part of the cast. Kumar went to meet Raj Khosla at Mehboob Studios, where he found him playing chess with Atmaram. When Raj introduced the two and told his father that he would be signing a film with Pawan Kumar, Atmaram smiled and said, '*Woh toh theek hai*, *lekin* picture complete *kar dena*. That's alright, just complete the picture.' They all had a good laugh over it then, but these words proved prophetic. When a location near Chena Creek in Ghodbunder was chosen for the film, Raj took ages to visit the site. It was months before the shoot actually began.

After shooting for about a year and a half, Raj decided that the story wasn't working. All outdoor footage and work were scrapped. A new writer was brought on board, changes were made and shooting started afresh with the new script. Once the shoot was concluded, the edit process took a little less than a year. 'By this stage, Raj ji had just lost interest in his work. He had been making films for 30 years!' said Pawan Kumar.[5] Raj had always liked to work at a leisurely pace and looked for ways to procrastinate. But at this point in time, this tendency intensified further. He would try to find any and every excuse to defer work.

Johnny Bakshi mentioned an instance of this in his tribute:

> Before leaving for a big outdoor schedule, Raj ji would call the direction and production department to his house to finalise the requirements and details. We were called at 11 a.m. When we reached there, we were informed that saheb was having his massage and will join us soon. Meanwhile, we were served lassi. By the time he emerged from his bedroom at 12:30, we had

> consumed three to four glasses. When he joined us, he would talk about everything but work and about 1:15 pm he would suggest, 'Let us have lunch before we start work. So there will be no break later, plus we cannot work on empty stomachs.' At 2 pm, lunch would be ordered and finished by 3 pm. His next trick, 'Boy, I will have forty winks and then start – totally fresh.' And he would go back to the bedroom. We would leave without any work. The moral of the story was: Raj Khosla cannot work because he has not eaten, Raj Khosla cannot work because he has eaten.[6]

But despite how long *Maati Maangey Khoon* was in production, Pawan Kumar does not find any malice on Raj Khosla's part: 'It was not as if he had any ill feeling. He meant well. It's just that it had now become his nature [to try to avoid or to defer work].'[7] But when he did choose to focus, Raj Khosla could still slip into his element. *Maati Maangey Khoon* had some brilliant music. Raj had worked with Pancham on five films (including his production *Do Chor*), two more than his father S.D. Burman. Among these, *Do Chor*, *Sunny* and *Maati Maangey Khoon* (arguably) have the best songs. But while the other two have many popular songs, *Maati Maangey Khoon* features a few underrated gems.

Possibly the most popular song of the soundtrack is 'Ye dil, ye paagal dil mera', also known as 'Awargi'. As always, Raj was a dominant force in shaping the soundtrack. While the composers for his films did their jobs according to their talent and capabilities, Raj Khosla always had the last word. He was present during recordings, and often interacted with the singers, as confirmed by Lata Mangeshkar and Asha

The soundtrack of *Maati Maangey Khoon* (1984).

Bhosle during their interviews for this book. He happened to have listened to Ghulam Ali's 'Awargi' in the early 1980s. The original tune was composed by Ghulam Ali himself, and the lyrics were by Mohsin Naqvi. Raj insisted that Pancham include the song in the film's soundtrack. Ghulam Ali had been trying to get a visa to India for a while.[8] Even the famous 'Chupke chupke raat din' in *Nikaah* (1982) could not be recorded for the film. An earlier recorded version was used.

When Ghulam Ali finally got the visa in 1983, a dinner was organized at the house of Reena Roy, the heroine of the film. Producer Pawan Kumar recalled how Raj, in his inimitable style, asked Ghulam Ali to record the song for his film. He said to Ghulam Ali, a fellow Punjabi, 'Maharaj, *tussi te samundar ho. Ek boond humein bhi de do.* Maharaj, you are the very ocean. Do spare a drop or two for us.'

R.D. Burman recorded the song afresh in Mumbai. About Ghulam Ali's experience of recording the song, Aniruddha Bhattacharjee and Balaji Vittal write:

> Ghulam Ali, used to singing with a harmonium, sarangi and a tabla, was initially uneasy in front of the mike. Pancham said, 'Ghulam Ali is a terrific singer, but when Raj Khosla insisted that we record a song of his with our orchestra, we knew it would be difficult, and it was. Though his percussionist was good, performing in front of an orchestra with a mike was difficult for him.'[9]

'Awargi' became a sort of theme song for the film. It keeps recurring throughout the film, accentuating the hero's loneliness and highlighting his relentless struggle.

Maati Maangey Khoon features as many as four exquisite *mujras*, impeccably performed for the screen by Rekha. Three of them are by Lata Mangeshkar, while the absolutely fabulous

'Mere ghungroo mujhe de do' is by Asha Bhosle. 'Lo sahib phir bhool gayi main' has an old soul, which comes across in the tune as well as the lyrics. It also arrives at a crucial moment in the film. 'Sang sang ye saari duniya' is a devotional song in the *jogan* template,[10] which Khosla had earlier employed in *Anita*. Filmmaker Dharmesh Darshan says:

> He understood the *jogan* like nobody else. I believe he was influenced by the famous Kidar Sharma film *Jogan* (1950) of Dilip Kumar and Nargis. In many of his films, Raj ji had that *jogan* touch in his songs. Like the song in *Anita*, 'Main dekhoon jis or sakhi ri/ Samne mere saanwariya', where he deliberately adds that bit with her wearing the *bhagwa*. Even in 'Sona lai jaa re' from *Mera Gaon Mera Desh*, there are moments like that. Dharam ji becomes a *jogi* and Asha Parekh does the *jogi* movement. Which is not required in a dacoit drama, but he added it any way.

Every song in *Maati Maangey Khoon*, especially the *mujras*, have mini narrative arcs of their own. Despite so many alterations in the script and being a work in progress for so long, the film isn't incoherent. Shatrughan and Rekha's chemistry is one of its highlights. The other thing that works is the drive of the central character to reclaim his land, whatever the cost. But as luck would have it, *Maati Maangey Khoon*, like all Raj Khosla directorials at the time, was washed out at the box office.

Ever since Parveen Babi appeared on the cover of *Time* magazine in 1976 ('Asia's frenetic film scene' the cover screamed), there was a surge of curiosity in the West about Bollywood. Western TV networks began visiting the studios in Bombay, interviewing actors, filmmakers and crew. The film industry was only too glad to allow Westerners into their sets.

Dr Shan Chandrasekar, a broadcaster and the founder of ATN TV Canada, visited the sets of *Maati Maangey Khoon* with his crew and filmed the shooting. The footage is available on YouTube today. 'We are delighted to be at the sets of one of the finest motion pictures under production,' Dr Chandrasekar announces on camera, 'namely *Maati Maangey Khoon*, produced by two of our favourite friends – pioneer producers Mr Pawan Kumar, very well known in the community, as well as Dr Lakhan Sinha from the United States. This is being directed by one of the outstanding motion picture directors of India, none other than Mr Raj Khosla himself.'[11] Rekha, Sudhir and Shatrughan Sinha flank Chandrasekar in the frame. They are in costume, and it is obvious that the song 'Chhup ja chand' is being shot. As soon as he says 'none other than Raj Khosla', everyone starts clapping, the loudest of all Rekha herself, looking at Raj off screen.

Meraa Dost Meraa Dushman (1984)

The other film of Raj Khosla visited by a television crew was *Meraa Dost Meraa Dushman*. In the French documentary *Welcome to Bollywood* (1978), we see footage of the film being shot. Sanjeev Kumar, Mukri and Parveen Babi are in the frame and Raj Khosla is directing. We see Parveen requesting a rehearsal, Raj nodding and then instructing Mukri. Shortly after, he gives an interview to the film crew where he dissects the star system in Hindi cinema and its impact on production schedules. He says, 'We have a peculiar problem here where we can't work with a star at one go. We work in instalments. The stars work in as many as 15 or 16 films at a time. They divide their time in grades, according to their ability. So, normally a film which would take 80 shooting days to finish, will only be completed after several years. Star system, to that extent, is harming the film. Because we can't make a film at one go and the work suffers from a lack of continuity.' Ironically, *Meraa Dost Meraa Dushman* was completed and released in 1984, a full five years after Raj Khosla said those things.

Johnny Bakshi had produced two films with Mahesh Bhatt as director, both of which had flopped. To stay afloat, he needed an established filmmaker to helm his next project. He and Raj had history. The ever-accessible Raj Khosla instantly agreed to do his film – and if his team is to be believed, he did it for free.[12]

For the first time, a film of Raj's was billed in the credits as 'Raj Khosla's *Meraa Dost Meraa Dushman*'.[13] It was also an opportunity for him to indulge once more in one of his favoured genres: the dacoit film. Both in its title and content, the film has several parallels with *Mera Gaon Mera Desh.* Right before the climax, Shatrughan Sinha inspires the villagers to take up arms against the dacoits, just as Dharmendra's character had done in the 1971 film. Raj's favourite shooting destination formed a backdrop once more. The villagers of Cheerwa, Udaipur, were only too glad to welcome Raj Khosla and his team in their midst (*Maati Maangey Khoon* was also partially shot in Udaipur).

One of the striking aspects of Raj Khosla's way of working was how important his team was for him. It wasn't just about being comfortable working with a certain set of people. It was about relationships. Film after film, he worked with not only the same director of photography (Pratap Sinha), editor (Waman Bhonsle), choreographer (Manohar Naidu), screenwriter (G.R. Kamat) and dialogue writer (Rahi Masoom Reza), but also a set of actors who were integral to his cinema – K.N. Singh, Bhagwan Dada, Dhumal, Birbal, C.S. Dubey, Nawab, Trilok Kapoor and Col Raj Kapoor, aka Raj Bharti. Both Trilok Kapoor and Col Raj Kapoor were present in *Meraa Dost Meraa Dushman.* Col Kapoor played the bad guy yet again, a bandit called Bahadur Singh. It's an age-old story of friends turned foes, as the title promises.

The two leads were played by Shatrughan Sinha and Danny Denzongpa. This was the first and only film Denzongpa ever did with Raj Khosla. Sanjeev Kumar had an interesting and quirky role. He is an ex-serviceman who, it is hinted, ran away from the battlefield (he was shot in the back, hence the moniker 'Goli Chacha') and is hiding in the village. He demands respect from the villagers, who know he's a coward and mock him openly for it. But they also feed him and look after him. There is a moment of reckoning where he holds a gun and all hell breaks loose. Sanjeev Kumar plays this timid but angry soldier rather well.

The soundtrack of *Meraa Dost Meraa Dushman* (1984).

Johnny Walker played one of the dacoits. Geeta Behl also played a cameo as one of the girls Danny's character takes for a ride. Behl, the daughter of producer Sham Behl, was introduced in *Main Tulsi Tere Aangan Ki* as Deb Mukherjee's love interest. She had also played a pivotal role in *Do Premee*.

The original cast of *Meraa Dost Meraa Dushman* also included Parveen Babi, a friend of Bakshi's. Parveen was fighting her own battles, grappling with a serious mental condition. She experienced a major meltdown because of which she was sent overseas for treatment. Of all the films that were left incomplete because of her exit, *Meraa Dost Meraa Dushman* was one. Bakshi then roped in another friend of his to replace her: Smita Patil.

1984 turned out to be the year in which Raj Khosla had the most releases ever – *Maati Maangey Khoon*, *Meraa Dost Meraa Dushman* and *Sunny*. Their proximity could also be credited for their fate.

But *Sunny* was in a different league. It may have been Raj's last great film. It was also his last multi-starrer and his last success.

Sunny (1984)

After *Main Tulsi Tere Aangan Ki*, *Sunny* was another film in which Raj drew extensively from his life and relationships. *Sunny* represented the revival of a relationship that went back almost three decades. Waheeda Rehman and Raj Khosla had parted ways after they worked together on *Solva Saal*. With *Guide*, they had had the chance to work together again but her experience in *C.I.D.* and *Solva Saal* had left a bad aftertaste, and Waheeda refused to have anything to do with him. Because of this, Raj lost the opportunity to direct *Guide*, which then went to Vijay Anand.

Many years later, when *Sunny* was offered to Waheeda, it was too good a role to pass up. Also, her husband Shashi Rekhi advised her to let the grievance go.[14] It had been so long, he said, and people change. Besides, what's the point in harbouring old grudges? Amarjeet, the producer of the film, also helped convince her. Waheeda told Nasreen Munni Kabir later, 'Raj Khosla was a very good director. He filmed songs very well. We had our arguments, but he was a very nice person to spend time with… In later years, when we both became more mature, we put all our differences behind us.'[15]

According to Raj's assistant Inder Khosla, *Sunny* was supposed to be Sunny Deol and Amrita Singh's debut. Because of the delays in the film, Deol's *Betaab* (1983) was completed and released first. Amarjeet had earlier produced *Rocky*, Sanjay Dutt's debut vehicle, which was partly directed by Raj Khosla. So, when Dharmendra's son Sunny Deol had to be launched, Raj Khosla seemed like the obvious choice. The screenplay was written by Bobby Tapia, Amarjeet's brother.

Despite its title, *Sunny* is the story of two women who spar over one man and then, eventually, his son, Sunny. It was an apt title for a Deol launch. It was Raj who insisted that Dharam play Sunny's father in the film. Dharmendra was still doing lead roles in films, and it would have been odd for him to play the father of a grown son. So, they never shared screen space and Dharam's character was killed off in the first half, but he did play his son's father.

Much like Vijay Anand's character in *Main Tulsi Tere Aangan Ki*, Dharmendra's Inderjeet in *Sunny* leads a double life. On the one hand, he is the legally wedded husband of Gayatri (Waheeda Rehman). But he is also in a relationship with Sitara (Sharmila Tagore). Alcohol is his constant companion. Gayatri learns of the other woman in her husband's life and seethes with rage. Inderjeet loses his life in an air mishap. The childless Gayatri lures a pregnant Sitara to her home and convinces her that it is a safe space for her to deliver the baby. But once the child is born, Gayatri hides him and tells Sitara that her son was stillborn. A distraught Sitara leaves the house and Gayatri raises Inderjeet and Sitara's son, Sunny (Sunny Deol), as her own. As fate would have it, he meets and falls in love with Sitara's niece, a girl she's adopted. The two women meet again, this time rivals for the affection of a son.

For the first time since her debut in *C.I.D.*, where she was supposedly playing a femme fatale, Waheeda played a role with shades of grey. To avenge losing her husband to Sitara, Gayatri steals the other woman's son. And now that she has raised this boy, she will go to the ends of the Earth to keep him for herself. About shooting *Sunny*, Waheeda told me, 'As a director, he was still very good. But he used to get tired pretty soon. He used to say, "Pack up *kar lo*." When we pointed out that the scene wasn't over yet, he told us, "*Nahi yaar*, *bahut ho gaya*. I am fed up," and used to walk out. Maybe he was unwell.'

Sharmila Tagore has fond memories of *Sunny* for several reasons. She had idolized Waheeda Rehman for years, and was glad to get another opportunity to share screen space with her. I say 'another' because just two years before this, she had played Waheeda's daughter in Gulzar's *Namkeen* (1982). And now they were supposed to be rivals fighting over men. She remembered:

> Waheeda ji, Nutan and Meena Kumari ji were my role models. Meena ji I had met a couple of times. She used to visit the sets of *Mere Humdum Mere Dost*. I used to just gaze at her – her *ada*, her *nazakat*… Nutan, of course, I've worked with much later. She used to sing so well. But of the three, I always had a special place for Waheeda ji, which can't be explained in words. It was a fan moment when I got to work with her. It was not because of her acting. It was just because of the way she was.

Tagore also recalls Sanjeev Kumar and her ganging up to bug Waheeda about Guru Dutt on the sets of *Namkeen*. They playfully teased her, saying, 'something must have happened', even as Waheeda kept insisting otherwise.

The actress recounted fond memories of how Raj had directed her, especially during one of her confrontation scenes with Waheeda:

> He was very perceptive. During a scene with Waheeda ji, Raj ji said that your eyebrows look a little different. There's usually a gap [between them], he said, but in this scene they look thicker than usual. So, he said, I should go back and fix them. He would catch these little things, and he was a very sensitive director, really old school. If you wanted a little time, he would give you that time. He was not in a hurry. So you didn't just say your lines – you react and feel and then say your lines.

> This gave me space for expressing the emotion, you know, and I think that helped the film too.

Raj could elevate a predictable plot, Tagore added. 'He created moments – moments between Waheeda and I, moments between Dharam and I, between the kids and I… These built on the emotional strength of the film.'

Portions of the film – especially those in Sitara's house – were shot in Sadhana's apartment at Santa Cruz. Sadhana and Raj Khosla had continued to be friends, and when she was told his team was looking for a bungalow to shoot their film in, she agreed happily. The rest of the film, including Gayatri and Inderjeet's mansion and other scenes, was all shot in Mehboob Studios.

Tagore recalls a hilarious moment from the shoot. She was supposed to slap Sunny Deol in one scene. But just two days before shooting for it, she chipped one of her front teeth. There was no time to do it up properly because she was busy all day every day. Working with this limitation, her dentist patched her up with a glue shot. All she had to do was eat and chew carefully for a few days. And then, while shooting the climax of the film with Sunny Deol and emoting, the chip broke, flew out and lodged itself on Sunny's face. Regardless of the mishap, they completed the shot and then cracked up.

Sunny was a glorious moment in the history of the Raj Khosla–R.D. Burman partnership. Despite the boundless talent the two possessed, their collaborations till then had been rather underwhelming, barring a few exceptions. While both created timeless music with other people, somehow their work with each other was devoid of that quality. *Sunny* was a happy exception. One can almost see a whole different side to Anand Bakshi in his work with Pancham, and *Sunny* is a prime example.

The soundtrack of *Sunny* (1984).

Sharmila Tagore was made to listen to some of the songs, which were recorded before the shoot began, and she loved them. The music was also one of the reasons that she agreed to do the film. The one song in the album that could easily find itself among the very best songs from Raj Khosla's pantheon is 'Jaane kya baat hai', a soulful rendering by Lata Mangeshkar that still tugs at the heartstrings. The tune was originally composed by R.D. Burman for a Bengali non-film album released during Durga Puja in 1982, and went '*Chokhe naame brishti/ Buke othe jhor je*' (the lyrics were by Gauriprasanna Majumdar). This version was sung by Asha Bhosle.

The two renderings are nearly identical. Lata sang the song with her signature pathos, and her version has the advantage of instantly conjuring up the visuals. 'Jaane kya baat hai' is one of those Raj Khosla songs that tells a whole, rounded-off story, even though you don't have context about the characters or the rest of the film. Sunny steps out of the club after a game of squash and stops in his tracks as he sees a girl (Amrita Singh) singing on TV in the lobby. We have earlier seen Sunny's birth-mother Sitara (Sharmila) hum the same tune. He asks the guy at the desk, 'Who is she?', pointing at Amrita, but doesn't get an answer.

Intercut to the studio where the song is being recorded. We see musicians, and the camera crew filming her. Meanwhile, Sunny hops into a cab and heads out for the studio. The cab zips through the highway and the song continues. In the next shot, we find him now staring at her from the other side of a glass window.

The backdrop for the song was, in reality, the reception of Mehboob Studios. Raj had found a permanent home in Mehboob ever since the studio was founded in the 1950s and it continued to be his base of operations, much after he had left his office, now taken over by Johnny Bakshi. The reception from *Sunny* had been seen some 26 years ago in *Solva Saal*. Back then, there was no glass window. It had the 1950s-style wood panelling, with ancient intercoms lining the wall.

In 2007, 23 years after *Sunny*, Asha Bhosle re-recorded 'Jaane kya baat hai' as part of an album called *Asha Reveals the Real RD*. Her rendition, which strangely doesn't feature on music streaming platforms, was performed in a more leisurely fashion, and sounds more sombre and morose than the original.

The other well-regarded song from *Sunny* is the ghazal 'Aur kya ahd-e-wafa hote hain', which exists in two versions. One was picturized on Sharmila Tagore and sung by Lata Mangeshkar. The other one was filmed with Sunny Deol, with Suresh Wadkar voicing him. As Sunny starts singing, Sitara looks at him in astonishment, recalling the song shared in a private moment so many years ago. As he sings on, Sitara looks at him closely, and then it dawns on her. He is her son, a spitting image of his father. All of this unfolds during the song sequence, without even a single line of dialogue being uttered. In Manmohan Desai and Prakash Mehra universes, it's usually a locket, a mole or heirloom that connects estranged family members. In *Sunny*, Raj Khosla had the song. It also clears up just why Raj Khosla had insisted that Dharmendra play father to his son in the film.

While speaking about Raj, Suresh Wadkar, who also sang for *Sunny*, told me:

> Raj ji was present in every sitting and every recording, and used to share his *daad* [praise] on every line. It was a pleasure to sing for him – you wanted to give it everything you had, because he encouraged you. And he understood music, so you couldn't cheat him. But for the recording of 'Aur kya ahd-e-wafa', he couldn't be present because the song was recorded in Madras [now Chennai]. Pancham was recording the background

music for one of his films there. So we got a call from him saying that this song would be recorded there.

But another song, 'Meri yaad aayegi aati rahegi', was done in Mehboob Studios with Suresh Wadkar and Lata Mangeshkar. And Raj was there throughout, Wadkar recalled. 'Most other filmmakers would step out for a smoke or a walk during rehearsals,' Wadkar said, 'but not him. During rehearsals, Lata ji would stand at the door of the singers' booth at Mehboob. Just beside that, there was a big glass pane, against which stood Raj Khosla. We did at least two to four rehearsals, and he listened to each one intently. After the performance, he came to me and gave me a huge *jhappi* [hug]. It was awesome.'

'Meri yaad aayegi aati rahegi' is a sweet romantic duet, tailor-made to fit a young couple in their twenties. Raj Khosla had recently bought a penthouse on Carter Road. It had a gorgeous balcony and a garden that he loved tending to. Lovebirds Sunny Deol and Amrita Singh were filmed in the balcony of that penthouse, serenading each other.

Sunny had two other tracks: the zestful 'Teri yaad tera naam' and 'Hum aashiq hain mit jaayenge'. The latter was one of the *peti* songs, with a street singer playing a harmonium strapped to his shoulder, colloquially known as a '*peti*', and a dancer accompanying him. Raj had a similar set-up in *Kala Pani* where Dev Anand and Madhubala masquerade as performers trying to get into the head of the villain. But in *Sunny*, the setting is less sinister. Sunny hears the singers playing while swimming, and gets his man Friday (Birbal) to call them in. They prance around the edge of the pool, singing their ballad of love and rebellion as Sunny joins in, trunks and all.

According to Raj Behl, *Sunny* did above-average business. In fact, he recalls, 'We used to go to Gaiety-Galaxy [movie theatre in Bandra] to gauge the reaction [of audiences]. It used to be full, and people used to clap and cry. We threw a success party at Sea Rock on the completion of 50 days.' The *mahurat* of the film was also held at Sea Rock.

So, while it wasn't as big a blockbuster as *Dostana*, *Sunny* remains Raj Khosla's last win at the box office with a great, memorable soundtrack. It was now time for his swansong.

21

The End

One of the traits Raj had imbibed from his Guru was to keep his team happy. This was a constant till the end of his days, even when things had slowed down. His secretary Ved Prakash related an anecdote from Atmaram Khosla's last days. Ved Prakash, who was his new secretary, was supposed to get salary cheques signed by Raj. It was probably unusual for a production company in the 1970s and 1980s, but the employees at Raj Khosla Films were paid on the last day of the month.[1] This happened even when there was no work and no films under production. But in this particular instance, the most important man in their boss's life was on his deathbed. They were all in the hospital. Raj Khosla was distraught. Nothing made sense.

After some time, Raj himself asked Prakash about the salary payout. It was the second day of the month already. Prakash replied that he had arranged the payment for all staff members who belonged to the middle class. It was just the senior employees who would get their salaries a few days late. 'Raj ji said to me, "Mr Ved Prakash, when a man returns home on the first of the month, his wife waits for him to hand over the salary. You've committed a blunder. What I'm facing is my own personal problem. Why should they suffer? This is your first lapse. Please be mindful in the future." And he took all the cheques and signed them,' Ved Prakash told me.

Another story narrated by Johnny Bakshi exemplifies Raj's care for his team.[2] Once, when Johnny went on a trip to Hollywood, he sent a note to the filmmaker: 'Do you know why Hollywood makes better films than us? Well, because they work five days a week.' When Raj read the card, he immediately called a staff meeting. The note from Bakshi was read out in the meeting and Raj Khosla announced that they would henceforth not work on Saturdays. Sundays were already a holiday. Raj Khosla's perpetual impulse to find leisure and to take a break wasn't for him alone. He wanted his team to take it easy. But he also kept tabs on them.

Inder remembers that when they were in office and Raj wasn't likely to come, they waited for his call before stepping out. He would call religiously every day to check on his team, even when there were no films on the floor. His office functioned like one in any other industry. They took leaves, and when they needed financial assistance, they would be provided loans, which were adjusted against their subsequent month's pay. Raj had created a merry band of followers. The biggest of stars from the period knew his assistants and technicians. Even today, more than three decades after his passing, Raj Khosla's team gets due respect and attention wherever they go.

After *Sunny*, for about three or four years, there was a lull. Plans were made, projects were announced but nothing seemed to move. A project with Johnny Bakshi's son Brando in the lead was announced around 1986. It was called *Khanabadosh*, and had a stellar cast, including Dharmendra, Sanjay Dutt, Richa

Sharma (who was to marry Sanjay in 1987), Gulshan Grover, Anupam Kher, Brando Bakshi and 'a new heroine'. Humayun Mirza was the screenwriter and Rahi Masoom Reza was to write dialogues, while the music director was Kamal Makhdoom. This last name is significant because in a long line of composers who worked with Raj, right from Madan Mohan, S.D. Burman, O.P. Nayyar to Laxmikant–Pyarelal, Kamal would be the last. Raj told Sheila Vesuna in 1986 that *Khanabadosh* would also be autobiographical in nature. 'It's about loneliness,' he said. 'Again, I will not compromise with this film.' It never took off.[3]

Around this time, Mahesh Bhatt struck gold with *Naam* (1986). His first couple of films had come out a cropper, but now he was on a streak. *Arth* (1982) had run for 25 weeks and *Saaransh* (1984) had been critically acclaimed across the board. He was basking in the sunshine and that's when he ran into his boss, languishing in the dark. They were at Sea Rock hotel, the haunt for film folk those days. It was the favourite destination for success parties, premieres and *mahurat*s, until the 1993 bomb blasts ripped the hotel apart. Bhatt recounted:

> Unlike those who were in the arc lights or seeking the arc lights, he was somewhere in the distant corner, in the shadows. There was the roar of the ocean behind him. I went up to him and he said, 'Oh, hi… Make me a drink.' I followed his instructions and added soda, water and whiskey. I remember going with the glass and coming back. 'So… how does it feel riding the tide?' he said once I had handed over the drink, and I replied, 'Sir, this is not what I had asked for.' And genuinely so – I was 35–36 and had found dizzying success. Yet the angst, the anguish and the mystery of life gnaws your insides: what is this all about? Where is all this going? The larger questions, which you try to address through

your films, but they continue to haunt you. So I said, 'This is not what I asked for.'

He snapped at me, 'Shut up. Enjoy it! Ask me what it is to ask for it and not to get it.'

It was heartbreaking, a stark, bare exchange between two directors, one who was just making his presence felt and one who had seen dizzying heights once and was now ebbing away into the darkness of life.

There was another encounter from the time that Mahesh Bhatt recounted. One day, at the Mehboob Studios office that was once his and then went to Johnny Bakshi, Raj Khosla was swigging on his drink and talking to Bhatt. As soon as his glass became empty, he took it under the table, poured his drink, then placed it back on the table and added water to it. Mahesh said, 'Boss, nobody's here, it's just me. Why are you doing this?'

'I guess it gets into your body. I am not as bold as you are,' replied his mentor. And indeed, Mahesh was able to open up about his infidelity. He could talk about it, face his demons squarely. Raj found it difficult. He was burdened by his truth, and it was eating him up. Bhatt makes an *Arth* and bares his soul, warts and all. When Raj tries to do the same thing in *Main Tulsi Tere Aangan Ki* or even *Sunny*, he has to layer his truth and dress it up so that it's visible and yet hiding in plain sight. Clearly, it troubled him a lot.

This was the most difficult phase of his life. A man who rode the high horse of success for years together, without bothering to – or having to – look back, was now not in the highest of spirits. He had bought a sprawling penthouse on Carter Road but refused to move there, despite the insistence of his daughters. His drinking would commence in the morning and continue through the day, unless he needed to work. Despite allegations from various quarters, it is very unlikely that he allowed his state of inebriation to affect his work in any way. After *Sunny*, there were claims that he turned up drunk on the sets. Both Sharmila Tagore and Waheeda Rehman categorically denied ever seeing him drunk at work. He did often cancel shoots and try to wrap up quickly, but some of his greatest classics have survived this quirk of his. Many of his team members, and Raj Khosla himself, have asserted in various interviews that he had lost interest in cinema. But he still tried to get projects off the ground, discussed new ideas with his writers, read extensively and sang at the drop of a hat. He was massively interested in history and his favourite historical figure was Napoleon. In fact, he was a fan. He loved Paris because of Napoleon. In a 1975 interview, Raj confessed to reading *The Age of Napoleon* (this could either be the 1963 book by J. Christopher Herold or the 1975 book by Will and Ariel Durant). He was marking passages that appealed to him with a pencil, he said.[4] He was also reading Rousseau at the time. He always found reading stimulating, and possibly also the impetus for his creativity.

Somewhere between 1986 and 1987, Raj Khosla's old friend Vinod Khanna came back to town. He had had his fill of a spiritual sojourn with Osho, aka Bhagwan Rajneesh, and decided that it was time to get back to films. Raj offered to be the first to relaunch him. A film called *Parda* was hurriedly announced, with Vinod Khanna in the lead and a strapping young man named Dan Dhanoa as the antagonist. Dhanoa told me:

> I had met Raj ji at his office in Bandra. He was a kind, affectionate man. He told me, 'Beta, I'll get back to you.' And then later he did get through to me and signed me for this film. An action-packed movie was being planned. We even had a photoshoot, and a signing amount was given. The shoot began. They had put up a giant set in Mehboob Studios. I remember giving some

> dates and then the dates got cancelled. Now, unlike the heroes, us villains had many films happening at the same time. At times, we were shooting for two or three films a day. Once or twice when I was shooting in Mehboob Studios, I would go over to the set just to meet Raj ji or to see what's happening. I was given to believe that things were on hold because there were some issues with Vinod Khanna.

Raj Khosla kept assuring Dan that they would resume soon. But to no avail.

According to Sanatan Vinchi, Raj Khosla's erstwhile accountant who is still an integral part of Raj Khosla Films, when they tried to register *Parda* as a title, they realized it was already taken. So they settled for *Naqāb*. Inder Khosla, who watched the development from close quarters, revealed that the set had been erected, and some parts of *Naqāb* had been shot. One Saturday there was no sign of Vinod Khanna. After waiting for a while, Raj Khosla packed up by 5.30–6 p.m. Finally, Vinod got in touch. Inder Khosla said:

> Vinod Khanna said he was supposed to go receive Osho, who was arriving the next day. 'It's a Sunday tomorrow... I'll return by the morning flight on Monday and resume shooting,' Khanna told the director. Raj ji said, 'No issues. We don't shoot on Sundays. You take your time. Come back on when you can. We can shoot in the afternoon at around 2 p.m. if you like.' Vinod Khanna even offered to complete one of the pending scenes that very day. But Raj ji told him to relax and that he'll see him on Monday. But Vinod kept insisting on doing that one scene. Raj went over the scene with his assistants. 'I want you in complete formals, all shaved, pressed

> and ready,' he told Vinod. Vinod showered, shaved and turned up in a complete suit. They began shooting at 7 p.m., and wrapped up by nine. Raj instructed his team to schedule a shoot at 2 p.m. on Monday.

According to Khosla, Vinod showed no signs of having anything on his mind.

Monday. The crew was all set up and ready. Two p.m. came and went, but Khanna didn't turn up. They kept calling and enquiring. There was no trace of Vinod Khanna anywhere. Later, they got to know that the man had locked himself up in his room. They kept waiting for a couple of days. Inder Khosla recalled:

> On the third day, Raj ji went to see him. But Vinod was just lying in his bed, not talking to anyone. He said, 'Listen, I will strip the set down. No worries, no need to shoot. I'll take you abroad and get you looked at. I know some good doctors. You'll get better in no time. Don't you worry.' Vinod didn't respond for a while, and then said with a lot of difficulty, 'No. I won't be able to do it.' We held on for a few more days, and we deliberated. We discussed what to do. What would be the right course of action in this regard? Finally, it was decided to get in touch with Rishi Kapoor.

Rishi was having his lunch when Raj Khosla called him. 'I'll be there immediately, Raj saab,' Kapoor said, and within a short while, he was in Raj's office. By the time Rishi Kapoor came into the project, *Parda*, the action film, had been scrapped and a new story had taken its place. This was a Muslim social called *Naqāb*. Rishi Kapoor and Farha were the leads. The story was credited to Abid Surti.

Considering his diminutive frame, Abid Surti cuts an impressive – even imposing – figure. He is a novelist, screenwriter, comic book writer (he is the creator of the legendary Indrajal Comics hero Bahadur), cartoonist, painter, journalist, playwright and an untiring environmental activist. Speaking to me on the phone, Surti said:

> Raj Kapoor had taken my script. He loved one of my stories, which was appearing as a comic strip called *Inspector Azad* in the *Illustrated Weekly of India*. It was, in turn, based on my novel called *Daud*. Raj Kapoor had read *Inspector Azad*; he was a comic book fan. I [had previously] got a call from the office of RK Films. For two years, we worked on the script. RK studio was not doing so well because *Mera Naam Joker* [1970] was a big flop, and all his writers had taken leave of him [Raj Kapoor].

According to Surti, this was supposed to be RK Films' next project. But when *Bobby* (1973) was declared a blockbuster, Surti's project was kept on the anvil. It was then that he was contacted by Raj Khosla. A Gujarati journalist got in touch with Abid Surti and told him that Raj would like to meet. 'The man who got in touch with me had told Raj Khosla about the story that had earlier been picked up by Raj Kapoor. It was immediately finalized. But then someone informed him that a very similar film is being made by Feroz Khan. Khosla wasn't doing so well at this time. So he immediately dropped the idea and asked me if I had another idea to narrate to him. And then I told him the story idea that ultimately became *Naqāb (1989)*. But my original idea was completely altered in the final film,' Abid Surti insists.

The original story, Surti says, was about the Haj pilgrimage. Muslim socials – a genre of film that focused on costume dramas about nawabs and courtesans, usually set in the backdrop of Lucknow or Aligarh – were a rage in the 1960s and 1970s. *Pakeezah* (1972) and *Umrao Jaan* (1981) were huge recent successes. Surti's story was in the same tradition. It was a love story, but it also expounded on the Haj pilgrimage and its significance. Said Surti:

> I drew the love story from *The Woman in White*. The hero falls in love with a girl, but she's married off to the villain. That part I had taken from *The Woman in White*. The hero's mother wants to go for Haj, but he's been deferring it because he is in love with this girl. But now that she is married to someone else, he gives in to his mother's entreaties and prepares for the pilgrimage. The mother explains the spirit of this pilgrimage to her son and assigns him a set of tasks to repent for his sins. One of them is to seek forgiveness from all his enemies or anyone he has ever thought ill of. That's when he goes to this villain who married his lover. He discovers that the girl is being tortured by her in-laws. But he still seeks the man's forgiveness. But the villain says, '*Maaf karne waala toh sirf* Allah *hai*. The only one who gives forgiveness is Allah,' and refuses to comply. It is then that our hero decides to seek revenge, and rescue his girl. But this story was altered completely.

What finally became *Naqāb* was a fair bit of *The Woman in White*. And this is interesting to anyone with any inkling of Raj Khosla's filmography. *Woh Kaun Thi?* was said to be inspired from Wilkie Collins's Victorian-era novel, but there were some major differences, which we've covered in a previous chapter. *Naqāb*, though, shares a strong resemblance with the novel. There are the two sisters, the mystery surrounding one of them, and the hero setting about to rescue his lover from the clutches of a conniving husband. There's even a fleeting moment where, in the last of Raj Khosla's favourite Easter eggs, Imran (Rishi Kapoor) has a glimpse of the mystery woman and wonders aloud, '*Raaste mein jo mujhe mili thhi, woh kaun thhi*? The girl I saw on the way, who was she?' and Haya (Farah) quips, '*Woh Kaun Thi*? *Raj Khosla ki film thhi*! That was a Raj Khosla film!'

Bindu and Amjad Khan returned to the Raj Khosla fold with this film. For both of them, it was their third movie with the director. 'The film had some very difficult Urdu dialogues,' Bindu recalled, 'because Raj ji himself spoke Urdu very well, and was proficient in ghazals and *sher-o-shayari*. He was very literate and well read. But *uss waqt woh bahut* aloof *ho gaye thhe*. But at that time, he had become very aloof. He didn't want to meet people. I mean, we did meet socially, but you could see that he was not well. But much before that we used to go to his house, and he used to sing those Saigal songs. "*Tumko jo aata hai, tum bhi gungunao*. Hum whatever you know," he used to say. So we hummed along a little. It was so much fun!'

Amjad Khan had been in *Teri Maang Sitaron Se Bhar Doon* and *Maati Maangey Khoon*. He had an author-backed role in *Teri Maang*, where the bond between his Sultan Bhai and Nutan's Lalli remains one of the most endearing things about the film. *Maati Maangey Khoon* was one of the dime-a-dozen villain roles that he was doing those days. Amjad played the role of the patriarch in *Naqāb*. The role – and possibly, his health – needed him to stay in bed for most of the film.

Farah Naaz was destined to be the last Raj Khosla heroine and as usual, the plot not only revolves around her character(s), Raj also manages to make her look as divine as all his leading ladies of yore. She gets the best lines and the best songs. Raj said, 'Farah has a very sensitive role to play. Over the years it has become easy to understand who is sensitive and who is not. Of the new girls, I thought Farah would be best.'[5]

Raj Khosla was quite displeased with the outcome of his past few films. He spoke about his lapses whenever he had the opportunity. In an interview he said, 'In spite of the flops I have not lost my confidence. I don't mind talking about them. Napoleon won 84 battles and lost only Waterloo. Yet he talked of only Waterloo.'[6] With *Naqāb*, he wanted to put his best foot forward. Though it was his home production, he was strapped for resources. He didn't have quite enough to build the canvas that he had in his mind. Having to build a set (for *Parda*) and then dismantle it must have taken its toll. Sanatan Vinchi told me:

> *Naqāb* was first an action film, which then became a love story. We were supposed to shoot the film in Ooty. Raj ji and Tanny Khosla had gone to Ooty for location hunting. They came back, looked at the photos they had taken, and it struck them that all that lush greenery won't be there when they planned to shoot it. Let's shoot with artificial greens, someone said. Why do I have to settle for fake greenery? Why can't I shoot at Film City instead? So Ooty plans were cancelled. Now we were shooting at Film City.

Money troubles plagued the soundtrack of the film as well. Raj Khosla later told journalist Rajiv Vijayakar about *Naqāb*:

> This time I wanted to do my best, but the lack of financial resources crippled my creativity. I had to do without my regular music team, L-P and Anand Bakshi, because I did not want them to work for me for less than what they were getting. I had to sell my music to

> a company (T-Series) which was extremely money-oriented. They gave me cash on the spot, which I badly needed, pretended I was doing *them* a favour by giving them the music of *Naqāb*, and then sabotaged its sale.[7]

Naqāb, the album, didn't reach the listeners in the way that so many of Raj Khosla's other soundtracks did. The album wasn't as widely available. It is only when the internet and social media came about that things started to change a bit.

The soundtrack of *Naqāb* (1989).

Raj Khosla's swansong gets a bad rap for being forgettable. Very few watched the film and it didn't get any reviews. Even now, film buffs scarcely talk about it while discussing his films. But one of the aspects *Naqāb* cannot be faulted for is its lilting music. Raj Khosla couldn't afford Laxmikant–Pyarelal anymore, so he opted for a new, relatively untested composer.

Kamal Makhdoom hailed from Hyderabad and had given the music for an obscure film called *Bhatke Rahee* (1984). Obscure the film and its composer maybe, but Makhdoom had singers such as Asha Bhosle, Anuradha Paudwal, Shabbir Kumar and Suresh Wadkar on board. Film historian and music buff Pavan Jha says, 'He was a music teacher with a strong understanding of poetry, qawwali and classical music. He was assistant to a few musicians in the 1970s.'

Rajiv Vijayakar told me, 'When you travel in a Mumbai local, between Bandra and Mahim stations, as soon as you cross the flyover and enter the Mahim side, you see buildings on the right side which are three-storied and four-storied tenements. This man lived there in one of the flats. He earned his living teaching music to poor kids. That was Kamal Makhdoom. Someone told Raj Khosla about him, and that's how he was signed on for *Naqāb*.' According to Sanatan Vinchi, it was Faruk Kaiser, Raj Khosla's assistant as well as a lyricist, who brought Kamal to him.

The crowning glory of the film is a ghazal by Asha Bhosle, 'Na kisi ka dil mujhe chahiye'. With scores of ghazals in her eight-decade-long career in films, it would be a tall claim for this song to feature in Asha Bhosle's top 10 ghazals. But once you listen to it, the claim doesn't seem unreal. Faruk Kaiser's lyrics fit the song like an elegant glove. Another soulful track by Asha Bhosle, 'Rakhiyo mera naqab', has been rendered in three versions, all having slightly different lyrics, the other two being 'Beti nahin main teri' and 'Do phool meri kabr mein'. Asha's voice rings with pathos and an old-world charm that was quite lost by the time *Naqāb* came along. The soul of these songs belonged in the 1960s. The other solo she had was 'Jaaneman jaanewafa', a lively, melodious piece which became a bit of a misfit in the film as it was sung by the mystery woman haunting the valleys, a situation reminiscent of 'Naina barse' in *Woh Kaun Thi?*. Asha Bhosle was so enamoured of the music of *Naqāb* that later, she called up Raj Khosla and said, 'This is my second *Umrao Jaan*.' When she was interviewed for this book, Bhosle corroborated and stood by her statement.

Suresh Wadkar had a playful, cutesy duet with Asha Bhosle, 'Nainon se naina lad gaye'. But if this were a popular album – a status that it sorely deserves – Wadkar would be best remembered for 'Bolunga nahin mooh se'. While talking about *Naqāb* over the phone, the first thing Wadkar did was to hum the song. He recalled meeting 'Papa ji' (that's what he called Raj Khosla) during the rehearsal of a different song called 'Baith mere paas tujhe dekhta rahoon' from *Yadon ki Kasam* (1985) at Mehboob. The composers were Laxmikant–Pyarelal, and Raj Khosla was there to meet them. Throughout the three-four rounds of rehearsals,

Raj just stood there listening to him. 'Directors didn't bother about music so much. There were just a handful, like Raj Kapoor and Raj Khosla, who took this level of interest in songs,' Wadkar recounted. He also remembered an incident while taking a walk on Carter Road when Raj Khosla ran into him. He was in his car. Papa ji offered him a ride, and kept playing songs for him as they rode through the suburb. 'He kept saying, "Have you heard this?" and then played a song for me, often singing along himself. He sang really well. For *Naqāb*, he got a new music director, Kamal *bhaiyya*, who created tunes with a slightly older flavour. I remember rehearsing the song at Papa ji's office, and once at his home.' Raj Khosla's daughter Anita also recalled 'Bolunga nahin mooh se' being performed at home back in the day.

'Ishq hai sachcha baaki sab jhootha' is a standard-issue Mohd Aziz track, making optimal use of his histrionics. The song often gets featured on YouTube Shorts or Instagram Reels. Kamal Makhdoom himself lent his voice to a qawwali that went 'Ishq na kario koi'. Each of these songs, in true Raj Khosla fashion, never become ornaments and manage to nudge the narrative forward. Most of them, especially 'Na kisi ka dil mujhe chahiye', 'Jaaneman jaanewafa' and 'Rakhiyo mera naqab', had narrative arcs within the songs.

But the film had its weaknesses, and despite Raj trying his best to infuse life into the script, *Naqāb* doesn't work either as a Muslim social, a love story or a thriller. It was a washout at the box office, an outcome that sadly contributed towards the undermining of a fantastic soundtrack.

Just 20 days before *Naqāb* was certified, on 22 September, Raj Khosla was interviewed by Nasreen Munni Kabir for her documentary about Guru Dutt. It is one of two televised interviews of Raj Khosla that survive, the other being by a French crew during the making of *Meraa Dost Meraa Dushman*. Nasreen says, 'It was Lalli who introduced me to Raj Khosla.' Lalitha Lajmi, Guru Dutt's sister, was fondly called Lalli (incidentally – and ironically – Lalli was also the name of Nutan's character in *Teri Maang Sitaron Se Bhar Doon*). For the first time in three decades, Lalitha had an occasion to call on Raj Khosla. The three met at Marina, and Raj was delighted to have met Lalli after so long. Lalli was keen to meet him too. They had a long conversation about Guru Dutt, but this was not recorded. Nasreen came to Raj's office a few days later, and this time his recollections were recorded for her documentary. For a change, Raj Khosla had an opportunity to leave the grim present behind and revel in the glory days of the past. Nothing got him going like talking about his boss.

After the film was completed, Nasreen gave him a copy of her film to watch. She said:

> I spoke to him over the phone, I asked him, 'How do you like it?' and he said something very poetic. He said, 'How did you get Guru Dutt to act for you?' That was a big compliment. What he meant was that because of the choice of the film clips, it was as if he was working for the documentary rather than for his films. That comment from him I'm never going to forget.

On 10 March 1988, Raj Khosla had written a letter to a certain Mr Daga of Daga Pictures, Calcutta:

> My film 'Naqāb' is complete and I have finished the background music also. I am keen on releasing the film

> on 20th May which is 2 days after Idd. I would therefore request you to please remit me a sum of Rs. 1,50,000/- due to me, being the underproduction department, immediately on receipt of this letter.

To this, he added:

> There is an old proverb which says that friendship is more lasting than silver or gold, so I would request you to forget everything and remember our old friendship, which has its roots since C.I.D.[8]

Evidently, the plan to release in May of that year was scrapped. Sanatan Vinchi confirmed that Raj Khosla wasn't happy with the output and decided to reshoot parts of *Naqāb*, but Rishi Kapoor and Farah were both busy shooting at a farm near Delhi – this could be for *Hamara Khandan* (1988). So *Naqāb* had to wait till they were back. The re-shoot and post-production pushed the tentative release date even further.

Ved Prakash, Raj Khosla's man Friday, confirmed in his interview that even before *Naqāb*'s release, the director felt that something was amiss. Raj had this instinct, some alarm that went off somewhere when he felt that his film wasn't panning out the way he'd expected. He instructed Ved Prakash to go ahead with the publicity of the film without showing it to anyone. He wanted to sit with his team of writers and work on something new and better.

And indeed, though *Naqāb* was certified on 11 October 1988, Raj Khosla faced problems releasing the film in Bombay. The distributor who had offered to pick it up for the Bombay territory had abandoned the film. Similar challenges were faced in other parts of the country as well. Raj Khosla wrote to Mr Daga on 20 December 1988:

> I am in receipt of your letter dated 17th Dec'88 and was surprised to read the contents of the same, which implied that you are not interested in the picture 'Naqāb'. I do not want to go into details, for the simple fact that today you are talking utter nonsense about the picture. I would therefore request you to kindly send me a letter stating that you are not interested in the picture, so that we can refund your monies.

Obviously, Raj Khosla wasn't getting the kind of response he had hoped for *Naqāb*, and things just went from bad to worse with what transpired next. The alcohol binges didn't have to wait till the evenings anymore. Besides work, the only things that kept him busy were drinking, reading and his bouts of chess. Hrishikesh Mukherjee had become one of his favourite chess buddies. Hrishi da had hung up his boots by then, and the two wizened filmmakers had developed a friendship over the years. Raj Khosla often paid him a visit and the two would spar over 64 squares. One evening, as Raj stepped out of Mukherjee's house and was crossing over to the other side of the street to get into his car, an errant cyclist plunged into him out of nowhere.

Raj had a lot on his mind, and going by several accounts, was mentally disturbed because of what was unfolding in his personal as well as his professional life. The double life he was leading sat heavy on his lean shoulders. His films were either being shelved or not being released. With all this sitting on his chest, he was always a little lost, a little absent from the moment. It was then conceivable that he didn't sense the cyclist coming on him. The rider and his cycle rammed into him with full force, and his lean frame hit the divider hard. His thigh bone audibly cracked, and the pain was palpable.

He was rushed to Dr Thakker's Nursing Home, which was on the nearby Turner Road. The doctors first attempted to fix a bolt to realign the bones. But the director's thigh had swelled up and it kept getting worse, so he had to be taken to surgery. A metal rod was inserted through surgical procedure, and finally, the swelling was somewhat arrested. Healing was still a long way off. He had to be in the hospital for at least two weeks, after which, he had to still move around on a walker. The experience was sheer agony, both physically and psychologically. It wasn't only his body but his confidence that had taken a hit. *Naqāb* was still not getting picked up. It was only in August 1989 that the film was released with the help of a friend. It was released on the account of Raj Khosla Films. They weren't paid upfront but it was decided that money would trickle in when people bought tickets to watch the film. But, as fate would have it, the film was a washout.

Those days and weeks of languishing in bed and moving around with help added to the bottomless pit of miseries. Raj never quite got over the hurt and the anguish. The daughters did their best to get him out of his affliction. But it was as if he had given up. The next couple of years rolled by in agony. The Hindi film industry has perpetually suffered from a kind of short-term memory loss. The champions of the moment are celebrated but nobody bothers about the has-beens. As far as the industry was concerned, Raj Khosla had been firmly relegated to the dusty attic of the past. No one came to see him anymore. There was a whole new generation of stars on the horizon, and they didn't particularly line up to work with him. But despite his dwindling confidence and a relentlessly tortuous and tangled personal life, the desire to wield magic hadn't left him yet. Despite the wallowing and melancholy, despite being dealt a bad hand and the string of flops, Raj was never known to sit around, licking his wounds. On to the next film, then.

Around February–March 1991, journalist Rajiv Vijayakar had two sit-downs with Raj Khosla, for possibly his last interview. 'For the first meeting, he had called me to Otter's Club. I had to wait for 45 minutes because he was so busy playing with Hrishikesh Mukherjee that he completely forgot that he had called me there,' said Vijayakar. Vijayakar ended up spending around two-and-a-half hours with Raj Khosla over those two sessions. Raj was candid as usual, assuming complete responsibility for his failed films. 'With his "spade-is-a-spade" directness, he confided in me how he had ruined even interesting themes like *Teri Maang Sitaron Se Bhar Doon* and *Daasi*.' He spilled the beans about the *Naqāb* fiasco, coupled with the allegation that the music of the film was deliberately sabotaged. He also took a walk down memory lane, speaking fondly of his association with the legendary composers of the past, starting with N. Datta, moving to S.D. Burman, Madan Mohan, O.P. Nayyar and then finding some kind of a stability with Laxmikant–Pyarelal. '"After I worked with them, I did not need anyone else," he said,' narrated Vijayakar. While speaking, Raj Khosla broke down a few times. He wept quite often then. He just needed an excuse and tears would flow. He recalled Madhubala turning down the lead role for *Bombai ka Babu* because she was dying and didn't want the film to suffer, and started sobbing. As he watched Sachin Tendulkar go at it with his bat in a one-day international match on television, he told Vijayakar that the master blaster was gifted this bat by Gavaskar, and he never played without that bat. Even before he could finish the sentence, he started crying. The sensitive artist's heart was perpetually filled to the brim, often finding reasons to spill over.

It was during this interview that Raj told Vijayakar about his new film. It was a 'musical love story with a touch of suspense', he said, adding '... you will find the old Raj Khosla is back, in top form.' He also added that he was back to working with the Laxmikant–Pyarelal duo after seven years (the last film they had teamed up for was *Meraa Dost Meraa Dushman*). He told Vijayakar, 'I called Laxmi on new year's day [Diwali] and broke the news, that they would be doing my new film. And do you know what Laxmi said? "Waah, Raj saab, you have made our new year for us."'

Vijayakar last spoke to Raj Khosla in mid-April 1991. Raj had promised a third meeting to talk about his music and give the young journalist precious insights about the classic songs he had made with Lata Mangeshkar, Asha Bhosle, Mohammed Rafi and Laxmikant–Pyarelal. During the call, Raj Khosla postponed the meeting because he was neck-deep in working out the screenplay with Rahi Masoom Reza and Umesh Kalbagh (Umesh had just made a splash co-writing the screenplay for *Chandni* [1989] and had also assisted Basu Chatterjee on several of his films). 'We are making fantastic progress,' he told Vijayakar over the phone.

Around this time, Raj also had a one-hour meeting with his secretary Ved Prakash. Ved had applied for leave to visit his hometown. Amongst other things, he told Ved his plans for sharing the profits on his new film. 'I haven't been able to do much for my staff [at Raj Khosla Films]. I want to share the profits on my upcoming film with my entire team. Let's work on this once you are back,' he said. Santan Vinchi confirmed that a title called *Pak Daman* was registered. Manoj Kumar remembers discussing the idea of a new film called *Naya Suraj* with Raj. His son-in-law Romi Bhalla had been exploring a project with him, and they had Aamir Khan and Madhuri Dixit in mind as leads for the film. It isn't clear whether the project Raj Khosla mentioned to Rajiv Vijayakar and Ved Prakash was either of these films, or an entirely different project.

None of these discussions came to fruition. Raj Khosla was administered doses of Antabuse, a medication that is used to deter the patient from consuming alcohol. He didn't take well to it, and had to be put on drips in a private nursing home. Anita says:

> Basically, he just stopped eating. So he had to be sent to Eros, a private nursing home, and put on drips. But he stopped eating solids. He would just consume liquids and continued to drink whiskey whenever he could. He was at Eros for quite some time. When I went to meet him there, he said he was feeling better. He was actually more comfortable in the hospital than at home. I had gone there with a friend of mine, and he spoke very clearly. I thought all he needs is some rest. Then suddenly we got the news that he had to be sent to Jaslok.

At Jaslok, Raj Khosla was diagnosed with jaundice. His liver was finally giving away. His condition kept getting worse. His youngest daughter Sonia recalls visiting the hospital on 8 June 1991:

> He was sitting up, he was conscious. They were trying to stop him from drinking. And he was taken to a hospital in Bandra and then they took him to Jaslok and there they got to know that all his organs were failing. But he was all right when he spoke to me. There was something inside me that told me something serious is going to happen. I met him and all he was telling me was that he was sorry. He just kept saying sorry. Then he asked me to comb his hair.

The next day, on 9 June 1991, Raj Khosla was declared dead due to multiple organ failure. The city of Mumbai saw unprecedented rains that day. The heavens were falling apart.

The roads were submerged. It seemed like an impossible task to manage to get him home. His son in law G.M. Kapur recalls walking all the way from Mahalaxmi to Jaslok, wading through water. It was evening by the time they reached the hospital. They could only take him home the next morning. The next day, the funeral procession left from Marina at 3 p.m.

The man who had built whole careers, made films with some of the biggest stars this nation had seen, was on his last journey. His body was laid on ice. His grandsons, little Nikhil and Mukul, were assigned the task of applying salt on the blocks of ice and wiping the floor as the ice melted. Some of the industry bigwigs came to pay their last respects. Most could not make it. Yash Johar and Yash Chopra were there, so was his friend Vinod Khanna, and his last pair of leads, Rishi Kapoor and Farah. Deb Mukherjee also showed up. The young Dharmesh Darshan, who was working on his debut at the time, was dismayed at the poor turnout at the send-off to a giant of Indian cinema: 'It was the business of the film industry to be there. He was a man who contributed to every element of cinema, and created stars.' It was an eye-opener for the man who was about to slink into the director's chair himself.

The agony and the ecstasy were finally at an end. Probably the last skill that Raj had learned from his Guru was to exit in silence. And so he did.

Filmography

Raj Khosla as Director

Milap (1955)

Cast	Dev Anand, Geeta Bali, Johnny Walker, K.N. Singh
Producer(s)	T.R. Fatehchand, Goverdhan T. Fatehchand
Assistant Director(s)	Pramod Chakravorty, Bhappi Sonie, Goverdhan T. Fatehchand, B. Padmanabham
Music	N. Datta
Singer(s)	Mohd. Rafi, Lata Mangeshkar, Asha Bhosle, Geeta Dutt
Lyricist(s)	Sahir Ludhianvi
Writer(s)	Rajinder Singh Bedi, Nabendu Ghosh, Raj Khosla

_C.I.D._ (1956)

Cast	Dev Anand, Shakila, Waheeda Rehman, Johnny Walker, K.N. Singh
Producer(s)	Guru Dutt
Assistant Director(s)	Pramod Chakravorty, Bhappi Sonie, B. Padmanabham
Music	O.P. Nayyar
Singer(s)	Mohd. Rafi, Asha Bhosle, Shamshad Begum, Geeta Dutt
Lyricist(s)	Jan Nisar Akhtar, Majrooh Sultanpuri
Writer(s)	Inder Raj Anand
Cinematographer(s)	V.K. Murthy, Anwar Pabani

Solva Saal (1958)

Cast	Dev Anand, Waheeda Rehman
Producer(s)	Chandrakant C. Desai
Assistant Director(s)	Satish Kumar, B. Padmanabham, Bhappi Sonie
Music	S.D. Burman
Singer(s)	Mohd. Rafi, Asha Bhosle, Hemant Kumar, Sudha Malhotra
Lyricist(s)	Majrooh Sultanpuri
Writer(s)	Omkar Dogra, Raj Khosla
Cinematographer(s)	Dwarka Divecha

Kala Pani (1958)

Cast	Dev Anand, Madhubala, Nalini Jaywant, Jankidas
Producer(s)	Dev Anand
Assistant Director(s)	Prabhu Dayal, Satish Kumar, B. Padmanabham

Music	S.D. Burman
Singer(s)	Mohd. Rafi, Asha Bhosle
Lyricist(s)	Majrooh Sultanpuri
Writer(s)	G.R. Kamat, Bhappi Sonie
Cinematographer(s)	V. Ratra

Bombai ka Babu (1960)

Cast	Dev Anand, Suchitra Sen, Jeevan
Producer(s)	Raj Khosla
Assistant Director(s)	Satish Mehra, B. Padmanabham
Music	S.D. Burman
Singer(s)	Mohd. Rafi, Asha Bhosle, Manna Dey, Mukesh
Lyricist(s)	Majrooh Sultanpuri
Writer(s)	G.R. Kamat, Rajinder Singh Bedi
Cinematographer(s)	Jal Mistry

Ek Musafir Ek Hasina (1962)

Cast	Joy Mukherjee, Sadhana, Jankidas
Producer(s)	Sashadhar Mukherjee
Assistant Director(s)	Suresh Bedi, Sudesh Issar, B. Padmanabham
Music	O.P. Nayyar
Singer(s)	Mohd. Rafi, Asha Bhosle
Lyricist(s)	Raja Mehdi Ali Khan, S.H. Bihari, Shewan Rizvi
Writer(s)	Miss Q. Hyder, Raj Khosla, K.A. Narayan
Cinematographer(s)	Fali Mistry

Woh Kaun Thi? (1964)

Cast	Manoj Kumar, Sadhana, Prem Chopra, K.N. Singh
Producer(s)	M.A. Madhu, N.N. Sippy
Assistant Director(s)	Suresh Bedi, Sudesh Issar, B Padmanabham
Music	Madan Mohan
Singer(s)	Mohd. Rafi, Lata Mangeshkar, Asha Bhosle, Mahendra Kapoor
Lyricist(s)	Raja Mehdi Ali Khan
Writer(s)	Dhuva Chatterjee, Ehsan Rizvi
Cinematographer(s)	K.H. Kapadia

Mera Saaya (1966)

Cast	Sunil Dutt, Sadhana, K.N. Singh, Prem Chopra, Birbal
Producer(s)	Premji
Assistant Director(s)	Sudesh Issar, B. Padmanabham, Bolu Khosla, Viren Bole
Music	Madan Mohan
Singer(s)	Mohd. Rafi, Lata Mangeshkar, Asha Bhosle
Lyricist(s)	Raja Mehdi Ali Khan
Writer(s)	Akhtar-Ul-Iman, G.R. Kamat
Cinematographer(s)	V. Babasaheb

Do Badan (1966)

Cast	Manoj Kumar, Asha Parekh, Simi Garewal, Pran, Birbal
Producer(s)	Huda Bihari

Assistant Director(s)	Suresh Bedi, Bolu Khosla, Sudesh Kumar, B. Padmanabham
Music	Ravi
Singer(s)	Mohd. Rafi, Lata Mangeshkar, Asha Bhosle
Lyricist(s)	Shakeel Badayuni
Writer(s)	G.R. Kamat, Chandrakant, Masood Mashhadi, Virendra Sinha
Cinematographer(s)	V.N. Reddy

Anita **(1967)**

Cast	Manoj Kumar, Sadhana, I.S. Johar, Birbal
Producer(s)	Lekhraj Khosla, Raj Khosla (Raj Khosla Films)
Assistant Director(s)	Sudesh Issar, B. Padmanabham, Bolu Khosla, Viren Bole
Music	Laxmikant Kudalkar, Pyarelal Sharma
Singer(s)	Mukesh, Lata Mangeshkar, Usha Mangeshkar
Lyricist(s)	Arzoo Lakhnavi, Anand Bakshi, Raja Mehdi Ali Khan
Writer(s)	G.R. Kamat, Chandrakant, Raj Khosla, Virendra Sinha
Cinematographer(s)	V. Gopi Krishna

Do Raaste **(1969)**

Cast	Rajesh Khanna, Mumtaz, Balraj Sahni, Prem Chopra, Bindu, Kamini Kaushal, Mehmood, Birbal

Producer(s)	Lekhraj Khosla, Raj Khosla (Raj Khosla Films)
Music	Laxmikant Kudalkar, Pyarelal Sharma
Singer(s)	Kishore Kumar, Lata Mangeshkar, Mohd. Rafi, Mukesh
Lyricist(s)	Anand Bakshi
Writer(s)	G.R. Kamat, Chandrakant Kakodkar, Akhtar Romani
Cinematographer(s)	V. Gopi Krishna

Chirag (1969)

Cast	Sunil Dutt, Asha Parekh, Om Prakash
Producer(s)	Premji
Assistant Director(s)	Sudesh Issar, B. Padmanabham, Bolu Khosla, Viren Bole
Music	Madan Mohan
Singer(s)	Mohd. Rafi, Lata Mangeshkar
Lyricist(s)	Majrooh Sultanpuri
Writer(s)	G.R. Kamat, O.P. Dutta, Akhtar Mirza, Akhtar-Ul-Iman
Cinematographer(s)	V. Gopi Krishna

Mera Gaon Mera Desh (1971)

Cast	Dharmendra, Asha Parekh, Vinod Khanna, Laxmi Chhaya, Jayant, Sudhir, Birbal
Producer(s)	Lekhraj Khosla, Bolu Khosla (Khosla Enterprises)
Assistant Director(s)	Sudesh Issar, Ravi Khanna, Mahesh
Music	Laxmikant Kudalkar, Pyarelal Sharma

Singer(s)	Mohd. Rafi, Lata Mangeshkar
Lyricist(s)	Anand Bakshi
Writer(s)	G.R. Kamat, Akhtar Romani
Cinematographer(s)	Pratap Sinha

Kuchhe Dhaage (1973)

Dedicated to Raj's Mother

Cast	Vinod Khanna, Moushumi Chatterjee, Kabir Bedi, K.N. Singh, Nirupa Roy, Ritesh, Sona (Mrs. Haji Mastan)
Producer(s)	Anil Khosla, Raj Khosla (Raj Khosla Films)
Assistant Director(s)	Viren Bole, Vimal Chopra, Farooq Kaisser, Pravesh Sagar
Music	Laxmikant Kudalkar, Pyarelal Sharma
Singer(s)	Lata Mangeshkar, Hemlata
Lyricist(s)	Anand Bakshi
Writer(s)	G.R. Kamat, Raj Khosla, Akhtar Romani
Cinematographer(s)	Pratap Sinha

Shareef Budmaash (1973)

Cast	Dev Anand, Hema Malini, Ajit, Jeevan, Helen, Sudhir, Shatrughan Sinha, Jankidas, Birbal
Producer(s)	Dev Anand, Kalpana Kartik, Amit Khanna
Music	R.D. Burman
Singer(s)	Kishore Kumar, Lata Mangeshkar, Asha Bhosle

Lyricist(s)	Anand Bakshi
Writer(s)	Dev Anand
Cinematographer(s)	Fali Mistry

Prem Kahani **(1975)**

Cast	Rajesh Khanna, Shashi Kapoor, Mumtaz, Vinod Khanna, K.N. Singh
Producer(s)	Lekhraj Khosla, Bolu Khosla (Khosla Combine)
Assistant Director(s)	Viren Bole, Farooq Kaisser, Pravesh Sagar
Music	Laxmikant Kudalkar, Pyarelal Sharma
Singer(s)	Kishore Kumar, Lata Mangeshkar, Mohd. Rafi, Mukesh
Lyricist(s)	Anand Bakshi
Writer(s)	Jayant Dharmadhikari, Raj Khosla, Rahi Masoom Reza
Cinematographer(s)	Kaka Thakur

Nehle peh Dehlaa **(1976)**

Cast	Sunil Dutt, Saira Banu, Vinod Khanna, Prem Nath, Om Prakash, Ranjeet, Kamini Kaushal, Bindu
Producer(s)	Sunil Dutt
Assistant Director(s)	Faruk Kaiser, Viren Bole, Sarwar Hussain, Parvesh Sagar, Gopal Balii, Ved Makini
Music	R.D. Burman
Singer(s)	Kishore Kumar, Lata Mangeshkar, Asha Bhosle, Manna Dey, Aziz Nazran
Lyricist(s)	Anand Bakshi, Farooq Qaiser

Writer(s)	K.K. Shukla, Satish Bhatnagar
Cinematographer(s)	Ramchandra

Main Tulsi Tere Aangan Ki (1978)

Cast	Nutan, Asha Parekh, Vijay Anand, Vinod Khanna, Deb Mukherjee, Geeta Behl, Birbal
Producer(s)	Raj Khosla (Raj Khosla Films)
Music	Laxmikant Kudalkar, Pyarelal Sharma
Singer(s)	Lata Mangeshkar, Asha Bhosle, Mohd. Rafi, Shobha Gurtu
Lyricist(s)	Anand Bakshi (Amir Khusro)
Writer(s)	Raj Bharti, Chandrakant Kakodkar, G.R. Kamat, Rahi Masoom Reza, Suraj Sanim
Cinematographer(s)	Pratap Sinha

Do Premee (1980)

Cast	Rishi Kapoor, Moushumi Chatterjee, Om Prakash, I.S. Johar, Deven Verma, Geeta Behl, Roopesh Kumar, Aruna Irani
Producer(s)	Kundan A. Thadani
Assistant Director(s)	Raj Behl, Viren Bole, Inder Khosla, Pravesh Sagar
Music	Laxmikant Kudalkar, Pyarelal Sharma
Singer(s)	Kishore Kumar, Lata Mangeshkar, Mohd. Rafi, Asha Bhosle, Manna Dey, Anuradha Paudwal
Lyricist(s)	Anand Bakshi

Writer(s)	Raj Bharti, Gulshan Nanda, G.R. Kamat, Rahi Masoom Reza
Cinematographer(s)	Fali Mistry

***Dostana* (1980)**

Cast	Amitabh Bachchan, Shatrughan Sinha, Zeenat Aman, Prem Chopra, Amrish Puri, Helen, K.N. Singh
Producer(s)	Hiroo Johar, Yash Johar
Assistant Director(s)	Raj Behl, Viren Bole, Inder Khosla, Pravesh Sagar
Music	Laxmikant Kudalkar, Pyarelal Sharma
Singer(s)	Kishore Kumar, Lata Mangeshkar, Mohd. Rafi, Asha Bhosle
Lyricist(s)	Anand Bakshi
Writer(s)	Salim Khan, Javed Akhtar
Cinematographer(s)	Nariman A. Irani

***Daasi* (1981)**

Cast	Sanjeev Kumar, Rekha, Moushumi Chatterjee, Rakesh Roshan, Vikram Makandar, Leela Mishra
Producer(s)	Subhash Verma
Assistant Director(s)	Parvesh Sagar, Raj Behl, Inder Khosla
Music	Ravindra Jain, Rajesh Roshan
Singer(s)	Kishore Kumar, Lata Mangeshkar, Asha Bhosle, Manna Dey, Bhupinder Singh, Ravindra Jain
Lyricist(s)	Anand Bakshi, Ravindra Jain

Writer(s)	K.K. Shrivastava
Cinematographer(s)	Pratap Sinha

***Teri Maang Sitaron Se Bhar Doon* (1982)**

Cast	Nutan, Padmini Kolhapure, Raj Kiran, Amjad Khan, Shashikala, Vijay Arora
Producer(s)	Anil Khosla, Raj Khosla (Raj Khosla Films)
Assistant Director(s)	Raj Behl, Viren Bole, Inder Khosla, Pravesh Sagar
Music	Laxmikant Kudalkar, Pyarelal Sharma
Singer(s)	Lata Mangeshkar, Asha Bhosle, Manna Dey, Suresh Wadkar, Amit Kumar, Alka Yagnik
Lyricist(s)	Anand Bakshi
Writer(s)	Jyotin Goel, A. Kamal, G.R. Kamat, Rahi Masoom Reza
Cinematographer(s)	Pratap Sinha

***Maati Maangey Khoon* (1984)**

Cast	Shatrughan Sinha, Rekha, Raj Babbar, Reena Roy, Tanuja, Amjad Khan, Om Puri, Sudhir
Producer(s)	Pawan Kumar, Lakhan Sinha
Music	R.D. Burman
Singer(s)	Lata Mangeshkar, Asha Bhosle, Ghulam Ali
Lyricist(s)	Anand Bakshi, Mohsin Naqvi
Cinematographer(s)	Pratap Sinha

Sunny (1984)

Cast	Dharmendra, Sunny Deol, Amrita Singh, Waheeda Rehman, Sharmila Tagore, Birbal
Producer(s)	Amarjeet, M.L. Chugh, Bobby Tappia
Assistant Director(s)	Raj Behl, Viren Bole, Inder Khosla, Pravesh Sagar, A. Kamal
Music	R.D. Burman
Singer(s)	Lata Mangeshkar, Asha Bhosle, Suresh Wadkar, Anand Kumar
Lyricist(s)	Anand Bakshi
Writer(s)	Bobby Tappia
Cinematographer(s)	Pratap Sinha

Meraa Dost Meraa Dushman (1984)

Cast	Shatrughan Sinha, Danny Denzongpa, Smita Patil, Sanjeev Kumar, Johnny Walker, Geeta Behl
Producer(s)	Johny Bakshi
Music	Laxmikant Kudalkar, Pyarelal Sharma
Singer(s)	Kishore Kumar, Asha Bhosle, Suresh Wadkar
Lyricist(s)	Anand Bakshi
Cinematographer(s)	Pratap Sinha

Naqāb (1989)

Cast	Rishi Kapoor, Farha, Bindu, Amjad Khan, Vijayendra, Chand Usmani
Producer(s)	Raj Khosla (Raj Khosla Films)
Assistant Director(s)	Inder Khosla, Raj Behl, Milan Luthria

Music	Kamal Makhdoom
Singer(s)	Asha Bhosle, Mohd Aziz, Suresh Wadkar, Kamal Makhdoom
Lyricist(s)	Faruk Kaiser
Writer(s)	G.R. Kamat, Abid Surti
Cinematographer(s)	Pratap Sinha

Raj Khosla as Producer (with Anil Khosla, under the Raj Khosla Films Banner)

Do Chor (1972)

Cast	Dharmendra, Tanuja, K.N. Singh
Director(s)	B. Padmanabham
Assistant Director(s)	Mahesh Bhatt, Madhukar Pathak, S.B. Sharma
Music	R.D. Burman
Singer(s)	Kishore Kumar, Lata Mangeshkar
Lyricist(s)	Majrooh Sultanpuri
Cinematographer(s)	V.N. Reddy

Notes

1. Origins: Punjab to Bombay

1. Sheila Vesuna, 'The man who met his Waterloo with a bottle of Scotch,' *Asian Age*, 10 August 1995. Copy of article courtesy NCPA.
2. Rajiv Vijayakar, 'The Musical Genius of Raj Khosla,' *Screen*, June 2000. Copy of article courtesy NCPA.
3. Amborish Roychoudhury's interview with the family.

2. Baby Steps: Radio, Singing and Acting

1. Khalid Mohamed, 'What would life and movies be without women?,' *Filmfare*, May 1979. Copy of article courtesy NFAI.
2. 'Behind the Screen: Director Raj Khosla,' *Filmfare*, 8 February 1963. Copy of article courtesy NFAI.
3. Ibid.
4. Ibid.
5. Khalid Mohamed, 'What would life and movies be without women?.'
6. Pandit Sudarshan's son was the writer Shashi Bhushan, who went on to write iconic films like *Professor* (1962), *Anamika* (1973) and *Laawaris* (1981).

7. Jaswant (real name Syed Irshad Hussain) had married actress Geeta Bali's sister Hardarshan Kaur, and fathered Yogeeta Bali, who later became an actress and married Mithun Chakraborty.
8. Interview with Amborish Roychoudhury.
9. Vishwas Nerurkar, 'His Journey,' https://www.madanmohan.in/html/the_legend/his_journey/his_journey.html.
10. Sheila Vesuna, 'Any film that is autobiographical has got to click,' *Star & Style*, July 4-17, 1986. Copy of article courtesy NFAI.

3. Learning the Ropes

1. Dev Anand, *Romancing with Life: An Autobiography* (Penguin, 2011), 74.
2. K.N. Subramaniam, 'My films have kept me entertained too,' *Filmfare*, 16–30 June, 1981. Copy of article courtesy NFAI.
3. Dev Anand, *Romancing with Life: An Autobiography,* 159.
4. Ibid.
5. Nasreen Munni Kabir, *Guru Dutt: A Life in Cinema* (Oxford University Press, 2004), 31.
6. Ibid.
7. Ibid.
8. Rauf Ahmed, *Shammi Kapoor: The Game Changer* (Om Books, 2016).
9. Interview given to London-based journalist Bhartendu Vimal, https://www.youtube.com/watch?v=iMCax9rP_f4.
10. Nasreen Munni Kabir's interview with Raj Khosla, transcripts provided to Amborish Roychoudhury.

4. The Guru Dutt Years

1. Amborish Roychoudhury's interview with Lalitha Lajmi.
2. Ibid.
3. Ibid.
4. Yasser Usman, *Guru Dutt: An Unfinished Story* (Simon & Schuster, 2021) 112.
5. Dev Anand, *Romancing with Life: An Autobiography* (Penguin, 2011), 116-118.

6. https://asanyfuleknow.blogspot.com/2020/12/ibn-e-mariam-hua-kare-koi-ghalib.html.
7. Nasreen Munni Kabir, *Guru Dutt: A Life in Cinema* (Oxford University Press, 2004) 40.
8. Anirudha Bhattacharjee and Balaji Vittal, *S.D. Burman: The Prince Musician* (Westland, 2018) 82.
9. Nasreen Munni Kabir's interview with Raj Khosla, transcripts provided to Amborish Roychoudhury.
10. Ibid.
11. Yasser Usman, *Guru Dutt*, 137.
12. Nasreen Munni Kabir's interview with Raj Khosla.
13. Sathya Saran, *Ten Years with Guru Dutt: Abrar Alvi's Journey* (Penguin, 2011). As a matter of fact, Sathya Saran's account is one book where Raj Khosla makes frequent appearances.
14. Ibid, 9.
15. Ibid, 30–31.

5. Debut – *Milap*

1. Khalid Mohamed, 'What would life and movies be without women?,' *Filmfare*, May 1979. Copy of article courtesy NFAI.
2. Frank Capra, *The Name Above the Title: An Autobiography* (Dacapo Press, 1997), 182.
3. Rauf Ahmed, *Shammi Kapoor: The Game Changer* (Om Books, 2016).
4. Nasreen Munni Kabir, *Guru Dutt: A Life in Cinema* (Oxford University Press, 2004).
5. Raj Khosla's interview with Nasreen Munni Kabir, transcripts provided to Amborish Roychoudhury.
6. 'Scintillating Romance and High-voltage Drama in Filmart's "Milap",' *Filmfare*, 4 March 1955. Copy of article courtesy NFAI.

6. On the Rise – *C.I.D.*

1. Amborish Roychoudhury's interview with Nasreen Munni Kabir.
2. Amborish Roychoudhury's interview with Lalitha Lajmi.
3. Amborish Roychoudhury's interview with Nasreen Munni Kabir.

4. Some examples are: https://www.hindustantimes.com/bollywood/guiness-world-record-holder-jagdish-raj-passes-away-bollywood-mourns/story-qugJg4QJCnuLbaIHu2MjiI.html; https://www.news18.com/movies/this-yesteryear-bollywood-artist-holds-guinness-world-record-for-the-most-type-cast-actor-8578348.html; https://www.dailyo.in/arts/jagdish-raaj-police-inspector-typecast-actor-bollywood-34726.
5. Nasreen Munni Kabir, *Guru Dutt: A Life in Cinema* (Oxford University Press, 2004), 71.
6. Nasreen Munni Kabir, *Guru Dutt: A Life in Cinema* (Oxford University Press, 2004).
7. *In Search of Guru Dutt*, directed by Nasreen Munni Kabir (1989), 38:05.
8. Karan Bali, 'Dances With Sheila,' *Upperstall*, https://upperstall.com/features/dances-with-sheila/.
9. 'Milon Gupta Interview Live: Part 1', 25 November 2013, https://www.youtube.com/watch?v=MyDdsQZ2Vwg.
10. Raj Khosla's interview with Nasreen Munni Kabir, transcripts shared with Amborish Roychoudhury.
11. Manek Premchand, *Majrooh Sultanpuri: The Poet for all Reasons* (Blue Pencil Publishers, 2021).
12. Sheila Vesuna, 'Any film that is autobiographical has got to tick,' *Star & Style*, 4–17 July. Copy of article courtesy NFAI.

7. Walking Out of the Shadows

1. Sheila Vesuna, 'The man who met his Waterloo with a bottle of Scotch,' *Asian Age*, 10 August 1995. Copy of article courtesy NCPA.
2. 'Films in the Making,' *Filmfare*, 24 May 1957.
3. H.Q. Chowdhury, *Incomparable Sachin Dev Burman* (Blue Pencil Publishers, 2018).
4. Aniruddha Bhattacharjee and Balaji Vittal, *S.D. Burman: The Prince Musician* (Westland, 2018), 132.
5. Raju Bharatan's *Filmfare* article 'How Asha lost Dada to Lata' (1–15 December 1985), quoted in Aniruddha Bhattacharjee and Balaji Vittal, *S.D. Burman: The Prince Musician* (Westland, 2018), 132.
6. Lata Mangeshkar and Nasreen Munni Kabir, *Lata Mangeshkar... In Her Own Voice: Conversations with Nasreen Munni Kabir* (Niyogi Books, 2009).

7. Amborish Roychoudhury's interview with Asha Bhosle.
8. Sheila Vesuna, 'The man who met his Waterloo with a bottle of scotch.'
9. Raj Khosla, 'Me and my heroines,' *Filmfare*, 11 November 1966. Copy of article courtesy NFAI.
10. Sheila Vesuna, 'The man who met his Waterloo with a bottle of Scotch.'
11. Anitaa Padhye, tr. Vikrant Pande, *Goldie: The Man and His Movies* (Amaryllis, 2021).

8. Of Men from Bombay and Women from Bengal

1. Raj Khosla, 'Me and my heroines,' *Filmfare*, 11 November 1966. Copy of article courtesy NFAI.
2. Ibid.
3. Sheila Vesuna, 'The man who met his Waterloo with a bottle of Scotch,' *Asian Age*, 10 August 1995. Copy of article courtesy NCPA.
4. Hanif Zaveri and Sumant Batra, *An Actor's Actor: The Authorized Biography of Sanjeev Kumar* (Penguin Random House, 2021).
5. Ibid.
6. Nandini Ramnath, 'Picture the song: "Chal Ri Sajni" from "Bombai Ka Babu" is about a love that cannot speak its name,' *Scroll.in*, https://scroll.in/reel/857609/picture-the-song-chal-ri-sajni-from-bombai-ka-babu-is-about-a-love-that-cannot-speak-its-name.
7. Interview with Amborish Roychoudhury.
8. Nasreen Munni Kabir, *Conversations with Waheeda Rehman* (Penguin Random House, 2015).

9. *Ek Musafir Ek Hasina*, and the Beginnings of the Sadhana Phase

1. Shishir Krishna Sharma, 'Phir Wohi Dil Laya Hoon – Joy Mukerjee,' Beete Hue Din blog, https://beetehuedin.blogspot.com/2015/12/phir-wohi-dil-laya-hoon-joy-mukerjee.html.
2. *Maratha Darbar Agarbatti ke Sitare*, Radio Ceylon.

3. Khalid Mohamed, 'What would life and movies be with women?,' *Filmfare*, May 1979.
4. Interview with Amborish Roychoudhury.
5. 'Why O P Nayyar Was Angry With Film Director Raj Khosla and What Happened After Ek Musafir Ek Hasina,' https://www.youtube.com/watch?v=U6QUAfzaTFA.
6. Sheila Vesuna, 'The man who met his Waterloo with a bottle of Scotch,' *Asian Age*, 10 August 1995. Copy of article courtesy NCPA.
7. Sheila Vesuna, 'Any film that is autobiographical has got to click,' *Star & Style*, July 4–17, 1986. Copy of article courtesy NFAI.
8. Ibid.
9. Raju Bharatan, *A Journey Down Melody Lane* (Hay House India, 2017).
10. Raj Khosla, 'My style of movie making,' *Filmfare*, 23 February 1968. Copy of interview courtesy Nasreen Munni Kabir.

10. *Woh Kaun Thi?* The Woman in White? Or Not

1. It was to be their first film together; Raj Khosla's assistant Bhappi Sonie was to cast them in *Ek Phool Char Kaante* just one year later.
2. Nasreen Munni Kabir, 'RD Burman archival interview: "Only if you have a rapport with the director do tunes come to you",' *Scroll.in*, 28 June 2023, https://scroll.in/reel/1051667/rd-burman-archival-interview-only-if-you-have-a-rapport-with-the-director-do-tunes-come-to-you.
3. Khalid Mohamed, 'What would life and movies be without women?,' *Filmfare*, May 1979. Copy of article courtesy NFAI.
4. Access to interview provided to Amborish Roychoudhury courtesy Rajil Sayani.
5. Interview with Amborish Roychoudhury.
6. Ibid.
7. Sheila Vesuna, 'Any film that is autobiographical has got to click,' *Star & Style*, July 4–17, 1986. Copy of article courtesy NFAI.
8. Raj Khosla, 'Me and My Heroines,' *Filmfare*, 11 November 1966. Copy of article courtesy NFAI.
9. Punita Bhatt, 'The Sadhana Mystique,' *Filmfare*, July 1991. Copy of article courtesy Normah Ismail.

10. Sheila Vesuna, 'Any film that is autobiographical has got to click.'
11. Khalid Mohamed, 'What would life and movies be without women?,' *Filmfare*, May 1979
12. The composer and Lata Mangeshkar had a similar episode with another song 'Mairi, main kaase kahon' from *Dastak* (1970).
13. Amborish Roychoudhury's interview with Samir Kohli.
14. Suresh Mathew, 'Revisiting "Lag Ja Gale" and Bollywood's Obsession With a Classic,' *Quint*, 26 July 2018, https://www.thequint.com/entertainment/bollywood/lag-ja-gale-song-madan-mohan-interview-lata-mangeshkar-woh-kaun-thi-sanjeev-kohli#read-more.
15. Ibid.

11. *Mera Saaya* – What *Jhumka*?

1. Raj Khosla's interview with Nasreen Munni Kabir, transcripts shared with Amborish Roychoudhury.
2. The Nightingale granted a telephonic interview to Amborish Roychoudhury on 9 August 2021. She passed away on 6 February 2022.
3. Farhana Farook, 'Dil Dhoondhta hai...,' *Filmfare*, 25 Jun 2016, https://www.filmfare.com/features/dil-dhoondhta-hai-14138.html.
4. Sheila Vesuna, 'The man who met his Waterloo with a bottle of Scotch,' *Asian Age*, 10 August 1995. Copy of article courtesy NCPA.
5. Ibid.
6. Ibid.

12. *Do Badan Pyar ki Aag mein Jal Gaye*

1. Translation from https://omershafee.wordpress.com/2013/08/26/ek-chameli-ke-mandve-tale-by-makhdoom-mohiuddin/.
2. Sheila Vesuna, 'The man who met his Waterloo with a bottle of Scotch,' *Asian Age*, 10 August 1995. Copy of article courtesy NCPA.
3. Translation credit to Yasir Abbasi and Nuwayra Farooqi.
4. Translation credit to Yasir Abbasi and Nuwayra Farooqi.
5. Asha Parekh, with Khalid Mohamed, *Asha Parekh: The Hit Girl* (Om Books, 2017).

6. Ranjan Das Gupta, 'Blast from the Past - Do Badan (1966),' 14 October 2010, https://www.thehindu.com/features/cinema/Blast-from-the-Past-Do-Badan-1966/article15780054.ece.
7. Sheila Vesuna, 'The man who met his Waterloo with a bottle of Scotch,' *Asian Age*, 10 August 1995.

13. The First Bump in the Road

1. Interview with Amborish Roychoudhury.
2. Pyarelal's interview with Amborish Roychoudhury.
3. Khalid Mohamed, 'What would life and movies be without women?' *Filmfare*, May 1979. Copy of article courtesy NFAI.
4. It was the director who encouraged Hamid Ali Khan to set aside his long name and adopt the shorter 'Ajit' for the screen.
5. Sheila Vesuna, 'Any film that is autobiographical has got to click,' *Star & Style*, July 4–17, 1986. Copy of article courtesy NFAI.

14. Two Roads Diverged in a Wood

1. Chandrakant Kalyandas Kakodar vs The State Of Maharashtra And Ors on 25 August 1969, Supreme Court of India, https://indiankanoon.org/doc/25099/.
2. Ibid.
3. Sheila Vesuna, 'The man who met his Waterloo with a bottle of Scotch', *Asian Age*, 10 August 1995. Copy of article courtesy NCPA.
4. As told to Farhana Farook for *Filmfare*, 'Rajesh Khanna's Rooh is still in Aashirwad', 10 July 2015, https://www.filmfare.com/features/rajesh-khannas-rooh-is-still-in-aashirwad-9782.html.
5. 'Raj Khosla – By Rajesh Khanna, as told to Bunny Reuben,' *Star & Style*, 13 November 1970. Copy of article courtesy NFAI.
6. Ibid.
7. Interview with Amborish Roychoudhury.
8. Anirudha Bhattacharjee and Parthiv Dhar, *Kishore Kumar: The Ultimate Biography* (Harper Collins, 2022), 339.
9. R.M. Vijayakar, 'Waman Bhonsle Tribute: Superstar Scissorhands Passes Away at 89,' 27 April 2021, https://web.archive.org/web/20210428033214/https://www.indiawest.com/

entertainment/bollywood/waman-bhonsle-tribute-superstar-scissorhands-passes-away-at-89/article_d7bffd48-a779-11eb-bff2-a74160e4d101.html.

10. Sheila Vesuna, 'The man who met his Waterloo with a bottle of Scotch.'

15. What Do You Wish Me to Do With You?

1. Tarun Kumar Bhaduri, *Abhishapta Chambal* (Ananda Publishers, 2012).
2. Khalid Mohamed, 'What would life and movies be without women?,' *Filmfare*, May 1979. Copy of article courtesy NFAI.
3. Sheila Vesuna, 'The man who met his Waterloo with a bottle of Scotch', *Asian Age*, 10 August 1995. Copy of article courtesy NCPA.
4. Sheila Vesuna, 'Any film that is autobiographical has got to click,' *Star & Style*, 4–17 July 1986. Copy of article courtesy NFAI.
5. Interview with Amborish Roychoudhury.
6. Sheila Vesuna, 'Any film that is autobiographical has got to click.'
7. Ibid.
8. Radio interview with Ameen Sayani for *Saridon Kay Saathi*. Access to interview provided to Amborish Roychoudhury courtesy Rajil Sayani.
9. Johnny Bakshi, 'Raj days, revisited,' *Metro Plus*, 11 July 1994. Copy of article courtesy NCPA.
10. Sheila Vesuna, 'Any film that is autobiographical has got to click.'
11. 'Meena, the Second!,' *Bombay Journal*, 8 July 1973. Copy of article courtesy NFAI.

16. Of Threads, Thieves and Guns

1. 'Meena, the Second!,' *Bombay Journal*, 8 July 1973. Copy of article courtesy NFAI.
2. Sheila Vesuna, 'Any film that is autobiographical has got to click,' *Star & Style*, July 4–17, 1986. Copy of article courtesy NFAI.
3. Amborish Roychoudhury's interview with Raj Khosla's team.

17. Gentlemen Crooks and Poets in Love

1. He spoke about issues with his personal life in several interviews, including the March 1975 and May 1979 *Filmfare* interviews, given to K.N. Subramaniam and Khalid Mohamed respectively.
2. Sheila Vesuna, 'Any film that is autobiographical has got to click,' *Star & Style*, 4–17 July 1986. Copy of article courtesy NFAI.
3. Amborish Roychoudhury's interview with Sriram Raghavan.
4. K.N. Subramaniam, 'Director's the evil: Interview with Raj Khosla,' *Filmfare*, 7 March 1975. Copy of article courtesy Nasreen Munni Kabir's archives.
5. Subhash K. Jha, 'Happy Birthday Moushumi Chatterjee: A look through her journey in Indian cinema,' *Firstpost*, 26 April 2022, https://www.firstpost.com/entertainment/happy-birthday-moushumi-chatterjee-a-look-through-her-journey-in-indian-cinema-10599581.html.
6. Sheila Vesuna, 'Any film that is autobiographical has got to click.'

18. Tulsi and a Biker Gang

1. Interview with Amborish Roychoudhury.
2. Sheila Vesuna, 'Any film that is autobiographical has got to click,' *Star & Style*, 4-17 July 1986. Copy of article courtesy NFAI.
3. Episode on Sunil Dutt, *Jeena Isi Ka Naam Hai*, Zee TV.
4. *The Anupam Kher Show*, Colors TV, https://www.youtube.com/watch?v=JhBdJVqV-i0.
5. K.N. Subramaniam, 'Director's the evil: Interview with Raj Khosla,' *Filmfare*, 7 March 1975. Copy of article courtesy Nasreen Munni Kabir's archives.
6. Sheila Vesuna, 'Any film that is autobiographical has got to click.'
7. K.N. Subramaniam, 'My films have kept me entertained too,' *Filmfare*, 16-30 June 1981. Copy of article courtesy NFAI.
8. Asha Parekh and Khalid Mohamed, *Asha Parekh: The Hit Girl* (Om Books, 2017), 111.
9. https://youtu.be/c-rmFM223MM?feature=shared&t=360.
10. Rajiv Vijayakar, *Music by Laxmikant Pyarelal* (Rupa, 2021).
11. Khalid Mohamed, 'What would life and movies be without women?,' *Filmfare*, May 1979. Copy of article courtesy NFAI.
12 K.N. Subramaniam, 'My films have kept me entertained too.'

19. *Salamat Rahe Dostana Hamara*

1. Farhana Farook, 'Anita Khosla talks about father Raj Khosla,' https://www.filmfare.com/filmfare-flashback/anita-khosla-talks-about-father-raj-khosla-29005.html.
2. Karan Johar with Poonam Saxena, *An Unsuitable Boy* (Penguin India, 2017).
3 Rajkumar Keswani, Dastan-E-Mughal-E-Azam (Manjul Publishing House, 2020).
4. Sheila Vesuna, 'The man who met his Waterloo with a bottle of Scotch,' *Asian Age*, 10 August 1995. Copy of article courtesy NCPA.
5. Sheila Vesuna, 'Any film that is autobiographical has got to click,' *Star & Style*, July 4–17, 1986. Copy of article courtesy NFAI.
6. Amborish Roychoudhury's interview with Salim Khan.
7. K.N. Subramaniam, 'My films have kept me entertained too,' *Filmfare*, 16–30 June, 1981. Copy of article courtesy NFAI.
8. Ibid.
9. Interview with Amborish Roychoudhury.
10. Rishi Kapoor with Meena Iyer, *Khullam Khulla*: *Rishi Kapoor Uncensored* (HarperCollins, 2017).
11. Ibid.
12. Sonal Gera, 'Rishi Kapoor responds to Moushumi Chatterjee's 'arrogant' remark,' *Indian Express*, 13 May 2015, https://indianexpress.com/article/entertainment/bollywood/rishi-kapoor-responds-to-moushumi-chatterjees-arrogant-remark/.

20. And Then There Were Six

1. Yasser Usman, *Sanjay Dutt: The Crazy Untold Story of Bollywood's Bad Boy* (Juggernaut, 2018).
2. Mobin Ansari, 'Raj Khosla: A Profile,' *Nagpur Times*, April 1976. Copy of article courtesy NFAI.
3. Johnny Bakshi, 'Raj days, revisited,' *Metro Plus*, 11 July 1994. Copy of article courtesy NCPA.
4. Interview with Amborish Roychoudhury.
5. Ibid.
6. Johnny Bakshi, 'Raj days, revisited.'

7. Interview with Amborish Roychoudhury.
8. Amborish Roychoudhury's interview with producer Pawan Kumar.
9. Aniruddha Bhattacharjee and Balaji Vittal, *R.D. Burman: The Man, The Music* (HarperCollins, 2011).
10. A *jogan* is a female saint or a hermit, the feminine form of a yogi. It became a popular template to depict heroines like that: wearing a saintly saree, sporting a tilak and singing on a *dotara* or *ektara*. Raj used this template in several films, especially *Anita* and *Maati Maangey Khoon*.
11. https://youtu.be/-mx9l2bM-1w?feature=shared&t=421.
12. Amborish Roychoudhury's interview with Raj Khosla's team.
13. When a filmmaker became a big enough name for the audience to watch the film because of him, they'd sometimes announce their authorship of the film on the poster. It was a wonder that Raj didn't do it before. I presume it was Johnny Bakshi's handiwork to use Raj's name and see if he could pull crowds in.
14. Waheeda Rehman's interview with Amborish Roychoudhury.
15. Nasreen Munni Kabir, *Conversations with Waheeda Rehman* (Penguin Random House, 2015).

21. The End

1. Till just 15–20 years ago, most companies paid salaries only on the first week of every month, sometimes even extending to the second week. It was unusual that Raj Khosla's employees got their salaries even before the current month ended.
2. Johnny Bakshi, 'Raj days, revisited,' *Metro Plus*, 11 July 1994. Copy of article courtesy NCPA.
3. Sheila Vesuna, 'Any film that is autobiographical has got to click,' *Star & Style*, 4–17 July 1986. Copy of article courtesy NFAI.
4. Interview with Raj Khosla by K.N. Subramaniam, 'Director's the evil,' *Filmfare*, 7 March 1975. Copy of article courtesy Nasreen Munni Kabir's archives.
5. Sheila Vesuna, 'Any film that is autobiographical has got to click.'
6 Sheila Vesuna, 'Any film that is autobiographical has got to click.'
7. Rajiv Vijayakar, 'The eternal romantic', *Filmfare*, July 1991.
8. Copy of the letter provided to Amborish Roychoudhury courtesy Raj Khosla's family.

Acknowledgements

This book started its journey way back in 2021. Since then, I've lost quite a bit of hair, gained a daughter and some perspective. All this while, this giant of a man has been perched on my shoulder, whispering into my ear. Raj Khosla was a genius but also every bit as flawed and as broken as the rest of us. In my eyes, that makes him relatable. I hope everyone who reads this book is able to see that. Researching on a popular Indian filmmaker is significantly more complicated than when your subject is an acclaimed arthouse director. Instead of journals, academic papers and coverage by the foreign press, what you have are film magazines and gossip columns to fall back on. There are no documentaries to watch, no memoirs to read. But the National Film Archive of India (NFAI), Pune, was a treasure trove, and this book owes a lot to that institution. Same goes for the library at National Centre for Performing Arts (NCPA), Mumbai, which helped me source a plethora of interviews and articles about Khosla.

When so many people have contributed to the shaping up of this book, there is always that sinking feeling that some indispensable assistance is being unjustly forgotten.

Nasreen Munni Kabir's precious guidance, help and perspectives have enriched this book, in addition to providing some information about her meeting with Raj Khosla, as well as some archival material from her own collection. Pavan Jha, film historian, has been a big help in verifying and tracking down some stories, especially on Kamal Makhdoom. Anirudha Bhattacharjee was equally helpful in checking details of many Pancham compositions in Raj Khosla's films. Writer Gautam Chintamani helped decode some stories about *Dostana*. Mohan Siddharth, who was a constant companion in many of my interviews during this journey, helped with his invaluable inputs as well as by transcribing some of the interviews. Transcription is a crucial task in projects such as these where so many personalities are being interviewed. Lopamudra Maitra Bajpai, a researcher and a writer herself, extended invaluable assistance in this respect, and so did Madhu D. Roy, a friend's wife and a big help in my first book as well. Collector and film enthusiast Zaheer Hasan provided some articles and a poster.

But I would be committing a mortal sin if I fail to record my gratitude to Jitesh Pillai. I wouldn't be writing this book if it weren't for him. Raj Khosla's daughters Anita Khosla, Uma Kapur and Uma's husband, G.M. Kapur, are the pillars this edifice stands on. They provided many of the stories and anecdotes that make up this book, gave me access to valuable information, and to other family members and friends. I'd also like to thank Sunita Bhalla Khosla, Reena Kataria Khosla and Sonia Vinaik Khosla for their perspectives, which helped this book immensely. Raj Khosla's biggest asset was his band of protégés, his team. A lot of stories in this book would be unverified hearsay if not for the precious inputs from Inder Khosla, Sanatan Vinchi, and Raj Behl. I was also able to speak to his secretaries Lorna Desouza and Ved Prakash. Finally,

Mahesh Bhatt, access to whom I blatantly exploited, texting him in the wee hours of the night and asking lame questions. He always countered them with a helpful, thoughtful and elaborate response. No matter what I asked for, 'Anything for my boss!' was the constant refrain. I'd like to thank Anil Khosla, Suchi Amladi, Pawan Kumar, Mohan Churiwala, Ketan Anand, Pramod Khosla, Arun Bhalla, Pankaj Dheer, Ketan Anand, Tasneem Khan, Sumeer Sabharwal, Samir Kohli, Moti Lalwani, Amit Khanna and, of course, the late Lalitha Lajmi.

This book wouldn't be in your hands if not for the tireless support and encouragement from the good folks at Hachette India. Right from Poulomi Chatterjee, who set the ball in motion – and has since moved on – and the first editor Sonali Jindal to Sini Nair, who stood steadfast beside the book throughout its four-year journey, I owe my gratitude to all of them. Aditi Sengupta has enriched the book with her suggestion and edits. Above all, I am deeply thankful to Dipanjali Chadha who graciously, painstakingly went through the book page by page, word by word, putting up with my idiosyncrasies and giving it its final shape.

The stars, actors, writers and directors who have contributed to this book are a glittering roster. Her interview for this book was one of the last Lata Mangeshkar gave before she passed away. Asha Bhosle graciously sat through my ramblings and patiently allowed me to go film by film, and shared stories about them. Pyarelal Sharma represented the legendary Laxmikant–Pyarelal team as well as Anand Bakshi, all of whom teamed up with Raj Khosla to create some timeless classics. One can't thank them enough. Manoj Kumar, Waheeda Rehman, Dharmendra, Aamir Khan, Sharmila Tagore, Shatrughan Sinha, Mumtaz, Asha Parekh, Moushumi Chatterjee, Salim Khan, Bindu, Prem Chopra, Sriram Raghavan and Dharmesh

Darshan have all shared their memories of Raj Khosla and his films in this book.

Finally, I'd be remiss not to thank the subject of this book, Raj Khosla. It seems a little odd thanking someone who's no more but in my defense, Raj Khosla himself sought inspiration in people who were long dead: K.L. Saigal, Mirza Ghalib, Shakespeare and Napoleon.